THE PICKERING MASTERS

The Letters of Francis Jeffrey to
Thomas and Jane Welsh Carlyle

The Letters of Francis Jeffrey to
Thomas and Jane Welsh Carlyle

Edited by
William Christie

Published by Pickering & Chatto (Publishers) Limited
21 Bloomsbury Way, London WC1A 2TH

2252 Ridge Road, Brookfield, Vermont 05036-9704, USA

www.pickeringchatto.com

BRITISH LIBRARY CATALOGUING IN PUBLICATION DATA

Jeffrey, Francis Jeffrey, Lord, 1773–1850
    The letters of Francis Jeffrey to Thomas and Jane Welsh Carlyle. – (The
    Pickering masters)
    1. Jeffrey, Francis Jeffrey, Lord, 1773–1850 – Correspondence 2. Carlyle,
    Thomas, 1795–1881 – Correspondence 3. Carlyle, Jane Welsh, 1801–1866
    – Correspondence 4. Critics – Scotland – Correspondence 5. Authors,
    Scottish – 19th century – Correspondence
    I. Title II. Christie, William, 1952–
    828.8'09

ISBN-13: 9781851969821

This publication is printed on acid-free paper that conforms to the American
National Standard for the Permanence of Paper for Printed Library Materials.

Typeset by Pickering & Chatto (Publishers) Limited
Printed in the United Kingdom at the University Press, Cambridge

CONTENTS

In memory of
Ken Fielding

ACKNOWLEDGEMENTS

My greatest debts are to the Carlyle scholars: to the late Ken Fielding, who wholeheartedly supported the project back in 2003 when I began my transcription and who selflessly read and commented on early drafts; to Ian Campbell, another of the editors of that great scholarly enterprise, the University of Edinburgh/Duke University Press edition of *The Collected Letters of Thomas and Jane Welsh Carlyle* (now available as *Carlyle Letters Online*), for help with everything from odd words that were difficult to decipher to allusions that were difficult to trace; to David Sorensen, editor of the *Carlyle Studies Annual* and a senior editor on the Carlyle Letters Project, who took an interest when it looked as if I would have to abandon the work.

Randall Stevenson, my friend and Head of the English Department at the University of Edinburgh, is not a Carlyle scholar, but is always willing to read what I write. For this, for stimulating conversation over *his* coffee, and for sheer good fellowship, I will always be grateful.

Prior to the invaluable contributions made by scholars and friends at the University of Edinburgh, the project could never have been undertaken without the ungrudging assistance and indeed open encouragement of the staff at the National Library of Scotland – of Iain Brown, the Principal Curator in the Manuscript Collections Division, in the first instance, but also of the many librarians who preside over the manuscript room at George IV Bridge Road.

And prior to this again, the Institute for Advanced Studies in the Humanities at the University of Edinburgh is to be thanked for two visiting fellowships (in 2003 and 2007), when the project was begun and completed under director John Frow and acting director Karina Williamson, respectively, with my presence at the Institute solicitously managed on both occasions by Anthea Taylor.

I am also indebted to Professor Geraldine Barnes, Head of the School of Letters, Art, and Media at the University of Sydney, for kindly offering the vital financial assistance that saw the completion and publication of the project.

Mark Pollard at Pickering & Chatto has been keen about the project from the beginning and helped to make it all worthwhile.

Finally, thanks to my wife Patrice and daughter Ellen for sharing the research trips to the UK with me – for being there, and for allowing me on occasion not to be there.

LIST OF ABBREVIATIONS

Carlyle Letters	*The Collected Letters of Thomas and Jane Welsh Carlyle*, ed. C. R. Sanders, K. J. Fielding, I. Campbell, et al. (Durham, NC: Duke University Press, 1970–) [now online: http://carlyleletters.dukejournals.org/].
ER	*Edinburgh Review*.
Life of Jeffrey	Lord [H.] Cockburn, *Life of Lord Jeffrey, with a Selection from His Correspondence*, 2 vols (Edinburgh: Adam and Charles Black, 1852).
NLS	National Library of Scotland.
Reminiscences	T. Carlyle, *Reminiscences*, ed. K. Fielding and I. Campbell (Oxford: Oxford University Press, 1997).

JEFFREY AND THE CARLYLES:
AN INTRODUCTION

Edin^r 13 Feby 1830

My Dear Carlyle

I am glad you think my regard for you a <u>Mystery</u> – as I am aware that must be its highest recommendation – I take it in an humbler sense – and am content to think it natural that one man of a kind heart should feel attracted towards another – and that a signal purity and loftiness of character, joined to great talents and something of a romantic history, should excite interest and respect. (below, p. 47)

I

The Thomas Carlyle who knocked on Francis Jeffrey's door at 92 George Street, Edinburgh, early in February of 1827 was not a young man. Though only newly married and recently settled at Comely Bank in the suburbs of the capital with his new wife, Jane Baillie Welsh, Carlyle was thirty-two.[1] And though of humble, country origins – he was born in the village of Ecclefechan in rural Dumfries-shire to James Carlyle, a stonemason turned small farmer, and his wife Margaret – this was by no means his first time in the big city, having been there as a university student eighteen years before in 1809. Carlyle at thirty-two, however, was as yet comparatively unknown, if not unpublished. His major publications – a translation of Goethe's *Wilhelm Meister's Apprenticeship* (1824) and a *Life of Schiller* (1825) – had not brought his name before the English-speaking reading public, probably because German thought and literature simply did not interest them enough. Carlyle was an ambitious man and never doubted his own ability, but he must at this time have doubted his chances of success, and he had just added a young wife to his responsibilities.

Francis Jeffrey, on the other hand, was fifty-three years old. He had for many years been one of Edinburgh's leading advocates and, along with Walter Scott, was its star literary attraction. 'Of all the celebrated characters of this place', wrote John Gibson Lockhart as 'Dr Peter Morris' in *Peter's Letters to His Kinsfolk*, 'I understand that Jeffrey is the one whom travellers are commonly most in a hurry to see.[2] He was still editor of what, in spite of some attenuation of its effectiveness, was still the leading periodical of the day: the *Edinburgh Review*. For this he received £700 per number – a staggering £2,800 a year[3] – on top of which he could pay himself upwards of £25 a sheet (£100 for an article of 32 pages) for his own contributions. And this without taking into account his income as an advocate. At Craigcrook, the celebrated country estate whose lease he purchased from the publisher Archibald Constable in 1815, Jeffrey entertained his close friends amongst Edinburgh's legal and professional elite as well as every visiting celebrity and dignitary, especially (though not exclusively) if they shared his liberal, reformist political convictions.

In the republic of letters, in other words, Jeffrey and Carlyle could hardly have been further apart. Notwithstanding this discrepancy, Carlyle bit the bullet and introduced himself. Having been given a letter of introduction to Jeffrey by Bryan Waller Procter ('Barry Cornwall'), 'Last week', Carlyle wrote to his mother in February 1827, 'I went up one evening and delivered it':

> The little man received me in his kindest style; talked with me for an hour, tho' very busy, on all possible things; and really proved himself by much the most agreeable citizen of Edinburgh that I had ever met with. I am sorry the man is so immersed in Law; otherwise it is possible enough we might even become *friends*. He invited me repeatedly to come to the 'Court' any morning, and he would introduce me to various people, among others to Sir Walter Scott. I have not gone yet, being a little careful of such introductions. He also spoke about writing in his Review; but I told him he must first read the *German Romance* to see what manner of man I was, and then we might determine if I could suit him. We parted in the friendliest style, mutually tolerant of each other. In a week or two, we may perhaps meet again.[4]

What clinched it for Carlyle – as he recalled forty years later in his *Reminiscences* – was that Jeffrey bothered with a 'formal return-call', a visit to the younger couple at Comely Bank, 'which gave a new speed to intimacy'.[5] There were calls and return calls between them that soon involved Mrs Charlotte Jeffrey and an unlikely friendship was underway – one that would fall apart seven years later, in 1834, though it was resurrected after a fashion and they would remain on speaking and visiting terms until Jeffrey's death in 1850.

It is characteristic of Carlyle and surely a part of his attraction that he was incapable of fawning to anyone. Certainly, he did not especially enjoy or admire what he called the '"mob of gentlemen" talking insipidities and giving dinners' that was the literary culture of professional Edinburgh.[6] Jeffrey, however, was different: 'a rare phenomenon', Carlyle assured Anna Montagu, 'and among the best of that rather unhappy race, Men of Letters now extant'.[7] Jeffrey's kind attentions were neither forced nor condescending, and the conversation shared by the two men was marked by 'an unembarrassment and frankness of hitting and repelling, which did not quite beseem our respective ages and positions'.[8] The unlikely friendship so speedily struck up between the two of them was enough briefly to reconcile Carlyle not just with Edinburgh, but even (as Jeffrey himself might puckishly have suggested) with his fellow human beings. Sitting down to write his *Reminiscences*, Carlyle remembered

> pleasant strolls out to Craigcrook (one of the prettiest places in the world), where, on a Sunday especially, I might hope, what was itself a rarity with me, to find a companionable human acquaintance, not to say one of such quality as this. He would wander about the woods with me, looking on the Firth, and Fife Hills, on the Pentlands and Edinburgh Castle and City, – nowhere was there such a view – perhaps he would walk most of the way back with me; quietly sparkling and chatting ... If I met him in the streets, in the Parliament House or accidentally anywhere, there ensued, unless he were engaged, a cheerful bit of talk and promenading. He frequently rode round by Comely Bank in returning home; and there I would see him, or hear something pleasant of him.[9]

Like his later reminiscences, Carlyle's letters at the time are flooded with an endearing light and warmth. Jeffrey was 'a man meant by Nature to be an intellectual Ariel', Carlyle told Procter, 'with a light etherealness of spirit'.[10] His response to Jeffrey's attentions and affection was in turn genuinely affectionate: 'Jeffrey and I continue to love one another, like a new Plyades and a new Orestes', Carlyle wrote to his brother John just over a year after he had first introduced himself, 'such often is my feeling to the little man'.[11]

More practically, Carlyle needed Jeffrey's introduction to an intelligent literary public. Large reviews like Jeffrey's *Edinburgh* were the logical places for an ambitious historical and cultural commentator like Carlyle to seek publication. This was an area of their relationship in which Carlyle could feel more equal. It is true that Jeffrey's emotional and intellectual investment in the *Edinburgh* was waning after twenty-five years. As a commissioning editor, moreover, he had always been hamstrung by the jealousy of his most prolific contributor, Henry Brougham, who tried as far as possible to keep significant speculation in the hands of himself and Jeffrey, and of one or two others amongst the original 'set'. Still, Jeffrey needed new and striking writers no less than Carlyle needed the opportunity to exploit the open secret of periodical anonymity to further his reputation. In his *Reminiscences*, Carlyle recalls with evident delight that his opening critical essays in the *Edinburgh Review* – the first on Jean Paul Richter and the second on German writing more generally – had 'set many tongues wagging, and some few brains thinking'.[12] To this day, Carlyle's magisterial and provocative essays 'Signs of the Times' (1829) and the later 'Characteristics' (1831) (written for Macvey Napier after Jeffrey's retirement from the editorship in July 1829) are amongst the *Edinburgh*'s most important original contributions to cultural thinking.

II

No account of Jeffrey's friendship with the Carlyles can proceed for long, however, without running up against the obvious differences between the two men – just as no reading of these letters can proceed for long without running up against their mutual exasperation.[13] Their feeling for each other, as Carlyle himself realized from the beginning, would always be marked by a certain ambivalence. 'That wonderful little man is expected here very soon', Carlyle wrote to his brother John on 25 August 1828, 'He takes no little interest in us; writes often, and half hates half loves me with the utmost sincerity'.[14] When I alluded earlier to the *unlikeliness* of the friendship between them, I meant more than just the obvious imbalance in background, status, wealth and age. Carlyle himself, we infer from the letter of Jeffrey's I have used as an epigraph to this introduction, thought of their relationship as a 'mystery'. And so it remained, in spite of Jeffrey's attempt to demystify it and to redefine it in terms of familiarity and sociability.

Indeed, it was lucky that the two men liked each other so well because there were few things on which the two of them could agree. A postscript Carlyle added to a letter of Jane's to Anna Montagu a month and half after he and Jeffrey first met hints at an impasse between the two men that would never be overcome throughout their long, vicissitudinous relationship and would require at times all the mutual toleration they could muster. It was an impasse that is only inadequately described as 'intellectual', 'philosophical' or 'political', and even the more capacious, if elusive term 'ideological' seems partial. It embraced *all* these things, certainly, but what comes across most strongly is the powerful temperamental difference between the two men: 'I saw Mr Jeffrey, and talked with him boldly for an hour; a man of the kindliest and richest nature, which the perverse utilitarianism of the time has all his life been striving vainly to spoil. Me he seemed to look upon as an enthusiast, distracted nearly, but amiable in my distraction'.[15] 'He has but one fault but that one is a thumper', Carlyle wrote to Anna Montagu again, in late November 1827: 'O that law had never been invented, or that Francis Jeffrey had never been a lawyer!'.[16] Carlyle's exasperation was fuelled, no doubt, by his own unhappy experience as an Edinburgh law student, but he was not the first to identify in Jeffrey and the *Edinburgh Review* an ethical arbitrariness and equivocation symptomatic of the legal profession shared by the main players. It is Jeffrey's morally dubious success as an advocate that informs Carlyle's portrait in the *Reminiscences*, beginning as it does with the highly tendentious anecdote of the honey-tongued Jeffrey's pleading the innocence of a known murderess. 'One thing struck me, in sad elucidation of his forensic glories: I found that essentially he was always as if speaking to a jury'.[17] Sometimes, as when he wrote to Procter in January 1828, Carlyle's complaint was less vocationally specific:

'Alas! that Mammon should be able to hire such servants'.[18] Between them, Jeffrey's professional success and enormous wealth suggested a pact with the world and the devil which, in the ascetic Carlyle's opinion, amounted automatically to intellectual and ethical disqualification.

III

For all his worldliness, however, Jeffrey could still elicit from one of the most grudging of all critical commentators a genuine affection and respect – even, though far less often, something resembling admiration. This remained true throughout the years of their comparative estrangement and it is this – this regard he felt, in spite of himself as it were, for a bartered soul – that was for Carlyle the mystery of their relationship. The high point came during 'the four intimate days talking' of the Jeffreys' visit in September 1830 to Craigenputtoch, the isolated farm to which the younger couple had withdrawn in late May 1828 (below, p. 67). However reconciled Carlyle may have been to Edinburgh by the good company belatedly offered by Jeffrey, he had in his heart long before they had met committed himself to withdrawing to the farm in Dumfriesshire inherited by Jane on her father's death (with rent paid to her mother, Grace Welsh). After six to eight months of close friendship with Jeffrey, Carlyle and Jane had spent two days with the Jeffrey family at 24 Moray Place in Edinburgh before setting out for Craigenputtoch, where they would remain on and off until in the middle of 1834 when they settled in the house now identified with them at number 5 Cheyne Row, Chelsea, in London.

Jeffrey had always, and openly, disapproved of the move to Craigenputtoch, largely for Jane's sake – and since their introduction to each other, Jeffrey and Jane had discovered an untraceable, and probably spurious, family connection. In objecting on Jane's behalf, Jeffrey, as it turned out, was proved right. But with the accession of the Whigs in November 1830, Jeffrey, too, would migrate – not to the Scottish countryside, however, but to the opposite extreme from the Carlyles: to London, and to the frenetic legal, political and bureaucratic life of the Lord Advocate of Scotland (Scotland's highest political administrator). In the meantime, he made a point of writing to and (more to the point) of visiting Carlyle and Jane in the obscurity and loneliness of Craigenputtoch. To this day, the journey remains a difficult one. Though like many of his generation Jeffrey made a habit of strenuous physical exercise, touring and climbing in the Highlands at every opportunity, to have transported his family over terrain at times 'barely passable'[19] to such remote and (compared with Moray Place) inhospitable accommodation is surely remarkable, in itself an act of love. Both the Carlyles were grateful for the recognition and attention that on each occasion Jeffrey had gone out of his way to bestow, and never more so than in September 1830. 'Jeffrey was more than usually friendly and interesting', Carlyle wrote to his mother soon after their departure, 'and we were left, with real regret'; to Anna Montagu he wrote, 'a more interesting and better man; a sadder and wiser; than I had ever seen him'.[20]

It is arguable that the first significant turning point in the friendship came only a month after this visit, with Jeffrey's comments in a letter of 28 October 1830 on Carlyle's uncompleted history of German literature. In response to a substantial draft, Jeffrey wrote in what was a characteristically uncompromising and insensitive mode: 'I have now read nearly all your M.S. – and confess that I have great doubts whether it will readily find a purchaser – just because I fear, if it were published, it would not readily find many readers'; 'If your work is ever printed, you will deal most unfairly by yourself if you do not alter and correct it unsparingly – but this idle prologue must at all events be suppressed – or you make sure of damnation' (below, pp. 73, 74). Carlyle was not surprisingly stung by the letter's 'long, unasked, abusive and almost ill-bred Criticism'. His way of coping was to dismiss Jeffrey's negativity as symptomatic of mental depression, and of the imaginative limitations of a man who, though essentially kind hearted, was personally lonely and culturally redundant:

> On reading Jeffrey's Letter, the first thought was naturally to *wash him away*, which could be done with unspeakable ease, I believe; but reflecting then on the man's intrinsic kindliness, also on his sufferings and even miseries some of which I have seen into, it appeared clear enough that he had been only in a sad fit of depression, whence his acetous fermentation of small beer; so I wrote him one of my friendliest Letters, and mean to be as kind to the worthy little Poet as is possible for me, let him kick against the pricks as he may. A warm loving heart, yet now when he is growing old, I question if there is on Earth one real Friend for him, only millions of Commensals and Compotators, and perhaps he feels this! Let us pity the poor white man; – and rejoice that *Dilettantism* will ere long be kicked out of Creation, in all probability for a century or two.[21]

Occasional compliments notwithstanding, Carlyle never had any faith in Jeffrey as a critic. Even when Carlyle was at his most friendly and respectful, Jeffrey was 'a good man and a bad critic'.[22] He never thought of Jeffrey the man of letters as anything other or greater than *successful* – a social distinction merely, not a personal or intellectual one.

IV

But it was more than this, more than just Jeffrey's wealth and success. The truth is that each represented – and subsequently came more and more to represent – what the other considered a prevailing cultural disease. This antipathy was no less a part of their mutual attraction, it seems, than of their mutual repulsion.

The most intransigent characterization of this impasse came later, in the *Reminiscences*, where in terms so characteristic of the culture wars of the immediate post-Napoleonic period Carlyle recalls that Jeffrey 'seemed bent on, first of all, converting me from what he called my "German Mysticism," – back merely, as I could conceive, into dead Edinburgh Whiggism, Scepticism, and Materialism'.[23]

For our purposes, it is difficult not to read the tension between these two men on the threshold of Victorian England as a Carlylean 'sign of the times'. The other side of the constitutional gaiety and lightness which Carlyle celebrated in Jeffrey during the honeymoon of their friendship – a lightness for which he found an objective correlative in Jeffrey's diminutive stature and physical sprightliness – is insubstantiality, superficiality and inconsequence. 'In conversation he is brilliant (or rather sparkling)', wrote Carlyle in his notebooks at the time: 'lively, kind, willing either to speak or listen, and above all men I have ever seen, ready and copious. On the whole exceedingly pleasant in light talk. Yet alas light, light, too light! He will talk of nothing *earnestly*.'[24] Jeffrey, on the other hand, worked away at what he saw as Carlyle's *gravitas* and self-importance, mocking and nagging:

> You may talk as long as you like about a false principle of pride or honor – and the necessity of having a right creed as to your relations with the universe – but you will never persuade anybody that the regulation of life is such a mighty laborious business as you would make it, or that it is not better to go lightly thro' it, with the first creed that comes to hand, than to spend the better part of it in an anxious verification of its articles — If you were only amusing yourself with these paradoxes, I should have no objection – but you take them so dreadfully in earnest that it vexes me – for it will neutralise half the fame, and all the use of your talents – and keep aloof from you most of the men who are fittest for your society — and so much for my renewed testimony ag[ains]t mysticism. (Jeffery to Carlyle, 4 January 1829, below, p. 34)[25]

The two of them would recur to this impasse obsessively in their dealings with each other over the years, with a good deal of acrimony and even contempt at different times.

Early on in the relationship, it seemed as if their very different tastes suited not just Jeffrey's agonistic social needs, but his editorial needs as well: 'he was to all appearance anxious that I would undertake the task of Germanizing the public', wrote Carlyle to his brother John in the middle of 1827, 'and ready even to let me do it "con amore", so I did not treat the whole Earth not yet Germanized as a "parcel of blockheads"'.[26] If Jeffrey was prepared to tolerate Carlyle's 'Germanizing', however, it was only on his own, strict terms, as Carlyle would discover in his dealings with the *Edinburgh* over the next two years, before Jeffrey resigned the editorship on becoming Dean of the Faculty of Advocates. In the vocabulary of Jeffrey's letters, 'German' and 'Germanic' remain part of a family of pejoratives – one that includes 'mysticism' and 'mystical'; 'affectation', 'jargon', 'extravagance', 'dogmatism' and 'exaggeration' – accusations repetitively and indiscriminately levelled at Carlyle from the very beginning.[27] 'Jeffrey evidently has a high opinion of me, and even seems to like me well', Carlyle wrote to his brother Alexander in September 1827, 'tho' he thinks I am a little extravagant or so; or as he calls it "too German"'.[28]

Throughout the conversations and letters that passed between them, Jeffrey hammered away at what he saw as the Carlyle's antisocial 'mysticism' and arrogant spiritual and moral elitism. Renowned for his magisterial dismissal of contemporaries like William Wordsworth, Walter Scott, John Thelwall and Thomas Moore, Jeffrey reserved a special impatience for Carlyle, with whose ideas and writings he always bordered on a kind of histrionic exasperation. For Jeffrey – and it was a truth he took every occasion to force-feed Carlyle – Carlyle's writing was too unconventional and mannered, likely to offend the very readers he was seeking to address. Jeffrey never read anything that Carlyle wrote, either as his editor or later as an interested reader, without open annoyance at its style and violent objections to its ideas. Reading Jeffrey's response to Carlyle's essay on Burns, to his history of German literature, to *Sartor Resartus*, to *The French Revolution* and to *Past and Present*, we discover that Jeffrey found Carlyle's writings variously misinformed and self-indulgent, arrogant and sometimes naive, even while never for a moment thinking them less than original and highly intelligent. Jeffrey never doubted Carlyle's genius, in other words, he just did not like anything Carlyle thought and wrote!

As it was with Carlyle's style, so was it with Carlyle the man. Jeffrey found Carlyle personally too prickly and uncompromising for the institutional positions for which the younger man sought his assistance. With the very first position for which Carlyle requested his intervention, for example, the chair of Moral Philosophy at the new University of London, Jeffrey was quick to point out the 'difficulties in the way of your appointment':

> You are, to say it in one word, a <u>Sectary</u> in taste and literature – and inspired by some of the zeal by which Sectaries are distinguished – a zeal, that is, to magnify the distinguishing doctrines of your sect, and rather to aggravate than reconcile the differences which divide them from the votaries of the Establishment – and I confess I doubt whether the patrons of the new University either <u>will</u> or <u>ought</u> to appoint such a person to such a charge. (Jeffrey to Carlyle, 6 [September] 1827, below, p. 4)

Here we confront what the letters reveal to have become, for both of them, a major issue and a major stumbling block. Jeffrey was generous even to a fault with the offers he pressed on Carlyle and with the help he gave to Carlyle's family and friends, but he was also the occasion of intense frustration in Carlyle's life over the seven years of their familiarity. Jeffrey's position in society and in the literary world held out the promise of publication and advancement that even someone as aggressively independent as Carlyle could not ignore. Whatever the state of their fluctuating personal feelings for Jeffrey, Carlyle and Jane remained constantly aware of the possible advantages accruing from a friendship with the editor of the influential *Edinburgh Review*, who in renouncing that Olympian position became, first, Dean of the Faculty of Advocates, then Lord Advocate of Scotland. It should be apparent to any reader of these letters that there were more bonds between the two men than the single one identified by Fred Kaplan of 'mutual recognition that Jeffrey must help Carlyle as best he could',[29] but Kaplan is right to stress that it *was* a bond and that it had been there from the beginning. Even if Jeffrey had not made any promises – and his letters confirm that he was generous with assurances that he would find *some* occupation or broker *some* publishing breakthrough for Carlyle, just as he was generous with offers of money – his very standing in the literary and political worlds promised the younger couple real advantages.

From this point of view, however, the Carlyles' relationship with Jeffrey was one of recurrent frustration. Reading the letters – Jeffrey's to the Carlyles and the Carlyles' to friends and family – we find ourselves time and again caught up in the project of Carlyle's career, only to be disappointed as time and again Jeffrey's mediation comes to nothing. (Jeffrey was not surprisingly far better able to help Carlyle's brother, the more sociable John, than he was to help Carlyle himself.) It was the same with the publication of Carlyle's history of German literature, and the same with the various professorial chairs that fell vacant: first at London, then at St Andrews, then at Edinburgh. A letter Carlyle wrote to Jane during his protracted stay in London in August and September of 1831, trying to interest publishers in his *Sartor Resartus* and gain preferment of some form or other, gives some insight into this frustration. Jeffrey had already held the manuscript of *Sartor* for over a week, promising to read it between what was an impossibly busy parliamentary schedule. Having missed Jeffrey one day (27 August), Carlyle 'returned' on the next:

> found the family Coach at the door, and all in the act of drawing on gloves to go out, except the Duke; with whom, after some gabblement with the others, I had the unwonted satisfaction of a private conversation – for ten minutes. The poor little dear is so hurried he cannot help it; besides he has little or nothing to *say* that were of moment. – Inquiring for Teuflk [i.e., *Sartor Resartus*] as I was privileged to do, the Critic professed that he had 'honestly read' 28 pages of it (surprising feat!) that he objected to the dilatoriness of the introductory part (as *we* both did also), and very much admired the scene of the sleeping City: farther that he would write to Murray that very day (as I gather from Empson he has since done) to appoint a meeting with him, and if possible attain some *finish* with that individual at least. He (Jeffrey) would look through the Book farther in the interim &c &c Alas! What could I do, but consent to let him have that 'other week,' tho' nigh *three* are now gone, and next to no way made, beyond ascertaining that way is highly difficult to make ... Jeffrey and

I spoke about the 'place under Government.' *Davon wird Nichts* ['Nothing will come of it']. 'All filled up'; 'applicants'; 'economical Ministry' &c &c: all which the Devil is welcome to, if he like. *Aide-toi, le ciel t'aidera* [roughly translated: 'the Lord helps them that help themselves']. I think of these things with considerable composure; at times with a certain silent ferocity.[30]

Jeffrey, to give him his due, did talk to the publisher John Murray about *Sartor Resartus* and, while expressing the grave misgivings he always expressed about Carlyle's work, did in fact gain Murray's agreement to publish. But Murray had obviously deferred too readily to Jeffrey for his own comfort and was soon seeking an excuse to absolve himself of the commitment he had made. Carlyle's desperate attempts to get the book published (it would eventually be published serially in *Fraser's Magazine* over two years later), like his various attempts to use Jeffrey to gain a salaried position, expose the tension that was never far away: 'I think of these things with considerable composure; at times with a certain silent ferocity'.

V

What mutual forbearance remained after the mortification of receiving Jeffrey's criticism of his history of German literature was severely tested by this trip of Carlyle's to London in August and September of 1831. Carlyle felt locked out. 'Of Jeffrey I may repeat that I can get little good', he wrote to Jane on 24 August, 'he really has no leisure to think of anything but his politics; so that I never get the smallest private talk with him. Indeed, how can he help me? Where, then, lies our help, Dearest? Be God thanked, with ourselves!'[31] Resentment at Jeffrey's failure to help with the important problem of a livelihood even leads to petty exploitation on the anxious couple's part: 'Throw the poor Duke a word sometimes', Carlyle writes to Jane on 29 August 1831, 'for his franks are very precious'.[32] Jeffrey's being a member of parliament meant that letters sent with his endorsement or 'frank' could be collected without payment, a not inconsiderable saving when you add up the amount of letter-writing that went on amongst the Carlyles and their family and friends. The franks again were the only benefit Carlyle could see in the relationship with Jeffrey when he wrote to Jane two days later, as his disappointment over his manuscript and his prospects expressed itself in ways that were becoming progressively more resentful:

On the whole, were it not for the franks (which *are* an immense blessing) I might as well discontinue my attendance at Jermyn Street [where the Jeffreys resided], where positively there is no good to be got, not so much as a serious word. The man is really, I suppose, very busy; farther I take his friendship for me, as I have all along done, to be perhaps three parts palabra, and one part half-sentiment, half-goodwill.[33]

Then there was the episode of the Edinburgh Observatory job. One of the final chapters in the history of their mutual 'neglect – or alienation' (Jeffrey to Jane, 28 December 1832, below, p. 126) came in early 1834 and involved, typically, yet another frustrated bid for preferment on Carlyle's part. Jeffrey's inability or disinclination to further his career seemed to Carlyle symbolized by the irritable, again exasperated response that he received from Jeffrey on 14 January 1834 to his soliciting Jeffrey's assistance with the job of Professor of Astronomy at the University of Edinburgh, which came with a post at the Edinburgh Observatory:

> It is best to tell you at once that I do not think there is the least chance of your getting the chair of astronomy, and that it would be idle to make any application – ...
>
> I am very sorry for this – but still more sorry for certain expressions of dissatisfaction in your letter – They revive and encrease the deep regret I have always felt at your not having the occupation and consequent independence of some regular profession – That of a <u>Teacher</u> is no doubt a most useful and noble one – But you cannot actually exercise it, unless you offer to teach what is thought worth learning – and in a way that is thought agreeable – and I am afraid you have not fulfilled either of those conditions – You know I do not myself set much value on the paradoxes and exaggerations in which you delight – and at all events I am quite clear that no man ever did more to obstruct the success of his doctrines by the tone in which he promulgated them – It is arrogant, vituperative – obscure – anti-national and inconclusive – likely enough to strike weak and ill conditioned fancies – but almost sure to revolt calm, candid and thinking persons – It sounds harsh to say this – but I say it as a witness – and as you begin to experience the effects, you may perhaps give more credit to my testimony than you used to do – You will never find (or make) the world friendly to your doctrines, while you insist upon dragooning it into them in so hyperbolical a manner. – (below, pp. 143–4)

Jeffrey's letter issues from a man who has been inundated with often quite arbitrary requests for preferment and representation since his assumption of the Lord Advocacy, requests that were especially annoying in the light of his own personal experience with jobbing. For years, as a young lawyer, he had been victim of the stranglehold exercised by the Scottish Tories over administrative and professional offices; now he had become the target of Whig hopefuls unashamedly pressing their claims for administrative positions and sinecures, 'left to the mercies of every county, city, parish, public body or person, who had an interest or fancy to urge'.[34] Yet he is at the same time embarrassed at the possible imputation that he is himself guilty of jobbing with his own ex-secretary, Thomas Henderson, for as Carlyle rightly inferred the Observatory job had already gone Henderson's way. There can be no doubt that Carlyle had considerable mathematical and scientific ability – we should bear in mind what Jeffrey had himself perhaps forgotten, that Carlyle had taught mathematics after leaving the university. Equally, however, there can be no doubt that Henderson's qualifications for the job were vastly superior to Carlyle's, who had not thought through either the job itself or his own experience before appealing to Jeffrey.

'On the whole', concluded Carlyle, after summarizing what he called the 'polite Fish-woman shriek' of Jeffrey's letter in a letter of his own to his brother John of 25 February 1834, Jeffrey 'makes it plain to me that in him of all men there is not the faintest shadow of help for me'.[35] Carlyle defended himself to his mother by pitying Jeffrey for his involvement in that 'Den of Discord and Dishonesty' that was the public, political world Jeffrey had chosen to inhabit.[36] It was clear the friendship was stretched to breaking point, however, and in spite of his asking for Jeffrey's help yet again in early February – this time in a second bid for the Chair of Rhetoric at Edinburgh – Carlyle let it be known that he was in no hurry to answer Jeffrey's letters.[37] It was not anger, Carlyle insisted to John – 'Why should I seem to the man to be what I am not, angry with him'[38] – but whatever it was proved insurmountable. In a letter to Jane of 21 May 1834 he formally lowered the curtain on the drama of their relationship:

> The Duke, now plain Mr Jeffrey, but soon to be Lord Jeffrey, is still here for a week: he had left his address for me with Mrs Austin; I determined to call some morning in passing, and did it on Monday. Reception anxiously cordial from all three; hurried insignificant talk from him still at the breakfast table; kindness playing over 'iron gravity' from me. I felt it to be a farewell visit, and that it should be 'hallowed in our choicest mood.' The poor Duke was so tremulous, he bade me 'good *evening*' at the door; immense *jerking* from Mrs Jeffrey, yet many kind words, and invitations back; silent smiling *Unbedeutendheit* [trifles] from Miss, who is grown no beauty, but a numb *blowse* [fat-faced girl], with, I think, a large shelf-underlip. And so ends our dealing with bright Jeffreydom; once so sparkling cheerful, now gone out into darkness.[39]

VI

If, for Jeffrey, Carlyle's fault from the beginning was a German extravagance, for Carlyle, Jeffrey, too, even in the early days, had a fatal flaw – he was too French, too eighteenth-century:

> There was something of Voltaire in him; something even in bodily features: those bright-beaming, swift and piercing hazel-eyes, with their accompaniment of rapid, keen expressions in the other lineaments of face, resembled one's notion of Voltaire; and in the voice too there was a fine, half-*plangent*, kind of metallic ringing tone, which used to remind me of what I fancied Voltaire's voice might have been: '*voix sombre et majesteuse*,' Duvernet calls it ... You could not define Jeffrey to be more than a potential Voltaire; say '*Scotch* Voltaire'.[40]

This might seem unexceptionable enough, but we should be careful not to allow the haze of memory and sentiment to mask the deep antipathy that Carlyle felt for the Enlightenment and all its ways. 'The Eighteenth Century, it is well known, does not figure to me as a lovely one', says Carlyle at the very opening of his massive *History of Frederick the Great* (1858–65). The comparison of Jeffrey with Voltaire was patronizing and, ultimately, dismissive. 'The Eighteenth', after all, 'was a *Sceptical* Century',[41] and Voltaire 'the paragon and epitome of a whole spiritual period', with 'his inborn levity of nature, his entire want of Earnestness. Voltaire was by birth a Mocker, and light *Pococurante*'. Again, Voltaire 'is no great Man, but only a great *Persifleur*; a man for whom life, and all that pertains to it, has, at best, but a despicable meaning; who meets its difficulties not with earnest force, but with gay agility'.[42]

The *'spiritual paralysis'* represented by the eighteenth century[43] would become more and more central to Carlyle's idiosyncratic historiography during the years after he first met Jeffrey:

> That the last century was a period of Denial, of Irreligion, and Destruction; to which a new period of Affirmation, of Religion, must succeed, if Society is to be reconstituted, or even to continue in existence: this with its thousand corollaries is a proposition for which the thinking minds of all nations are prepared.[44]

> In France or England, since the days of Diderot and Hume, though all thought has been of a sceptico-metaphysical texture, so far as there was any Thought, we have seen no Metaphysics; but only more or less ineffectual questionings whether such could be. In the Pyrronhism of Hume and the Materialism of Diderot, Logic had, as it were, overshot itself, overset itself.[45]

Again and again, Carlyle adverts to the blight cast over European cultural and intellectual enterprise by the ideas and ethos of an overlong eighteenth century, of which Jeffrey and the Edinburgh Whigs, Sceptics and Materialists of his own age were an extension. Though sanguine enough to believe the blight 'now almost passed away',[46] Carlyle nonetheless saw himself as duty-bound to diagnose and remedy it. All his major articles and books, if they are not actually set in the eighteenth century – 'Burns', 'Voltaire', 'Boswell's Life of Johnson', 'Diderot', *The French Revolution, Frederick the Great* – return at some stage to vilify the intellectual life of the period and to urge (or celebrate) Europe's recovery from it: the many studies of German literature, for example, 'Characteristics', *Sartor Resartus* and *On Heroes, Hero-Worship, and the Heroic in History*.

At one stage, Jane Welsh Carlyle attributed the breakdown of Jeffrey and the Carlyles' relationship in 1834 to Jeffrey's having taken offence at an article Carlyle had written on Diderot and published in the *Foreign Quarterly Review* in 1833.[47] In the article, Carlyle welcomes the collected works of Diderot as 'the Acts and the Epistles of the Parisian Church of Antichrist'; 'the Antichristian Canon'.[48] Years before Matthew Arnold willed poetry to supersede religion, Carlyle was complaining that 'The History of Literature, especially for the last two centuries, is our proper Church History; the other Church, during that time, having more and more decayed from its old functions and influence, and ceased to have a history'. This inversion of values he traces to (amongst other things) 'the unutterable confusion worst confounded of our present Periodical existence; when, among other phenomena, a young Fourth Estate (whom all the three elder may try if they can hold) is seen sprawling and staggering tumultuously through the world'.[49] Later in the article, the reference to Jeffrey and his 'dead Edinburgh Whiggism, Scepticism, and Materialism' is, as Jane suspected, unequivocal:

> With great expenditure of words and froth, in arguments as waste, wild-weltering, delirious-dismal as the chaos they would demonstrate; which arguments one now knows not whether to laugh at or to weep at, and almost does both, – have Diderot and his sect perhaps made this apparent to all who examine it: That in the French System of Thought (called also the Scotch, and still familiar enough everywhere, which for want of a better title we have named the Mechanical), there is no room for Divinity; that to him, for whom *intellect*, or the power of knowing and believing, is still synonymous with *logic*, or the mere power of arranging and communicating, there is absolutely no proof discoverable of a Divinity ... For so wonderful a self-swallowing product of the Spirit of the Time, could any result to arrive at be fitter than this of the ETERNAL NO?[50]

If Jeffrey had been inclined to take offence at Carlyle's association of the Scottish with 'the French System of Thought', however, as Jane thought he had, he would have done so much, much earlier than 1833. The 1828 essay by Carlyle on Burns that Jeffrey had edited for the *Edinburgh*, for example, had been an implicit refutation of Jeffrey's own controversial article on Burns of 1809, in which he had criticized Burns's 'admiration of thoughtlessness, oddity, and vehement sensibility' and the 'pitiful cant of careless feeling and eccentric genius'.[51] Carlyle's Burns, on the contrary, was a Carlylean hero and martyr to the soulless rationalism of his Gallicized compatriots:

> It is curious to remark that Scotland [in the eighteenth century], so full of writers, had no Scottish culture, nor indeed any English; our culture was almost exclusively French. It was by studying Racine and Voltaire, Batteux and Boileau, that Kames had trained himself to be a critic and philosopher; it was the light of Montesquieu and Mably that guided Robertson in his political speculations; Quesnay's lamp that kindled the lamp of Adam Smith ...
>
> The heart, not of a mere hot-blooded Verse-monger, or poetical *Restaurateur*, but of a true Poet and Singer, worthy of the old religious heroic times, had been given him [Burns]: and he fell in an age, not of heroism and religion, but of scepticism, selfishness and triviality, when true Nobleness was little understood, and its place supplied by a hollow, dissocial, altogether barren and unfruitful principle of Pride.[52]

Again, in an essay on Novalis for the *Foreign Review* of 1829, Carlyle confirms that 'the plummet of French or Scotch Logic, excellent, nay indispensable as it is for surveying all coasts and harbours, will absolutely not sound the deep-seas of human Inquiry'.[53]

It is perhaps not surprising that Jeffrey's social and literary conservatism made reading Carlyle's *Sartor Resartus* difficult, not to say impossible for him. If he persevered, however, he would have heard from the voice of Diogenes Teufelsdröckh, Carlyle's serio-comic German professor of everything-in-general, an early, sustained attack on himself and the other Whig lawyers and reformists who were the children of the Scottish Enlightenment. Just as what Jeffrey represented in the intellectual and social scheme of things was the butt of so much of Carlyle's early polemic, so was it the butt of Carlyle's apocalyptic satire:

> Thou wilt have no Mystery and Mysticism; wilt walk through thy world by the sunshine of what thou callest Truth, or even by the Handlamp of what I call Attorney Logic; and 'explain' all, 'account' for all, or believe nothing of it? Nay, thou wilt attempt laughter; whoso recognises the unfathomable, all-pervading domain of Mystery, which is everywhere under our feet and among our hands; to whom the Universe is an Oracle and Temple, as well as a Kitchen and Cattle-stall, – he shall be a (delirious) Mystic; to him thou, with sniffing charity, wilt protrusively proffer thy Handlamp, and shriek, as one injured, when he puts his foot through it? – *Armer Teufel!* ['poor Devil!'] Doth not thy Cow calve, doth not thy Bull gender? Thou thyself, wert thou not Born, wilt thou not Die? 'Explain' me all this, or do one of two things: Retire into private places with thy foolish cackle; or, what were better, give it up, and weep, not that the reign of wonder is done, and God's world all disembellished and prosaic, but that thou hitherto art a Dilettante and sandblind Pedant.[54]

'What's the use of virtue?', Jeffrey's close friend Sydney Smith had aped him, rhetorically, in a letter written some years earlier: 'What's the use of wealth? What's a guinea but a damned yellow circle? What's a chamber pot but an infernal yellow sphere? The whole effort of your mind is to destroy.'[55] It was not, as it happens, and Jeffrey was, if anything, too scrupulous about the uses of virtue. But Jeffrey was, indeed, sceptical, consciously resisting that 'reign of Wonder' and admiration that the Romantics would restore to our apprehension of the world. He had no faith in Carlyle's gods and heroes and little faith in faith itself.

VII

What Carlyle identified as Jeffrey's eighteenth-century scepticism and philosophical materialism certainly had its ideological dimension. 'Yet is his path not my path; nor are his thoughts my thoughts: it becomes more and more clear to me that we shall never do any good together', Carlyle wrote to Jane on 11 September 1831, 'frivolous Gigmanity *cannot* unite itself to our stern destiny.'[56] 'Gigmanity' or 'Gigmen' were the philistines in the Carlyles' special vocabulary: everything that was narrow and utilitarian, and thus unimaginative, in the modern Mechanical Age. As Jeffrey, in his role as Lord Advocate of Scotland, struggled with the Scottish counterpart of the Great Reform Bill, he became for Carlyle the dead Edinburgh Whig again, an exemplar (with Jeremy Bentham and Henry Brougham) of sterile rational reformism. 'His environment here is as stupid fully as it was in Edin*r*', Carlyle wrote to Jane after catching up with Jeffrey in London: '*trivialitas trivialitatum, omnia trivialitas*!'[57] Carlyle is Ecclesiastes looking down on the unregenerate, as Carlyle would impersonate Ecclesiastes again throughout *Sartor Resartus*.

For Carlyle, the surest sign of Jeffrey's spiritual unregeneracy was his determination to take an active part in contemporary political events – in short, his public ambition. Convinced that Jeffrey's political career had taken off at a time when he was no longer capable of sustaining the pressure, let alone of rising to it, Carlyle's comments on Jeffrey's elevation to the Lord Advocacy in November 1830 were essentially those of the later *Reminiscences*: 'In the *House*, I doubt he will NOT prosper, his health is too weak, and even his voice'.[58] This had nothing to do with Jeffrey's personal integrity, as it happens; two months later Carlyle could still refer to him as 'the *worthiest* public man in all broad Scotland'.[59] But none of the occasional comments passed on Jeffrey's integrity meant that Carlyle actually *approved* of the Advocate's politics, or of politics as it was then being practised in Britain. Quite the reverse. Carlyle, to quote Ian Campbell, 'saw less and less hope for the country, as it approached the convulsion of the reform movement of the early 1830s'.[60]

Turning from their intellectual allegiances to their respective cultural and political visions, in other words, we are confronted yet again by that very real incompatibility or impasse that is always liable to manifest itself in their dealings with each other. As Carlyle's political and historical vision began to take clearer shape over the early years of the 1830s, so, too, he became alienated from Jeffrey and from all that Jeffrey represented:

> And what are your whigs and Lord Advocates, and Lord Chancellors, and the whole host of unspeakably gabbling Parliamenteers and Pulpiteers and Pamphleteers; – if a man suspect that 'there is fire enough in his belly to burn up' the entire creation of such! These all build on Mechanism: one spark of Dynamism; of Inspiration, were it in the poorest soul, is stronger than they all. As for the whig Ministry, with whom Jeffrey might appear to connect me, I partly see two things: first that they will have nothing in any shape to do with me, did I show them the virtue of a Paul, nay the more virtue the less chance, for virtue is Freewill to choose the Good, not Tool-usefulness to forge at the Expedient: secondly that they, the Whigs, except perhaps Brougham and his Implements, will not endure.[61]

Not only was Jeffrey as Lord Advocate directly responsible for the Scottish counterpart of the famous Reform Bill of June 1832, but in its totality the reform movement and the Bill that consummated it might be said to have symbolized Jeffrey's whole political and editorial career.[62] Carlyle certainly thought so when in his *Reminiscences* he accused Jeffrey and the *Edinburgh* of having accelerated the development of a blind democracy. The older, more conservative Carlyle looked back on nearly seventy years of the nineteenth century to identify in the periodical editor and reforming politician a symptom and a cause of the democratic levelling that threatened the spiritual hierarchies he felt called upon to defend. In Carlyle's ageing, apocalyptic vision, Jeffrey was Carlyle's own 'antitype' (to use Rosemary Ashton's word),[63] if not the anti-Christ itself:

> Jeffrey was perhaps at the height of his reputation about 1816; his *Edinburgh Review* a kind of Delphic Oracle, and Voice of the Inspired, for great majorities of what is called the 'Intelligent Public'; and himself regarded universally as a man of consummate penetration, and the *facile princeps* in the departments he had chosen to cultivate and practice. In the half-century that has followed, what a change in all this ... Jeffrey was by no means the Supreme in Criticism or in anything else; but it is certain that there has no Critic appeared among us since who was worth naming beside him – and his influence, for good and for evil, in Literature and otherwise, has been very great. 'Democracy,' the gradual uprise, and rule in all things, of roaring, million-headed, unreflecting, darkly suffering, darkly sinning 'Demos,' came to call its old superiors to account, at its maddest of tribunals: nothing in my time has so forwarded all this as Jeffrey and his once famous Edinburgh Review.[64]

But we have already seen that the lineaments of this portrait of Jeffrey as a sceptic and a leveller were there from the beginning. Carlyle's version of early nineteenth-century history was the product of a long-standing antagonism between the two friends – of his distrust of, not to say contempt for, Jeffrey's worldliness and Whiggism. Jeffrey's political career enforced the realization of an unlikeness that became harder and harder for Carlyle to ignore. It was to his brother John that he complained early in 1831 of 'the whole host of unspeakably gabbling Parliamenteers and Pulpiteers and Pamphleteers' in the political London of the early 1830s. It was to John, again, that he wrote late in 1832 with all the freedom of having one month earlier discharged a long-standing debt to Jeffrey:

> The Advocate acknowledges his debt cleared: it is the only thing we have heard of him for a great while. I imagine, our relation is a good deal cooled; and may now be visibly to him, as it has long been visibly to me, a rather fruitless one. His world is not our world: he dwells in the glitter of saloon chandeliers, walking in the 'vain show' of Parliamenteering and Gigmanity, which also he feels to be vain; we in the whirlwind and wild-piping Battle of Fate, which nevertheless, by God's grace, we feel to be not vain and a show, but true and a reality. Thus may each, without disadvantage, go his several way. If Jeffrey's well-being ever lay within my reach, how gladly would I increase it! But I hope better things for him; tho' he is evidently declining in the world's grace, and knows as well as the world that his Political career has proved a nonentity. Often have I lamented to think that so genial a nature had been (by the *Zeitgeist*, who works such misery) turned into that frosty unfruitful course ... So there we leave it, –[65]

What Carlyle confided to his journal on 16 May 1832, therefore, with the passage of the Reform Bill imminent, gives as clear an indication as any of the gulf between the two:

> The only reform is in thyself. Know this O Politician, and be moderately political.
>
> For me, I have never yet done one political act; not so much as the signing of a petition. My case is this. I comport myself wholly like an alien; like a man who is not in his own country; whose own country lies perhaps a century or two distant.[66]

Jeffrey, in his turn, had his own impatience with the Carlyles' (anti-)politics, as with Carlyle's writing and cultural vision more generally – the impatience of the political pragmatist slaving away at what he was convinced, in spite of all the sorry compromises required by due process, offered a blueprint for a better future: 'you profess to take no interest in politics! – and to think it a fit thing for a man with a head and heart, to occupy them about the conditioned and the "unconditioned" and such gibberish – O fie! – Your brothers['] blood cries up from the earth ag[ains]t such idleness' (Jeffrey to Carlyle, 1 August 1830, below, p. 62).

VIII

The relationship between Francis Jeffrey and Thomas and Jane Welsh Carlyle did not finally collapse until 1834, though it almost certainly would have collapsed earlier had not Jeffrey's commitment to it forced a continuation. It is clear that the relationship was becoming more one-sided and that even Jeffrey was less earnestly attentive, his letters fewer, and not just because of his official duties. The relationship was revived again three years later in 1837 by Carlyle's sending Jeffrey a copy of his recently-published *The French Revolution*. As a friendship, however, it could hardly be expected to have recovered its original intensity. The last letter that Jeffrey wrote to the Carlyles – and presumably theirs to him – was within months of his death, but after a major illness suffered in 1841 Jeffrey seemed to the Carlyles quickly to become an old man: frail, anxious and overly emotional. Still, David Alec Wilson is right to remind us that they 'never quarrelled or missed a chance of coming together as long as Jeffrey lived', and that even 'strangers who happened to witness their reunions used to remark how much they liked each other'.[67]

A letter that Jeffrey wrote to his friend and fellow *Edinburgh* reviewer Henry Brougham in 1837 captures something of Jeffrey's excitement at the revival of the friendship, and thus of the genuine affection he had always harboured for Carlyle and the genuine concern he felt for Carlyle's deserved success, even while it betrays the deeper incompatibility that would always frustrate them:

My Dear Chancellor – If you have seen that strange, but most original book, which my antient friend Carlyle has put forth on the French revolution, you will, I am sure, forgive me for smuggling a few congratulatory and admonitory lines to him, under your cover. He is half crazy, and intractable – but is a man of Genius – and I wish you could look at his book – and mention it, to any good judges – who may have more leisure than you – and half as much indulgence – Your friend H[enry]. Taylor knows about him – and I am sure will countersign my certificate – He has a very nice enthusiastic wife too – who will be unspeakably gratified by any success of his – and whom I should be delighted to gratify – There! – the murder is out – and you may do your pleasure.[68]

IX

'The murder is out' – between we two predatory males, that is. Brougham is being led to believe that Jeffrey's real motive in promoting Carlyle's book is to ingratiate himself with Carlyle's wife. It was not, but it does remind me that up to this point I have talked exclusively of the ideas and needs of the two men. Yet the reader will notice that, as the years go by, Jeffrey in his letters turns more and more directly to Jane, until the bulk of them are written exclusively to her. If Jeffrey and Carlyle's relationship was frustrating to them and in some ways puzzling to us, on the face of it at least Jeffrey's relationship with Jane Welsh Carlyle is even more difficult to characterize. That there was a good deal of gallantry on Jeffrey's part – as there was in his attitude to women generally – and a good deal of flirtation on both their parts is apparent as soon as she ceases to be 'Mrs Carlyle' and becomes 'Jane' and 'Jeanie'. And this is indeed exceptionally early on in their relationship, especially when one considers contemporary conventions and the fact that the wives of many of Jeffrey's intimate friends amongst his contemporaries remained 'Mrs' all their lives. Here the age difference explains a great deal – that and the imputed family relationship between them (that vague and capacious relation of 'cousin'), though it is just as likely that the relationship was 'discovered' to excuse the impulse to familiarity. Jeffrey emphasized the age difference and 'Jeanie' or 'coz' soon becomes 'My Dear Child'. Here Jane was at the double disadvantage of being both younger and female (Carlyle is only occasionally patronized in this way). Indeed, it is interesting to note that Jane's later understanding of the termination of her and Jeffrey's relationship in the mid-1830s was her decisive renunciation of his projection of her as infantile. 'Since Jeffrey was pleased to compliment me on my "bits of convictions"', she wrote to Carlyle on 10 August 1845, 'I have not had my '*rights of WOMAN*' so trifled with!' – as she had recently by Carlyle himself, that is. '*He* payed the penalty of his assurance in losing from that time forward my valuable correspondence', she concludes.[69]

There is, however, no reason to doubt that Jane and Jeffrey had shared a familiarity and a confidence that amounted to more than his talking down to her. Much of it was play, at times even adolescent and in Jeffrey's case obsessive, as in his constantly and fetishistically recurring to the picture of Jane given to him by her mother (to be returned in 1834 after they had fallen out). In November 1833, even after a year of only very occasional correspondence, Jane herself had a picture of Jeffrey framed which she had had in her possession for four years.[70] But the peculiar mixture of amorousness, paternalism and sibling familiarity in Jeffrey satisfied obvious needs and Jane found Jeffrey's attentions no less flattering than cloying. Reading so focused a collection of letters as these it is always well to remember that, like all literate people of their day only more so, the two of them conducted an extensive correspondence and played other games with other friends and relatives. And Jeffrey's gallantry, as I said, was notorious, and might have been scandalous had it not been laughable. One letter will serve, written from London by the seventy-year-old Judge in the Court of Session to his friend Henry Cockburn on 26 March 1843. In it, Jeffrey records a round of 'sexual' successes on the previous day:

> I called on my friends the Cayleys (and kissed the 3 daughters); then Lady T. Lister (whom I kissed also); then to the Carlyles, whom I did not find; then to Lady Hollands, and to Macaulays, and Lord Melbourne's. – Dined at the Monteagles with the Aubrey de Vere's; my excellent friend Stephens, Millman, John Mills and the Bishop of Norwich, whom I carried down in a cab to the Berry's, where I kissed both them and Lady C. Landseer, in the midst of an admiring crowd ... And so, after breakfasting with Macaulay, and making him read a bit of his History, I went up to Lockharts to see Lady Gifford (kissed her and her daughter) & called on Dickens.[71]

There can be no doubt that, had Jane been at home, she too would have received her quota of kisses, though in the context it is hardly flattering.

Still, there is occasionally about Jeffrey's letters to Jane a confidence and an emotional abandon that is unique in his correspondence, even in one committed to his friendships as Jeffrey was and more and more given to emotional abandonment. One finds in Jeffrey's correspondence with both the Carlyles, but especially with Jane, an uncharacteristic narrowness of reference. Many of the letters are almost exclusively personal, often trivially so, in their banter and description. 'Jeffrey writes faithfully and fully', Jane wrote to Eliza Stodart on 16 January 1831, 'but his local information never passes the garden-walls of Craig-crook'.[72] This was in part because what for Jeffrey were the most immediately accessible topics, especially throughout the early 1830s – the people and incidents and issues of his political life – were of no interest to either of the Carlyles. News about these found its way into most of the other letters Jeffrey wrote, not least into the almost daily diary he maintained in his correspondence with Cockburn. But the main reason was that Jeffrey rather enjoyed – indeed, part of him shared

– the Carlyles' indifference to his own power and fame, in spite of his occasionally chiding them for it. Just as he took vicarious pleasure in their retreat from public life, so he used his relationship with Jane as an escape from this world. There were times when he tried to make an everywhere out of the little room of his correspondence with Jane.

Whether there was ever anything more between them than that, however, is doubtful. As blind as he so often was to Jane's emotional needs, Carlyle does get this one right in his *Reminiscences*:

> He was much taken with my little Jeannie, as he well might be; one of the brightest and cleverest creatures in the whole world; full of innocent rustic simplicity and veracity, yet with the gracefullest discernment, calmly natural deportment; instinct with beauty and intelligence to the finger-ends! He became, in a sort, her would-be openly declared friend and quasi-lover; as was his way in such cases. He had much the habit of flirting about with women, especially pretty women, much more the both pretty and clever; all in a weakish, mostly dramatic, and wholly theoretic way ... I believe he really entertained a sincere regard and affection for her, in the heart of his theoretic dangling, which later continued unabated for several years to come, – with not a little quizzing and light interest on her part, and without shadow of offence on mine, or anybody else's.[73]

Neither is there any reason to doubt Jeffrey's love for his wife, Charlotte, or the integrity of the nuclear family that Cockburn went out of his way to protect. On this, Cockburn himself should have the last word:

> In 1813 Love performed his greatest feat in making this loather of deep water cross the Atlantic, in order to marry Charlotte, one of the daughters of Charles Wilkes, banker in New York, an Englishman, nephew to the famous John. There has been one child, a daughter, of this marriage; who, with her mother, has accompanied Jeffrey everywhere he has gone. The three are inseparable.[74]

So they were in 1835 when Cockburn wrote this and so they remained. The man whose own childhood family had been devastated by the loss of a loving mother when he was thirteen, and who in the space of three years (1802–5) had lost a first child, his closest sister Mary, and his first wife Catherine (née Wilson), clung more closely to his immediate family than any other public man amongst his contemporaries. Indeed, the reason why none of the letters from Thomas and Jane Welsh Carlyle to Francis Jeffrey has survived to complete this correspondence is that they were sacrificed to the closeness of this family. Jeffrey's daughter Charlotte, who in 1838 had married the lecturer, later editor of the *Edinburgh Review*, William Empson, destroyed them after J. A. Froude's controversial publication of Carlyle's *Reminiscences*, which had publicized her mother's nervous twitching and her own physical unattractiveness and social awkwardness.

X

Both family and friendship were quite literally *vital* to Jeffrey ('the life of our life'), who could write to Carlyle in all honesty that, in spite of his own wealth and success, he had

> never placed them in competition with the indulgence of the kind affections – I have never ceased to hold that the true treasure of existence was love – I have never wavered in that faith – never, for many minutes, been unconscious of its sustaining and redeeming power – I feel therefore in my inmost heart that I can never have enough of love – and that the best of all gifts is given me when pure and thoughtful hearts are resolutely willing to ally themselves with mine (26 September 1830, below, p. 69).

Carlyle may well have had this letter in mind when he wrote to Leigh Hunt in May 1833 that, though personally alienated from Jeffrey, he could still assure Hunt of a fair hearing:

> Jeffrey has not written to me for many months: indeed till two weeks ago I was in his debt in that point. Whatever you may have written to him, I do not think he will in the long run misunderstand it, still less take it ill. He affects indeed the philosophy of a man of the world, and has no settled *creed* of any higher sort: but there is a perpetual noble contradiction to it in that poetical heart of his. He loves all men, and especially loves the love of all men.[75]

Jeffrey was familiar and sociable by disposition, as well as by philosophical and political conviction (it is worth reminding ourselves of the importance of sociability in the long running 'science of man' of the Scottish Enlightenment). The consolation and resolution offered by ordinary, familiar affections – distinguished here from the passions and imagination of the gifted – more and more became central to his life and thought, as scepticism about religious and cultural enthusiasms was central to his philosophy, and toleration of religious and cultural differences central to his politics. Often enough, especially in the later years (and this is borne out by the letters that follow), it is impossible to distinguish this faith in the ordinary human affections from rank sentimentality. If the novels of that other distinguished friend of his old age, Charles Dickens, had not come along, Francis Jeffrey might have had to invent them.

Notes:

1   Sources for the information contained in this introduction and in the footnotes to the text of Jeffrey's letters are identified in the List of Abbreviations. I am especially indebted to the editorial material in *Carlyle Letters*.
2   *Peter's Letters to His Kinsfolk*, 3 vols (Edinburgh: Blackwood, 1819), vol. 1, p. 52.
3   For Constable's accounts, see NLS, MS 672, ff. 98–9.
4   *Carlyle Letters*, vol. 4, p. 190.

5   *Reminiscences*, p. 360.

6   *Carlyle Letters*, vol. 2, pp. 245–6.

7   *Carlyle Letters*, vol. 4, p. 282.

8   *Reminiscences*, pp. 362–3.

9   *Reminiscences*, p. 363.

10 *Carlyle Letters*, vol. 4, p. 305.

11 *Carlyle Letters*, vol. 4, p. 341.

12 *Reminiscences*, p. 360.

13 The letters referred to here do not include any directly from the Carlyles to Jeffrey, proba-
    bly destroyed by Jeffrey's daughter Charlotte in a fit of pique at Carlyle's characterization
    of her in his *Reminiscences*. Fortunately, Carlyle's and Jane's copious correspondence with
    family and other friends – and, at times, with each other – enables us to recover their
    responses to Jeffrey's letters and to the issues they raise.

14 *Carlyle Letters*, vol. 4, p. 399.

15 *Carlyle Letters*, vol. 4, p. 222.

16 *Carlyle Letters*, vol. 4, p. 282.

17 *Reminiscences*, p. 370.

18 *Carlyle Letters*, vol. 4, p. 305.

19 I. Campbell, *Thomas Carlyle*, rev. edn (Edinburgh: Saltire Society, 1993), p. 70. Com-
    pare *Reminiscences*, p. 365.

20 *Carlyle Letters*, vol. 5, pp. 167, 185.

21 *Carlyle Letters*, vol. 5, p. 190.

22 Carlyle to Goethe, 22 January 1831, *Carlyle Letters*, vol. 5, p. 222.

23 *Reminiscences*, p. 362.

24 *Two Note Books of Thomas Carlyle, from 23d March 1822 to 16th May 1832*, ed. C. E.
    Norton (1898; Mamaroneck, NY: Paul A. Appel, 1972), pp. 174–5.

25 Cf. Carlyle in his *Reminiscences*: 'we had ... more than ever a series of sharp fencing, night
    after night; which could decide nothing for either of us, except our radical incompatibility in
    respect of World-Theory, and the incurable divergence of our opinions on the most impor-
    tant matters. "You are so dreadfully in earnest!" he said to me, once or oftener' (p. 369).

26 *Carlyle Letters*, vol. 4, pp. 228–9.

27 All Jeffrey's early letters to Carlyle will be seen to bear this out, but see, for example, Jef-
    frey's letter of 23 September 1828 below, p. 21, defending his editorial 'retrenchments' to
    Carlyle's article on the poet Robert Burns.

28 *Carlyle Letters*, vol. 4, p. 256.

29 F. Kaplan, *Thomas Carlyle: A Biography* (Ithaca, NY: Cornell University Press, 1983), p.
    129.

30 *Carlyle Letters*, vol. 5, pp. 376–7.

31 *Carlyle Letters*, vol. 5, pp. 363–4.

32 *Carlyle Letters*, vol. 5, p. 380.

33 *Carlyle Letters*, vol. 5, p. 382.

34 *Life of Jeffrey*, vol. 1, p. 355.

35 *Carlyle Letters*, vol. 7, pp. 78, 103.

36 28 January 1834, *Carlyle Letters*, vol. 7, pp. 85–6.

37 See, for example, Carlyle to his mother, 11 February 1834; to his brother Alexander,
    18 February 1834; to his brother John, 25 February 1834, *Carlyle Letters*, vol. 7, pp.
    95, 98, 103.

38 *Carlyle Letters*, vol. 7, p. 165.

39   *Carlyle Letters*, vol. 7, pp. 176–7.

40   *Reminiscences*, p. 383.

41   T. Carlyle, *On Heroes, Hero-Worship, and the Heroic in History*, ed. M. Engel, M. K. Goldberg and J. J. Brattin, The Norman and Charlotte Strouse Edition of the Writings of Thomas Carlyle, 1 (Berkeley, CA: University of California Press, 1993), p. 147.

42   Carlyle, 'Voltaire', in T. Carlyle, *Critical and Miscellaneous Essays*, 4 vols (London: Chapman and Hall, 1857), vol. 2, pp. 1–56, on pp. 5, 18, 22–3.

43   Carlyle, *On Heroes*, p. 147.

44   Carlyle to [Gustave] d'Eichthal, 9 August 1830, *Carlyle Letters*, vol. 5, p. 136.

45   Carlyle, 'Characteristics', in *Critical and Miscellaneous Essays*, vol. 3, pp. 1–33, on p. 31.

46   Carlyle, 'Voltaire', in *Critical and Miscellaneous Essays*, vol. 2, p. 5.

47   *Carlyle Letters*, vol. 7, p. 42.

48   Carlyle, 'Diderot', in *Critical and Miscellaneous Essays*, vol. 3, pp. 189–242, on p. 189.

49   Carlyle, 'Diderot', in *Critical and Miscellaneous Essays*, vol. 3, pp. 207–8. The essay in which Matthew Arnold foresees the supersession of religion by poetry is entitled 'The Study of Poetry'.

50   Carlyle, 'Diderot', in *Critical and Miscellaneous Essays*, vol. 3, pp. 229–30. Compare the 'ETERNAL NO' here with 'The Everlasting No' of his satirical credo, *Sartor Resartus* (see T. Carlyle, *Sartor Resartus: The Life and Opinions of Herr Teufelsdröckh in Three Books*, ed. M. Engel and R. L. Tarr, The Norman and Charlotte Strouse Edition of the Writings of Thomas Carlyle, 2 (Berkeley, CA: University of California Press, 2000), Book II, ch. VII).

51   Jeffrey, review of Cromek's *Reliques of Robert Burns*, *ER*, 13:36 (January 1809), pp. 249–76, on pp. 253–4.

52   Carlyle, 'Burns', in *Critical and Miscellaneous Essays*, vol. 1, pp. 195–240, on pp. 218, 235.

53   Carlyle, 'Novalis', in *Critical and Miscellaneous Essays*, vol. 2, pp. 57–97, on p. 97.

54   *Sartor Resartus*, p. 53.

55   *The Letters of Sydney Smith*, ed. N. C. Smith, 2 vols (Oxford: Clarendon Press, 1953), vol. 1, pp. 95–6.

56   *Carlyle Letters*, vol. 5, p. 417.

57   *Carlyle Letters*, vol. 5, p. 429.

58   *Carlyle Letters*, vol. 5, p. 203.

59   *Carlyle Letters*, vol. 5, p. 217.

60   Campbell, *Thomas Carlyle*, p. 71.

61   Carlyle to his brother John, 4 March 1831, *Carlyle Letters*, vol. 5, p. 244.

62   See B. Fontana, *Rethinking the Politics of Commercial Society: The Edinburgh Review 1802–1832* (Cambridge: Cambridge University Press, 1985), *passim*.

63   R. Ashton, *Thomas and Jane Carlyle: Portrait of a Marriage* (London: Pimlico, 2003), p. 79.

64   *Reminiscences*, p. 382.

65   *Carlyle Letters*, vol. 6, p. 246.

66   *Two Note Books of Thomas Carlyle*, pp. 274–5.

67   D. A. Wilson, *Carlyle*, 6 vols (London: Kegan Paul et al.; New York: E. P. Dutton, 1923–34), vol. 2: *Carlyle to 'The French Revolution' (1826–37)* (1924), p. 355.

68   NLS, MS 1809, ff. 102–3.

69   *Carlyle Letters*, vol. 19, p. 137.

70   *Carlyle Letters*, vol. 7, p. 35.

71 NLS, Adv. MSS 9.1.11, ff. 41–2. *All* the kisses, incidentally, have been removed from Cockburn's transcription of this letter in his *Life of Lord Jeffrey*, vol. 2, pp. 379–80.
72 *Carlyle Letters*, vol. 5, p. 208.
73 *Reminiscences*, pp. 360–1.
74 NLS Adv. MSS 9.1.8, f. 2.
75 *Carlyle Letters*, vol. 6, p. 375.

CHRONOLOGY

Year	Francis Jeffery	Thomas and Jane Welsh Carlyle	General
1773	FJ born (23 October) in Edinburgh.		Walter Scott 2 years old; William Wordsworth 3 years old.
1776			American Declaration of Independence.
1781	FJ attends Edinburgh High School (to 1787).		
1786	FJ's mother dies suddenly.		
1787	FJ attends University of Glasgow (to 1789).		
1788			George Gordon (Lord Byron) born.
1789	FJ studies law at University of Edinburgh (to 1790).		Fall of the Bastille initiates French Revolution.
1791	FJ to Queen's College, Oxford (to 1792).		
1792	FJ studies law at Edinburgh again (to 1793).		
1793	FJ attends trial of Thomas Muir, transported for sedition.		Louis XVI of France executed; England and France declare war.
1794	FJ admitted to practise at Scottish bar.		Robespierre executed.
1795		TC born (4 December) in Ecclefechan.	'Gagging Acts' passed in parliament to limit freedom of association and speech.
1796	FJ absents himself from meeting of Faculty of Advocates which votes to deprive Henry Erskine of deanship.		Britain threatened with invasion.
1797		TC's brother Alexander born.	

Year	Francis Jeffery	Thomas and Jane Welsh Carlyle	General
1798	FJ walking tour through Cumberland and Wales.		Irish uprising; Napoleon invades Egypt; Wordsworth and Coleridge publish *Lyrical Ballads*.
1799			Napoleon becomes First Consul of France.
1800	FJ attends lecture course on chemistry.		Union of Great Britain and Ireland.
1801	FJ marries Catherine (Kitty) Wilson; contemplates applying for chair of History at Edinburgh.	TC's brother John born; JWC born Jane Baillie Welsh (14 July) in Haddington.	Prime Minister William Pitt resigns; Addington ministry begins.
1802	Foundation of *Edinburgh Review*; FJ's son born and dies next month.		Peace of Amiens (with France); Napoleon becomes Consul for life; French army invades Switzerland.
1803	FJ becomes editor of *ER*.		Britain declares war on France.
1804	FJ's sister Mary dies.		Code Napoléon; Pitt's second ministry.
1805	FJ's wife Catherine dies.		Battle of Trafalgar; Henry Dundas (Lord Melville) forced to resign.
1806	FJ duels with Thomas Moore.	TC attends Annan Academy (to 1809).	Pitt dies; Ministry of All the Talents formed; Charles James Fox dies.
1807			Slave trade abolished; war of the Iberian peninsula begins.
1808	FJ and Henry Brougham's 'Don Pedro Cevallos' article published in *ER* to public outcry.		Convention of Cintra.
1809		TC walks to Edinburgh to begin his studies at the university (to 1813).	*Quarterly Review* founded; Byron's *English Bards and Scotch Reviewers* published.
1811			Prince of Wales declared Regent.
1812	FJ rejects offer of a seat in Parliament.		*Childe Harold's Pilgrimage* first published; PM Spencer Percival shot; US declares war on Britain over trade routes; Napoleon invades Russia.

Year	Francis Jeffery	Thomas and Jane Welsh Carlyle	General
1813	FJ to America to marry Charlotte Wilkes; meets US Secretary of State Monroe and President Madison.		Wellington's peninsular campaign successful; Southey becomes Poet Laureate.
1814	FJ returns from America; daughter Charlotte (Charley) born.	TC begins teaching at Annan Academy.	Treaty with Austria, Prussia, and Russia; Napoleon defeated, exiled on Elba; Wordsworth's *The Excursion* published; Scott's *Waverley* published.
1815	FJ purchases lease of Craigcrook, north-west of Edinburgh; tours the Continent.		Napoleon escapes; the Battle of Waterloo.
1816	FJ's article on 'Beauty' published in *Encyclopædia Britannica*.	TC accepts teaching post at Kirkcaldy Burgh School, Fife.	Byron goes into exile.
1817		TC abandons his intention to enter Presbyterian ministry.	*Blackwood's Edinburgh Magazine* founded.
1818		TC back at university studying natural philosophy.	
1819		TC begins to learn German.	Byron *Don Juan* first published; Peterloo Massacre.
1820	FJ addresses 'The Pantheon Meeting' (first public political assembly in Edinburgh in 25 years); installed Lord Rector of University of Glasgow.	TC writes review of Pictet's theory of gravitation, sends it to FJ for *ER*, and hears nothing (no trace exists).	George III dies; Cato Street conspiracy; Scottish insurrection; trial of Queen Caroline; *London Magazine* founded.
1821	FJ re-elected Lord Rector of Glasgow (according to form); rejects overtures to secure him a seat in parliament.		Napoleon dies.
1822		TC gains post as tutor in Buller family.	Castlereagh's suicide.
1824		TC's translation *Wilhelm Meister's Apprenticeship* published.	Byron dies.
1825		TC's *Life of Friedrich Schiller* published in book form.	
1826		TC and JWC marry (17 October) and settle at Comely Bank in Edinburgh.	Bankruptcy of Archibald Constable and collapse of Walter Scott's finances; University of London founded.

Year	Francis Jeffery	Thomas and Jane Welsh Carlyle	General
1827		TC's *German Romance* published.	
	FJ meets TC for first time (early February); TC's 'Jean Paul Friedrich Richter' published in *ER*; TC and JWC first dine at Craigcrook (September).		
1828	Carlyles with the Jeffreys at Moray Place before leaving for Craigenputtoch (May); FJ visits TC and JWC (November); TC's 'Burns' published in *ER*.		Repeal of Test and Corporation Acts; Wellington becomes PM.
1829	FJ elected to Dean of Faculty of Advocates; hands editorship of *ER* to Macvey Napier.	TC's 'Voltaire' and 'Novalis' published in *Foreign Review*; TC works on history of German literature.	Catholic Emancipation Act.
	TC's 'Signs of the Times' published in *ER*; FJ meets TC in King's Arms Inn, Dumfries, on his way to England; with JWC visits Mrs Richardson (August); TC and JWC visit FJ at Craigcrook (October).		
1830	FJ appointed Lord Advocate of Scotland when Whigs come into power.	TC writing for *Foreign Review* and *Fraser's Magazine*; TC's sister Margaret dies (June); begins *Sartor Resartus*.	Death of George IV and accession of William IV; revolution in France (Charles X succeeded by Louis- Phillippe, Duke of Orleans); resignation of Wellington; Whigs form government under Earl Grey.
	FJ at Craigenputtoch with TC and JWC (September).		
1831	FJ becomes MP for the Forfarshire Burghs; maiden speech in House of Commons; loses seat on electoral technicality (March); given Malton electorate (April); parliament dissolved; elected for Malton again (June); brings Scottish Reform Bill before House of Commons (July–September); seriously ill (September–October).	TC publishes poetry and prose in *Fraser's*; his 'Taylor's Historic Survey of German Poetry' published in *ER*; TC to London with *Sartor* (August); TC meets John Stuart Mill; JWC to London (October); TC's 'Characteristics' published in *ER*.	Rioting over defeat of reform legislation.
	FJ arranges for *Sartor* to be published by John Murray but TC's negotiations with Murray break down.		
1832	Reform Ministry resigns (May) and is later restored; FJ's Scottish Reform Bill finally passed; FJ elected MP for Edinburgh (December).	TC's father dies (January); TC writes reminiscence of his father; TC's 'Biography' and 'Boswell's Life of Johnson' published in *Fraser's*.	Great Reform Bill through Lords (June); cholera in Scotland; Walter Scott dies; Goethe dies.

Year	Francis Jeffery	Thomas and Jane Welsh Carlyle	General
1833	FJ and wife to London (February); Scottish Burgh Bill through parliament (August); public dinner held in FJ's honour in Edinburgh (November).	TC's 'Diderot' published in *Foreign Quarterly Review*; Emerson visits Craigenputtoch (August); TC offered use of Barjarg library; *Sartor* published in instalments in *Fraser's* (September 1833–August 1834).	Factory Act passed; Oxford Movement initiated.
	TC and JWC in Edinburgh, FJ a constant visitor (January).		
1834	FJ returns to London (February); elected Judge of Court of Session, takes seat (May, June).	TC to London, finds 5 Cheyne Row, Chelsea (May); JWC to London; TC begins work on *The French Revolution*.	The 'Tolpuddle Martyrs' transported; Melbourne resigns as PM; Robert Peel forms Tory ministry.
	FJ alienated from TC and JWC.		
1835		First volume of *The French Revolution* accidentally burnt (March), TC begins rewriting; completes vol. 1 (September).	Peel resigns as PM; Melbourne forms Whig ministry.
1836		*Sartor* published in Boston.	Chartist movement begins (to 1848).
1837		TC's *The French Revolution* published (May).	Death of William IV; Victoria assumes throne.
	FJ writes to TC on receiving his *French Revolution* and the two are reconciled.		
1838	FJ's daughter Charlotte (Charley) marries William Empson.	TC's *Sartor* published in England.	First trans-Atlantic steamship crossing.
1839	FJ's granddaughter Charlotte (Tarley) born.	TC's *Chartism* published.	
1840			Victoria marries Prince Albert of Saxe-Coburg-Gotha.
1841	FJ suffers severe, protracted illness (relieved of judicial duties until May 1842); granddaughter Margaret born.	TC's lectures *On Heroes, Hero-Worship, and the Heroic in History* published.	
1842		JWC's mother Grace Welsh dies.	Copyright Act extends copyright to 42 yrs (or 7 yrs after death).
1843	FJ's *Contributions to the Edinburgh Review* published; granddaughter Nancy born.	TC's *Past and Present* published.	The Disuption of the Church of Scotland.

Year	Francis Jeffery	Thomas and Jane Welsh Carlyle	General
1845		TC's edition of *The Letters and Speeches of Oliver Cromwell* published in 2 vols.	Irish Famine begins (to 1851).
1846		Expanded edition of TC's *The Letters and Speeches of Oliver Cromwell* published in 3 vols.	
1848			Louis Phillippe abdicates, France becomes a republic under Louis Napoleon; Marx and Engel's *Communist Manifesto* published.
1850	FJ dies (26 January); wife Charlotte dies (May).	TC's *Latter Day Pamphlets* published.	Wordsworth dies.
1851		TC's *Life of Sterling* published.	
1852		TC begins work on his *History of Frederick the Great*.	
1858		TC's *History of Frederick the Great* vols 1–2 published (final vols, 5–6, published 1865).	
1866		JWC dies (21 April); TC writes the remainder of his 'reminiscences' (to 1868), including that of FJ (January 1867).	
1881		TC dies (5 February); Froude's edition of TC's *Reminiscences* published.	

EDITORIAL NOTE

Many phrases and some quite long passages from the letters published here for the first time have previously appeared in scholarly studies. The most generous selection is that of David Alec Wilson in *Carlyle to 'The French Revolution'* (1924), the second of his six-volume life of Carlyle. Of all Carlyle's biographers, Wilson has been the most sympathetic to Jeffrey and that is reflected in the extent and nature of his quotations from these letters. It was also, perhaps tellingly, the last time the letters themselves were collectively available to biographers. Wilson obviously had all but a dozen or so in his possession at the time of writing his biography – a gift from Jeffrey's daughter Mrs Empson, he says in his Preface, though Charlotte Empson had been born in 1814. Immediately after Wilson's work, the collection was broken up for some reason, with about three-fifths going to the National Library of Scotland to be bound and catalogued as MS 787. These letters have been readily available since the 1920s, more recently on microfilm. The other two-fifths disappeared altogether, however, only to re-emerge at Christies in 1985 when the National Library of Scotland bought them to complete their collection. These late arrivals are now held loose and uncatalogued as Acc. 8964 and have not proved nearly as accessible to scholars. The catalogued letters (MS 787) are generally but by no means exclusively earlier and later letters, with the 'lost' letters (Acc. 8964) representing a sequence in the middle, from May 1830 to December 1833. Otherwise the division of the letters appears to have been without rationale. In the case of three letters, half ended up in one accession and half in the other, and they had to be pieced together again for this volume.

The disintegration of the collection and the fact that Wilson quotes so generously from the letters has discouraged scholars from reviewing or republishing them. So has Jeffrey's handwriting. What Wilson does transcribe, he transcribes with the accuracy of one who has had to make himself familiar with a hand so appalling that it was a standing joke amongst all Jeffrey's friends and correspondents. On this and other issues to do with Jeffrey's letters, Algernon Moncrieff's introduction to James Taylor's *Lord Jeffrey and Craigcrook* is worth quoting at length:

Jeffrey's correspondents had a still greater trial in his handwriting, of which he used to say that he had three kinds – one which his friends and the printer could read, one which the printer could read but his friends could not, and the third class completely illegible to both. In May 1822 Jeffrey was desirous of a visit from Sydney Smith, and wrote to him to invite him to come. Sydney's reply was, 'We are much obliged by your letter, and should have been still more so had it been legible. I have tried to read it from left to right, and Mrs. Sydney from right to left, but neither of us can decipher a single word of it.' Nevertheless, the task of deciphering Jeffrey's letters was generally amply repaid by the contents. We shall never see such letters again – lively, affectionate, full of strong feeling, lighted up with gleams of fancy and merriment, and a crisp, concise succession of sentences. They have all the qualities which letters ought to have.[1]

Elsewhere, Sydney Smith suggested that Jeffrey adopt the motto *Mens sine manu*.[2] Indeed, 'so excellent, & so illegible' were Jeffrey's letters that for his own sake, and the sake of posterity, Henry Cockburn had his daughter Jane and others transcribe the 427 letters that he personally received from Jeffrey in his lifetime.[3]

From an editorial point of view, the challenge of Jeffrey's handwriting has led, very occasionally, to an inspired guess, enclosed within square brackets and preceded by a question mark, and on even fewer occasions to an interrogative gap. One or two words have driven me insane, but I have only rarely had to resort to these desperate measures. Certainly there are far fewer than I imagined I would need when I began my transcription, and I now feel confident about my readings.

Part of the reason why Jeffrey's handwriting is so difficult to decipher is because he composed and wrote at an incredible speed. In order to preserve a sense of this I have, in line with the vast majority of recent editions of famil-iar letters, retained the writer's own punctuation as far as possible. Like Byron, for example, Jeffrey had little time for nice distinctions like commas, full stops, semi-colons and colons. He resorted instead to the short dash for almost all his punctuation, except where he would spare his reader with a long dash. These dashes admittedly differ in length, especially from one letter to another, but it seemed not just simpler but also more faithful to represent them in a few forms only. Where for Jeffrey the end of a line obviated the need for any punctua-tion I have occasionally inserted a dash in square brackets for readers without the benefit of the original page in front of them. The only manipulation I have allowed myself is very occasionally with indentation before a new paragraph, for indentation, too, sometimes disappears in order to allow him to get more words on the page. Where one sentence ends mid-line with the usual dash, especially with a long one, there can be no doubt the next line is intended to begin a new paragraph, however flush against the left-hand margin it may be. Sometimes, however, I have had to guess. All I can say is that my intention has never been one of formalizing Jeffrey's prose because I do not see that as my job.

Words or phrases enclosed within angular brackets (< >) represent words written above the line (or, rarely, beneath or beside it).

Finally, a word about footnotes. Their main function is to explain contemporary or literary allusions and to identify the people referred to. Occasionally, however, I have elaborated a context, with the narrative of Jeffrey's relationship with the Carlyles in mind. When I do this, I quote more often than not from the Carlyles' own letters, sometimes at length. I hope I have avoided a Menippean excess, but this seemed to me justified by the loss of all the Carlyles' letters to Jeffrey. What it has also done is to deepen my debt to the encyclopaedic *Collected Letters of Thomas and Jane Welsh Carlyle*.

None of these letters is to be found in the closest thing we have in print to a collection of Jeffrey's letters: Cockburn's *Life of Lord Jeffrey*. Cockburn's *Life* formally reproduces substantial parts of 211 letters as its second volume and, in its first, quotes more or less liberally from many others. By my calculations, it represents about a twentieth of the extant letters of Francis Jeffrey and it is hoped that this volume will be the beginning of their collective publication.

Notes:

1   J. Taylor (ed.), *Lord Jeffrey and Craigcrook: A History of the Castle* (Edinburgh: David Douglas, 1892), p. 34.
2   *The Letters of Sydney Smith*, ed. N. C. Smith, 2 vols (Oxford: Clarendon Press, 1953), vol. 1, p. 171.
3   See NLS, Adv. MSS 9.1.8, f. 3.

1827

TO THOMAS CARLYLE

date [June 1827]*
from Edinburgh

My Dear Sir

I have been looking with some impatience for the article you gave me reason to expect about this time for the Review[1] – If it could be sent to 92 Geo. St before 3 o'clock today, I should have the pleasure of taking it with me to Craigcrook[2] for my recreation on Sunday – If this should be too troublesome it would be very agreeable if I were to find it on my return here on Monday before 12. I venture to name these early periods chiefly because when I had the pleasure of seeing you in your own house some days ago, you mentioned that you had pretty nearly completed your task — But I hope you will not suspect me of any disposition to plague you by my importunity — or of any other feeling but obligation – at whatever time it may suit you to favour me with your contribution —

Believe me, With Very Sincere Regard – Your obliged and Faithful
F. Jeffrey

92 Geo. St –
Saturday Morn[g]

I mean, the very first morning I have an hour's leisure, to bring Mrs Jeffrey to wait on Mrs Carlyle – and to settle about your both coming to see us at Craigcrook

---

* See the textual note to the next letter.

National Library of Scotland, MS 787, f. 3.

1. The short article on the German writer Jean Paul, entitled 'Jean Paul F. Richter', that in late May or early June Carlyle agreed to contribute to the June 1827 number of the *Edinburgh Review*. See *ER*, 46 (June 1827), pp. 176–95. 'I engaged as it were for paving the way' – to a larger contribution to the October 1827 number – 'to give him [Jeffrey] in this present publication some little short paper; I think, on the subject of Jean Paul, tho' that is not quite settled with myself yet', wrote Carlyle to his brother John on 4 June. In the same letter, Car-

lyle recalls meeting Jeffrey recently in the courts at Parliament House: '"The Article? Where is the Article?" seemed to be the gist of his talk to me' (*Carlyle Letters*, vol. 4, p. 228).

2.   Jeffrey's country estate, three miles north-west of the centre of Edinburgh, where the successful advocate spent many of his weekends and vacation periods. 'In 1815 Jeffrey set up his rustic household gods at Craigcrook, where all his subsequent summers have been passed', wrote Henry Cockburn in his *Memorials of His Time*: 'This was scarcely a merely private arrangement. It has affected the happiness, and improved both the heads and the hearts of all the worthy of this place' (H. Cockburn, *Memorials of His Time* (Edinburgh: Adam and Charles Black, 1856), p. 294). Very early on in their relationship, after having visited Jeffrey at Craigcrook for the first time on 10 September 1827, the Carlyles dubbed Jeffrey 'the Duke of Craigcrook', which Jeffrey effectively became in 1834 when he was appointed Judge in the Court of Session and assumed the title of Lord Jeffrey.

TO THOMAS CARLYLE

date [early July 1827]*

from Edinburgh

My Dear Sir

I am very gratified by your note, and will not let you wait till Saturday to learn that I am not at all frightened at your Teutonic fire – and shall receive your larger exposition of the faith that is in you, with all respect and thankfulness – I feel at once that you are a man of Genius – and of original character and right heart – and shall be proud and happy to know more of you – I fairly tell you that I think your taste vicious in some points – and your opinions of the real value and talents of your German idols erroneous[1] – But I know I am very ignorant of them – and think I can say with truth that I am neither bigotted nor intolerant – It will be a real pleasure to me to discuss these matters with a person of your intelligence candour and good temper – and I make no doubt that the result will be far more to my advantage than yours

I wish I had leisure to enter upon it now – But I pass my days in a fever of frivolous occupations which must appear very absurd and unnatural to you – and of which – tho' I bear it gaily – I perhaps do not think very differently — By and bye however I shall have more time to myself – and it is a serious disappointment to me to find that you are going to leave this neighbourhood just as my holidays begin —

If I can possibly get away from the court by 3 o'clock tomorrow, Mrs J. and I will call at your house – when I hope we may arrange some longer meeting – In the mean time

Believe me always

Your obliged and Faithful

F. Jeffrey

92 Geo. St

Thursday Evg

---

* Pencil marking on the document in the NLS declares this the 'Earliest of the Jeffrey Letters', dating it '?July 1827', but the familiarity of this letter and the reference in the former letter

to Carlyle's article on Richter make their order less clear cut – even if, as David Alec Wilson writes, this one 'cannot be later than the beginning of July' (D. A. Wilson, *Carlyle*, 6 vols (London: Kegan Paul et al.; New York: E. P. Dutton, 1923–34), vol. 2: *Carlyle to 'The French Revolution' (1826–37)* (1924), p. 28).

National Library of Scotland, MS 787, f. 1.

1.   This disapproval of the 'Germanic' – of what Jeffrey sees as its intellectual and emotional exaggerations and affectations – is reiterated throughout his letters to Carlyle.

TO THOMAS CARLYLE

date 24 or 25 August 1827*
from [Edinburgh]

My Dear Sir

I am glad to see by your card that you are returned to these parts – tho' sorry to have missed your call — I am myself obliged to go tomorrow on business to Glasgow for a few days – but hope to see you and Mrs Carlyle before the end of the week –

I am a little anxious to know what progress you have made in your <u>opus majus</u> on German Genius and Literature[1] – and hope you can contrive to have it ready by the middle of next month – or soon after – Have you seen the new <u>Foreign Quarterly</u>?[2] – There is a long, and I think reasonable discourse on that subject in it – a propos of the works of one Hoffman, with whom I have not the honor to be acquainted – I especially agree with the critic on the subject of what he calls the <u>fantastic</u> style of the Germans – and ~~agree~~ <am of opinion> with him that it is nothing better than fantastic – and has not a deep moral meaning, or secondary sense, as you appear to imagine – But we shall have the benefit of your deliberate judgment on all these matters I hope by and bye —

In the mean time I hope you and your fair spouse have returned in health hope and happiness — I think I am decidedly better for my ramble — I prefix a draft, (dated Monday) for a paltry sum as our publishers acknowledgement for your paper on Richter – and am always

Very Affectly Yours

F. Jeffrey

* Postmarked 25 August.

National Library of Scotland, MS 787, ff. 5–6.

1.   The article on the 'State of German Literature' that Carlyle was preparing for the *Edinburgh Review*, which eventually appeared in *ER*, 46 (October 1827), pp. 304–51.

2.   As distinct from the other periodical devoted to foreign literature, the *Foreign Review*, though the two would merge in April 1830 under the former title.

TO THOMAS CARLYLE

date 6 [September 1827]
from Craigcrook

Craigcrook Thursday Evg 6th

My Dear Sir

I hope you do not think I require a day's deliberation to say that I shall be ready at all times to recommend you as a man of genius and learning – and sincerely gratified in being enabled to contribute in my way to your success – But still it requires some deliberation to answer your letter – and would require still more, if I did not think so highly both of your candour and your temper, as to feel quite secure that whatever opinion I form on the subject, I may safely and explicitly express –

I tell you therefore at once that I see difficulties in the way of your appointment[1] – You are, to say it in one word, a <u>Sectary</u> in taste and literature – and inspired by some of the zeal by which Sectaries are distinguished – a zeal, that is, to magnify the distinguishing doctrines of your sect, and rather to aggravate than reconcile the differences which divide them from the votaries of the Establishment – and I confess I doubt whether the patrons of the new University either <u>will</u> or <u>ought</u> to appoint such a person to such a charge – The very frankness and sincerity of your character tend to make this objection more formidable – If your admiration of the German models were a mere air or singularity adopted capriciously or to create a sensation it would be easy for you conscientiously to disguise or qualify it, so as not to let it very conspicuously affect your academic instructions – But I very greatly mistake you if this be the case, and indeed can fancy that I see you, as you read the surmise, swelling with all the virtuous indignation of one who would rather submit to martyrdom than renounce any article of ~~your~~ <his> philosophical and critical creed. Now I suppose you are aware that there is scarcely one of the patrons of the L.U. who adopt that creed – and probably but few of them who do not regard it as a damnable heresy – and, without supposing that they are as zealous in the opposite faith as you are in yours, do you think it likely that they will put it in the way of being impressed on the academic youths for whose instruction they are providing?

This however is <u>the</u> question for your consideration [–] In all <u>other</u> respects I have no doubt that you are fully qualified for the situation to which you aspire, and likely to do great honor both to yourself and the Establishment by the manner in which you would discharge its duties – As a man of virtue, temper, genius and learning, I shall most readily and warmly recommend you – but I know you would not wish me to disguise those singularities of opinion on which (tho' I think erroneously) I believe you most value yourself, and from which I foresee the obstructions to your success at which I have now hinted.

I ought also perhaps to mention that I heard long ago that the chair which you have in view was to be offered to my friend Thos Campbell[2] – and if the disagreements which I am aware have arisen between him and some of the directors are healed, I do not think it improbable that this offer will still be made – but I speak without any positive knowledge or information on the subject —

Tho' I am a little impatient to see your <u>conspectus</u> of German literature I should be very sorry that you should hurry yourself – only if you are ready nearly about the time I mentioned I think it likely that you may have the honor of leading the van in the new N° —

We shall be most happy to see you here whenever you have leisure – I am still in some fear of being sent to Harrogate – and being uncertain of my time in other respects I wish you and Mrs Carlyle would dine here on <u>Monday</u> next and come early — In the mean time let me know what you wish me to do for you in your [?   ] of ambition

      God bless you Very Faithfully Yours

      <u>F. Jeffrey</u>

National Library of Scotland, MS 787, ff. 7–8.

1.   To a chair at the new 'University of London', which was preparing to take its first 300 students in 1828. Having written initially to the late Francis Horner's brother Leonard in his capacity as coordinator of the new project, Jeffrey also tried to convince his friend and fellow reviewer Henry Brougham (one of the founders of the new university; see note 1 to the next letter) of Carlyle's fitness for the Chair of Moral Philosophy. See, as well as Jeffrey's next letter of 17 October 1827, Carlyle's letter to his brother Alexander (11 September 1827), and Jane's to John Carlyle (13 September 1827), and subsequent letters to other friends and family (*Carlyle Letters*, vol. 4, pp. 256, 259, and ff.).

2.   The Scottish poet, journalist and editor Thomas Campbell (1777–1844), famous for his long poems *The Pleasures of Hope* (1799) and *Gertrude of Wyoming* (1809). Campbell has been credited with the original idea of setting up a University of London.

TO THOMAS CARLYLE

date 17 October 1827

from Harrogate

Harrogate Wedy 17th

My Dear Sir

I believe I ought to have written to you before – tho' I am sure that I would have done so, if I had had anything favourable – or even anything decided, to tell you – I found Mr Brougham[1] singularly shy on the subject – and tho' I introduced it half a dozen times during the day I spent with him on my way here, he contrived always to evade it in ways that showed me that he had not at all made up his mind with regard to it, and did not wish to be pressed for an explicit answer even by an intimate friend — he had some pretext for this indeed in the reference I made very early to your paper in the forthcoming N°– of which of course I then had no ostensible copy – but I could perceive that he was rather alarmed at your German predilections – and said that this being a chair on which the eyes of all the enemies of the Institution would be very keenly fastened, either for censure or ridicule, it was particularly necessary to be cautious about it – and that he himself had an impression that it might be most prudent not to fill it up at all in the first instance – but to let the establishment settle down in public opinion, by the weight of the safer and less questionable doctrines of physical and practical science for which they are already provided – before risking it on the more ticklish ground of speculation — This is about all I could get out of him – but he promised to read your paper – and to think afterwards of what I had said to him – He passed thro' this place last Thursday – but having several visits to pay on his way to London would only arrive there I think today or tomorrow – I believe I ought to have ordered a second copy of your article to have been forwarded to his address so as to have met him there – but as he will meet with arrears enough of more pressing business on his arrival – and as we cannot hope that he will read that long dissertation the very moment it comes to his hand, I rather fancy there has been no time yet lost – as I set out for Scotland tomorrow it is too late for me to do anything myself, till I get home But if you are anxious to save time, there can be no impropriety in your getting a copy of the sheets from Ballantyne,[2] and sending them yourself to H. B. Esqre M.P. <u>Hill Street Berkeley Square London</u> – with a short line, merely stating that these are the papers of which I had spoken to him, and that both you and I will be anxious to know his opinion of them as soon as convenient – you must take care that the covers are not over an ounce weight – but I think if a sheet be carefully diced, and pared on the margins, it will go in one – as to your going yourself to London I am decidedly of opinion that it would be quite useless, till we have Mr B's reaction to our case – as <u>without</u> his assistance – or ag[ains]t his opinion I am clear that you have no chance whatever – I must add, <u>in confidence</u> – that he made very light of Irving's recommendation[3] – which I rather suspect would not be of much weight with any of the Directors –

I am a little startled at the notion of your Nithsdale retreat[4] – and my impressions (perhaps somewhat selfish) are certainly ag[ains]t it – I think it has been your misfortune not to have mixed sufficiently with intelligent men of various opinions, and open and intrepid minds – and that such a retirement as you meditate would aggravate all the peculiarities which in my humble opinion (you[?'ll *MS torn*] forgive the freedom) now fetter your understanding – and obstruct your career both of usefulness and distinction. – I am quite sure too that you will very soon tire of planting fir trees among granite rocks – and that you will either grow torpid and lumpish, or get dyspepsy again, by hard and unprofitable study

– till much learning and bad digestion bring on hypochondriacal derangement – and then you will infect your fair wife with the same distempers – and both of you will break your necks some foggy night over one of the said granite rocks! – Think better of this scheme then my good friend before you let it sink into your fancy – and do not cast away the fair chances of happiness that lie before you – merely because they lie on what you think a vulgar and jostling road, in pursuit of an unsocial and contemplative felicity, not made for men — Give my love to my dear cousin[5] – and ask her if she does not in her heart think my plan a wiser and <u>safer</u> one than yours? –

As we mean to visit Broughams mother on our way down – we shall be scarcely be at Craigcrook before Sunday night – and the sooner I hear of you after that the better – I hope for ten days or a fortnight's quiet there before my professional work begins – – I think I am rather better for my libations here – tho' my sleep has not been so bad for a long while – Mrs J. and Charly[6] are quite well and desire to be kindly remembered – The Review is going on briskly – tho' after some weeks –

Ever Very Affectly Yours
F. Jeffrey

National Library of Scotland, MS 787, ff. 9–10.

1. Henry Brougham (1778–1868), created first Baron Brougham and Vaux in 1830, was (with Jeffrey) the most prolific of the *Edinburgh* reviewers, a KC and MP who was at this time the effective leader of the Whigs in the House of Commons. As the most energetic member of the founding committee of the new University of London, Brougham's interest could well have secured Carlyle the chair he sought.

2. The printer James Ballantyne (1772–1833), responsible for printing the *Edinburgh Review*.

3. Edward Irving (1792–1834), a charismatic preacher, one-time tutor of Jane Baillie Welsh (i.e., the unmarried Jane Welsh Carlyle), and a career rival, role model and close friend of Carlyle's from his early days as a teacher at Kirkcaldy, who was also at one time a rival for Jane's affections. See Carlyle's *Reminiscences*, pp. 200–348.

4. Carlyle had announced his intention of retiring from Edinburgh to Craigenputtoch, an isolated farm 14 miles west-north-west of Dumfries in the Nithsdale division of Dumfriesshire. Jeffrey's discomfort was in keeping with his general distrust of provincial isolation.

5. Jeffrey and Jane 'discovered mutual old cousinships by the maternal side' (now untraceable) which allowed Jeffrey to refer to her familiarly as his cousin throughout the remainder of their relationship (*Reminiscences*, p. 361).

6. The two Charlottes: Mrs Jeffrey (neé Charlotte Wilkes), a native of America whom Jeffrey met in Edinburgh in 1811 during her tour of Britain and the Continent with her uncle and aunt, Louis and Frances Simond, and for whom he sailed to America in 1813; and Jeffrey's daughter Charlotte, later Mrs Empson (usually 'Charley', pron. 'Sharly'). Carlyle has some rather unflattering things to say about Charlotte Empson (née Jeffrey) in his *Reminiscences*, published immediately after his death in 1881 by J. A. Froude: 'The Daughter Charlotte had inherited her [mother's] nervous infirmity ["a certain nervous

tic or jerk of the head"], and indeed I think was partly lame in one arm. For the rest, an inferior specimen to either of her parents; an abstruse, suspicious, timid, enthusiastic; and at length, on the death of her parents, and of her good old jargoning Husband Empson (a long-winded *Edinburgh Reviewer*, much an adorer of Macaulay, etc.), became quite a morbid, exclusive character; and lives withdrawn ... Perhaps she was already rather jealous of *us*? She spoke very little; wore a half-pouting, half-mocking expression; and had the air of a prettyish spoiled child' (*Reminiscences*, p. 367). It may well have been this portrait that provoked Charlotte Empson into destroying all of the Carlyles' letters to her father.

TO THOMAS CARLYLE

date [?late October 1827]
from [Edinburgh]

My dear Sir

I send you the proof[1] – all but the 2 first lines – which are of no use, and would stop the press if they were sent – I should like to have this returned in the course of tomorrow – as we are rather behindhand, and must get on —

I hope to see you before you set out for the South[2]

The proof of course will be returned <u>to me</u>

Ever very Truly Yours
F. Jeffrey
Wed[y]

National Library of Scotland, MS 787, f. 11.
1. Proof sheets of Carlyle's article on the 'State of German Literature', *ER*, 66 (October 1827), pp. 304–51.
2. No such journey was made at this time. (Jeffrey probably refers to Carlyle's intention to go to London to further his bid for the chair at the new university.)

TO THOMAS CARLYLE

date 6 December 1827
from Edinburgh

My Dear Sir

I now prefix an draft for your heretical tractate on German literature[1] – I hear nothing of the London chair of Ethics – and suspect it will not be soon filled up – Have you got a copy of Wiffen's Tasso[2] yet? If you have not I will send you mine – which has just come here from the binder – and is a little too fine for ordinary use – If it was not a present from the author I would make one of it to my fair cousin — He has translated the whole poem – and also given a long – and somewhat [?washy] life — I never get out of court till near dark – and when I ride a [?　　　　　　　　　　　*] come home by lamp light – But I will come down to you some Sunday – for I think of you both very often – and with great kindness —

Ever very Truly Yours —
F. Jeffrey
24. Moray Place
Friday 6ᵗʰ

---

* Three or four words have been cut off here by Carlyle's removing the money draft referred to.

National Library of Scotland, MS 787, f. 16.

1.　Payment (a draft on an account) for Carlyle's review of German literature.
2.　Jeffrey was hoping Carlyle would review the translation of Italian Renaissance poet Torquato Tasso's *Gerusalemme Liberata* by Jeremiah Holmes Wiffen, *Jerusalem Delivered, translated into English Spenserian Verse*, which had gone into a number of editions since its first appearance in 1824.

TO THOMAS CARLYLE

date 24 [December 1827]
from [Edinburgh]

My Dear Sir

Tho' my holidays have not yet begun – for I am just returned from a Jury Trial – I have not been quite idle in making enquiries about the probability of your success at St. Andrews[1] – though I am afraid I have nothing very encouraging to report – The nomination I find is understood to be in substance with Dr. Nicol, the Principal[2] – an active, jobbing, popular man – who has placed most of the present Professors, and conferred obligations on all – and who, from having great influence with Lord Melville[3] in his day of power, has acquired an absolute ascendancy, over these grateful and obsequious Sages — If you can secure Nicol therefore, you may command their votes – and if he is against you, there is no hope in them — I do not well know thro' what channel you can approach him – and to say the truth I have but little hope of your finding favour in his eyes – He is a good-natured sensible, worldly man – and not without some sense of the propriety of bringing known talents and reputation to the aid of his declining college [–] But he is a cautious, prudent person – without genius or learning, and without reverence for them, – very zealous for <u>Moderation</u> in matters ecclesiastical[4] – and having a great contempt and distrust for all sorts of enthusiasm — It is not unlikely that he has already cast his eyes on some decent, manageable and judicious priest for this office – tho' I have not yet heard of any candidate but a young man at the Box – a Mr Kinnear[5] who is said to be given to study

Think over what sort of recommendations you could muster – and from what quarters? Your high religionists, like E. Irving, will do you no good – but harm – Men of rank and high tories I take it will weigh most in the scale – and after them men of repute for learning — I shall think of something to be done and pray tell me how you suppose I can be useful –

But do not run away to Dumfriesshire – tho' this Temple of Glory and Science should for the present be shut to you – You can be as quiet here as there – when the reading – or the studious fit is on you – and you surely may divert yourself as well – and certainly give more pleasure, when you can condescend to be social – and so God bless you – We are going to the country for two days on a visit – But after Friday I shall be home again – and comparatively at leisure

Love to my fair cousin – she must not let her lips grow pale – or I shall be obliged to prescribe for her

> Ever Very Truly Yours,
> F. Jeffrey.

24 Moray Place
Monday Evg 24th

How do you come on with Tasso? and do you think you can let me have an Italian article before the end of Jan^y?[6]

National Library of Scotland, MS 787, ff. 14–15.

1. The Chair of Moral Philosophy held by Thomas Chalmers at St Andrews was about to be vacated. Carlyle's application was unsuccessful, in spite of glowing recommendations from (amongst others) David Brewster, John Wilson, John Leslie, Bryan Procter and Edward Irving, and in spite of Jeffrey's doing all he could: 'The dear little "Duke" (Jane says, she could *kiss* him) has written me a paper, which might of itself bring me any Professorship in the Island', Carlyle to his brother John, 1 February 1828 (*Carlyle Letters*, vol. 4, p. 317).

2. Revd Dr Francis Nicol (usu. Nicoll; 1771–1835), Moderator of the General Assembly in 1809 and one of the leaders of the Moderates in the Church of Scotland, had been appointed Principal of the United College(s) of St Leonard and St Salvator (United College) at St Andrews in 1819.

3. Henry Dundas, first Viscount Melville (1742–1811) – a.k.a. Harry the Ninth – the MP and Lord Advocate of Scotland who managed Scotland in the late eighteenth century and kept the Whigs out of office.

4. Nicoll was one of the Moderates who dominated the General Assembly of the Presbyterian Church of Scotland and who for some decades now had been politically conservative.

5. Unidentified.

6. See note 2 to the letter of 6 December 1827, above. No article on Tasso and/or Italian literature was ever contributed by Carlyle.

TO THOMAS CARLYLE

date [27 December 1827]
from [Edinburgh]

My Dear Sir

Here is my <u>verdict</u> on your favour – It is, as you see, in the shape of a letter to Nicol – you are quite right to go on – and also not to care too much for the result – your great risk is from <u>Cook</u>[1] – if he were set aside I really think your chance fair enough — God bless you – my head and hands are too full of lesser matters, to let me expatiate more on philosophies – academic or practical – only remember it is a pleasure to me, to do you any service –

Very affectly yours

<u>F. Jeffrey</u>

Monday 27th

National Library of Scotland, MS 787, f. 18.

1. George Cook (1772–1845), son of a previous professor of Moral Philosophy at St Andrews and leader of the Moderates in the Church of Scotland. He would be appointed to a chair of Moral Philosophy at St Andrews two years later (*Carlyle Letters*, vol. 4, p. 317).

TO THOMAS CARLYLE

date [?30 December 1827]
from Edinburgh

Moray Place Thursday Evg

My Dear Sir

I have no time to write – but I have a letter from Dr Hunter[1] – There are no award candidates in the field of any mark or likelihood. Dr Cook is <u>understood</u> to be willing to take the place, if it is <u>offered</u> – but to be, for the present, averse to stoop to ask for it – Dr H. says it will not be <u>offered</u> – but that, if he solicits it, his claims will be formidable – He sees no objection to your coming forward – but advises me to write myself to Nicol – who is the <u>arbiter fortunarum</u>[2] — <u>I have written</u> to Nicol – and when he answers, you shall know what – and this is all, at this present – from your

trusty friend and obedt svt to command

Love to my pale coz. —

<u>F. Jeffrey</u>

National Library of Scotland, MS 787, f. 12.

1.   Probably Dr James Hunter (1772–1845), Professor of Logic, Rhetoric and Metaphysics at United College, St Andrews, who married the sister of Francis Jeffrey's first wife, Catherine (née Wilson), but also possibly his father, Dr John Hunter (1745–1837), a classical scholar, Professor of Humanity and Principal of United College.
2.   Latin: decider of fortunes.

1828

TO THOMAS CARLYLE

date [3 January 1828]
from Edinburgh

My Dear Sir

Here is Nicol's answer – which you see amounts to nothing – sincere as he boasts it to be – my own notion is that he reckons on Cook – and will support him if he appears – the roll of other candidates is not very frightful

Think what you will do – and command any services of mine – you see there will be no vacancy till Nov^r – so you may go over and drink punch with the professors after their spring vacation –

    Ever Yours
    F. Jeffrey

24 Moray Place
Monday Evg

Have you thought any more about Tasso?

National Library of Scotland, MS 787, f. 20.

TO THOMAS CARLYLE

date 27 June 1828
from Edinburgh

Edin^r 27 June 1828

My Dear Carlyle

Why do you not write to me? With all your rustic cares you must have at least as much leisure as I do – and besides, you promised – one or both of you – to let us hear from you within ten days after your arrival in your harborage[1] – It is rather mortifying to be so soon forgotten – and I will not tell you how often we have talked and wondered at your neglect of us nor how kindly we have been remembering you, in spite of it all — Well – but I hope you are happy – and that your health is good – and that you have no ennui – and yet a few occasional regrets for your separation from those who wished you to be nearer them – and some candid doubts now and then as to the absolute wisdom of the retreat you have so manfully made from the fret and stir of the breathing world in which they must yet a while pant on – tell me what you have been doing, and projecting – and with what you have been occupying that large discourse of Reason, looking before and after — We have summer at last – beautiful and balmy summer – and I am almost as glad of it for your sakes as my own – I did not like to think of you in a new chilly house on a moorish hill side, in that bleak cutting weather – but now I can think of you with some comfort, trotting about in the saucy breeze, and sitting calmly with open windows looking at the moon —— I have had rather a sweaty time of it in the courts – with some uneasiness about my poor voice – But I am scrambling thro', with a stout heart, and get to Craigcrook on Saturdays and Sundays – with more relish every time – We are in the full flush of summer there now – bowered up with roses and spicy shrubs – and surrounded with fresh foliage, and bleating lambs and chuckling blackbirds and thrushes — Moreover I have at last put forward another review – in which I fear there is not much in your way – I write little in it – but the first half of Lord Collingwood[2] which I hope my fair cousin will read for my sake There is a paper on History too, very scholarly and wisely written — Some horrid German blockhead has sent me an incomprehensible little pamphlett for you – about Kants philosophy – a childish – primer sort of thing of 20 pages – with a thick sealed letter – pray how shall I transmit them? – You will see there is to be a new London University[3] – under the especial patronage of the Bishops and the good Duke[4] – Perhaps they may want a Professor of Mysticism there – shall I speak for you to some of my orthodox friends? We have been burying Dugald Stewart[5] – and if I were a little more at leisure I should compose a small panegyric for him – for, tho' a bit of a humbug – he was a man of a lofty and pure mind — and could for the most part be understood – for which you of course will despise him — Why does not your wife write to me? I am afraid she is a false woman after all and thinks little of deluding poor young men to their ruin — However I forgive her – and love her very truly into the bargain – and feel a sincere interest and anxiety about her welfare and happiness. — Bid her tell me how she passes her time – and how the time passes – I sometimes ride past your deserted little mansion at Comely Bank[6] – and see vulgar heads at the windows thro' which your intellectual countenances used to smile on me – and now God bless you and good night for the morning light is coming in at my shutters, and I must go to bed — Let me know when you think I can do you any service – and believe me always Very Affectly Yours

F. Jeffrey

Tho' I mean this only to revive and refresh you, I may as well ask whether you have been thinking of doing anything for me in the reviewing way – with Burns – or Tasso or anything else? – The Teutonic Muse I think may be allowed to slumber for a season yet — —

National Library of Scotland, MS 787, ff. 22–3.

1. The Carlyles had stayed with the Jeffreys at 24 Moray Place in Edinburgh on 23 and 24 May 1828 before setting out for Craigenputtoch, the isolated farm (see note 3 to the letter of 17 October 1827, above) which would be their principal residence until they settled in London in the middle of 1834.

2. A review of Lord Collingwood on the naval service, *ER*, 47 (May 1828), pp. 385–418. Jeffrey may only have written the 'first half', but in 1843 he reprinted the whole article in his selected *Contributions to the Edinburgh Review*.

3. Jeffrey is referring to the establishment of King's College in London as a conservative counterpart to the more liberal 'University of London' (which would be renamed 'University College, London') at which Carlyle had earlier sought a chair.

4. Arthur Wellesley, first Duke of Wellington (1769–1852).

5. Dugald Stewart (1753–1828), the Scottish mathematician, philosopher, political economist and Whig ideologue who for thirty-five years was Professor of Moral Philosophy at the University of Edinburgh. Stewart's supporters included Tories like Walter Scott and philosophical radicals like James Mill, and his popularity is attested by the large memorial built in his honour that to this day dominates Calton Hill in Edinburgh. He was especially influential on the generation of Scottish liberal Whig intellectuals that grew to maturity in the 1790s (including Francis Horner, Henry Brougham, Thomas Brown and Henry Cockburn).

6. Then on the north western outskirts of Edinburgh, where the Carlyles had lived for twenty months before their departure for Craigenputtoch.

TO THOMAS CARLYLE

date 16 July 1828
from Edinburgh

Edin^r 16 July 1828

O ye of little faith! – and so you thought, because we lived sociably with our friends – and had some <little> regard to our own happiness and their's, and rather preferred understanding what we heard and read – we must necessarily be false and selfish, and incapable of any real regard for those, for whom we professed friendship! — I shall like mysticism I think now, less than ever – if it lead to misanthropy as well as extravagance, and make people suspicious as well as useless — I would not be prone to these sentiments for all that philosophy – old or new, or the philosophers stone itself – could bestow on me — But you are not in earnest I know in your distrust or your wonder – and all this is but an air to excuse your extreme indolence – and I forgive you for it – and there is an end —— I envy you a little now and then in a hot busy day – and wish I could lay me down and pant by your lovely waters – and hush my fretted pulse in your cool evening solitudes – But I press my temples, and close my eyes – and abstract my spirit from the continued fever – and call up visions of quiet and loveliness – and then I possess my soul again – and return to my task with cheerfulness and patience – and wait for the coming on of time – contentedly enough – If my health were quite entire I should not care at all – but I cannot always venture now to walk out before going to sleep in the dewy dawn – or even to read for half an hour in some sweet and soothing poem, after my dull task is over – washing its earthy stains from my brain in those waters of healing – and so I often go to sleep with my fancy defiled – and join toil to toil with a troubled sleep – and that is irksome – and is a profane dulling of a summers day ——

But why should I talk of myself? – unless to let you see how much I confide in you —— Sir Walter has acknowledged the medal[1] – & made a very pretty speech for Goethe – and called him one of his masters – and said civil things too of you – which is more than you deserve at his hands —— I have read most of my old love Mrs Richardson's poems[2] – and like them better than I expected – they are often very sweet and eloquent – The fault is that there is no great substance in them – and that most of them are spun out intolerably – but the good parts are very good —— I am in the very thick of a long term of Jury trials – wrangling awkward tedious pettifogging cases – which will keep me from my morning dreams and evening rambles for ten days to come – and send me pale and shaken to my shades after all – about the end of the month we run to Loch lomond for a fortnight[3] – and then return for a while to Craigcrook – about Sept[r] I think we shall probably tour Southend[4] – and purpose most relentlessly to take you on our way – But we shall give you fair notice of our approach – that, if you cannot receive us, we may at least contrive to have a meeting on your borders ——

Tell my fair cousin that I love her very dearly – and think of her many times every day – and that I am very proud of her postscript, and mean to answer it by a whole letter, as soon as I have a quiet hour – for I will not converse with her in this scratchy way – I hope she rides and runs about enough – and that the summer sun has brought the roses back to her cheeks again and living heat to her hands —— Tell me about reviewing – tho' after all you say about working for booksellers I am half afraid to ask you —— But mine is a free service I hope – and if you like it better you shall command – Lockharts Burns[5] is but a poor affair – but sensible and honest – And I can never read anything about Burns – without a melting and a burning in my blood – I hear of nothing new – Indeed I have read nothing but law manuscripts since I saw you – so that it will be a great refreshment to get a sheet <full> even of mysticism – make your letters double or triple if you have leisure – the longer the better —— My Charlottes send their love to you I assure you very sincerely – and so God bless you –

If there is anything I can do to serve you – in money matters – or anything else, pray tell me frankly and I shall answer with the same simplicity —

Ever Very Affctly Your's

F. Jeffrey

National Library of Scotland, MS 787, ff. 24–5.

1. Goethe had sent Carlyle six medals to be awarded to people who had served German literature in Britain. Carlyle's allocation of the medals – the recipients he contemplated included, with Scott (who received two of the medals), John Wilson, John Gibson Lockhart, Wordsworth and the unlikely choice of Jeffrey – is discussed in letters to Walter Scott on 13 April 1828, to his brother John on 16 April 1828, and to Goethe himself on 18 April 1828 (*Carlyle Letters*, vol. 4, pp. 354, 360, 364–5). Later Carlyle added William Taylor of Norwich – see the letter to Goethe, 25 September 1828 (*Carlyle Letters*, vol. 4, p. 406).

2. Caroline Richardson (1777–1853), the poet and novelist from Forge in Dumfriesshire. In his *Reminiscences*, Carlyle recalls Jeffrey's and Jane's visiting her during a trip the Jeffreys made to Dumfries to see the Carlyles: 'After breakfast, he went across with my Wife to visit a certain Mrs. Richardson, Authoress of some Novels; really a superior kind of woman and much a lady; who had been an old flame of his, perhaps twenty-five or thirty years before. "These old loves don't do!" said Mrs. Jeffrey, with easy sarcasm, who was left behind with me. And accordingly there had been some embarrassment, I afterwards found, but on both sides the gratifying of some good though melancholy feelings' (*Reminiscences*, p. 366).

3. Jeffrey made the journey to Scotland's largest loch as often as once every two or three years on average.

4. Presumably the village on the southern extremity of the Kintyre peninsula in Argyllshire.

5. John Gibson Lockhart (1794–1854), an Edinburgh lawyer, essayist and novelist, wrote a *Life of Robert Burns* in 1828. In his *Peter's Letters to His Kinfolk* (1819) and with John Wilson ('Christopher North', see note 3 to the letter of 3 November 1829, below) in *Blackwood's Edinburgh Magazine*, Lockhart mounted an aggressive challenge to the Edinburgh Whig cultural ascendancy of Jeffrey and his friends.

TO THOMAS CARLYLE

date 1 August 1828

from Craigcrook

Craigcrook – 1 Augt 1828

My Dear Sir

We set off early tomorrow morning for Loch Lomond – and I am too much hurried today, to do more than say that I sent you by yesterdays mail a packet containing Currie and Cromeks Burns[1] – and 3 volumes of travels together with your German correspondents letters – the book was forgotten – and really was not worth remembering — I was in such a bustle all day that I could not lay my hand on another book for you – But when I come back I dare say I shall be able to collect some —

You have misunderstood me about Sir Walter – his acknowledgements to you and Goethe were only verbal – and I have a letter of his to put on its course to Weimar ——God bless you – I hope you will be able to do something about Burns — But I really cannot consent to your <u>dechainement</u>[2] upon all the innocent harmonists of the age[3] – Felicia Hemans[4] is my delight – and for Moore[5] I have the most profound admiration – What you say of them – while it has that slight colour of Reason which no ingenuous man ever wanted, in the excess of his absurdity, is thoroughly unjust – and full of prejudice – and a right sense of excellence[6] – Apart from all that is <u>amatory</u> in any sense of the word, I will show you infinite passages in Moore, to which I defy you to find a match in Goethé and any of his followers — It is mere deadness to music and fancy not to see this – And for Felicia, she is as pure as rock crystal – and as gentle as a female fairy – a fie on your ungallant, unkind insensible prejudices – I would as soon tolerate an exclusive admirer of Pope as of your Germans [–] Do renounce paradox, and outlandish absurdity – and stand on your own feet – a true British man

Well – God help you – I have no time to say more but that I thank you from my heart for your kindness – and tell you you are safe at least in bestowing it —— Love to my fair cousin – I will write to her from the Lake —

> Ever yours
> F. Jeffrey

National Library of Scotland, MS 787, ff. 26–7.

1. James Currie, *The Works of Robert Burns, with an Account of His Life, and a Criticism on His Writings* (1800) and Robert Hartley Cromek, *Reliques of Robert Burns, consisting chiefly of Original Letters, Poems and Critical Observations of Scottish Songs* (1808). Jeffrey had reviewed Cromek's *Reliques* in *ER*, 13 (January 1809), pp. 249–76.
2. French: explosion; outburst.
3. See note 1, on Hooker, to the letter of 8 December 1828, below.
4. Felicia Dorothea Hemans (née Browne; 1793–1835), a poet widely celebrated in the 1820s who would go on to become the most popular poet of the nineteenth century. Jeffrey would review some of her poetry in the *Edinburgh Review* of October 1829 (see note 3 to the letter of 9 December 1829, below).
5. Thomas Moore (1779–1852), Irish poet and song writer, prominent particularly in Whig cultural circles. Jeffrey had begun by reviewing Moore savagely in 1806 (which led to a famously anti-climactic duel), before becoming a close personal friend.
6. This makes no sense in the context, and Jeffrey may have meant to write that Carlyle's attitude to the poetry of Hemans and Moore *wants* (i.e., *lacks*) 'a right sense of excellence', or I may be misreading his handwriting.

TO JANE WELSH CARLYLE

date 23 August 1828

from Craigcrook

Craigcrook 23 Augt 1828

My Dear Child

I could not write to you from the highlands – tho' I thought about you every day – Why I could not, remains a mystery to me at this day – as impenetrable as any of Goethe's – but the fact is certain – I was under a spell – and could not write at all – I went about in sunshine and in shower – rejoicing in the voices of the cataracts and dreaming away my days by calm waters and lonely vallies – with a forgetfulness of writing that seemed native to the scene – But I am back in my own den again – and begin to be thankful that heaven taught letters for the comfort of absent lovers – and other desiring persons [–] I half expected that you – or the master mystic – would have written to me before this time – I wrote to him I think from Glasgow – and want to know what he is doing [–] I wished much for him yesterday – when I had a Russian mystic with whom I could have matched him – a fine stout, obstinate, ambitious Muscovite – who has read all the unreadable works of the Germans – and thinks he is destined to separate the dross from the ore, and reveal the true secret of philosophy for the first time to the world – un pure Sclavonie[1] – He is a man of 50 – a mighty traveller – a speaker with all tongues – and very musical and melancholy —— Are you tired yet of your solitude? – and will you come again, and occupy your little room in Moray Place in Nov^r? – You will find it very gay with paper and paint – and the landscape without, and the welcome within, as you left them – But we are coming first to take you – I cannot yet calculate exactly at what time – for I am entangled with the review – and having played truant for so long at Loch lomond, must not quit my post now till my task is done — tho' I hope it will be soon after the middle of Sept^{er} – The weather is very sweet now – the full flush and splendour of autumn – with its broad lights – deep morning calms – and majesty of mingling colours – We are very tranquil and lovely too in these suburban shades – which you will scarcely allow to be the country – both town and suburbs being now pretty much discredited – we are all well – not but that I have intimations of my <u>tracheal</u> infirmity[2] – and broken slumbers still – Charlie is in perfect bloom and goes down twice a week to Lethe[3] on her poney – We came home by the falls of the Clyde[4] and paid some visits – which I daresay you think was very frivolous – But they diverted us – and did no harm —— Tell me how you occupy yourself – and what thoughts you cherish – of life and truth, and happiness and duty? My creed is a very humble and quiescent one on all these matters – it is to think action and effort no otherwise right than as they are necessary or agreeable – and, seeing in what a vast proportion of things we

<u>must be passive</u>, and submit to be borne on the stream of destiny, to learn to be contented with that lot – and to await patiently for the accidents of enjoyment and illumination, which, as well as the contrary – will come to us at any rate, and in spite of our little impotent struggles – in this life, or another – bad heresy this, in the eyes of your men of energy who expect [to *MS torn*] make discoveries as to their own notions and to acquire dominion over them – poor things! – I am sure my notions are the most natural – and I am persuaded you agree with me in your heart – and so will your husband too – when the fermentation subsides – and the intellectual fluid recovers its transparency ——

I have never written to Mrs Richardson about the poems – and I am afraid she may be mortified – If you are in any correspondence with her tell her that I admire them – and that I will write to her very soon — We all send our loves to you – My dear [?Curl][5] and all the rest – He has got a number of new words – and some pretty morsels of morality besides kissing in a very delicate manner –

God bless you my Dear Cousin
Very Affectly Yours
<u>F. Jeffrey</u>

National Library of Scotland, MS 787, ff. 78–9.

1.   Archaic French: Slav.
2.   The latter part of Jeffrey's career as a speaker in court and parliament was plagued by a susceptibility to tracheitis, an affliction which in its unpredictability was obviously exacerbated and complicated by anxiety. ('So much wine goes down it, so many words leap over it, how can it rest?' asked his friend Sydney Smith, *The Letters of Sydney Smith*, ed. N. C. Smith, 2 vols (Oxford: Clarendon Press, 1953), vol. 1, p. 472.) This and his varicose veins become common complaints in Jeffrey's letters to sympathetic friends, on which his friend and biographer Henry Cockburn (in a letter to Jeffrey's wife Charlotte of 2 February 1823) is instructive: 'He enumerated his disorders to me t'other day, beginning, like his model Job, at the sole of his foot, & ending with the crown of his head. But you know that all orators like to describe, & and that with all good describers the picture is stronger than the original' (NLS, Dep. 235, box 1). Compare also Jeffrey's self-mocking letter to Jane of 4 and 5 December 1833, below, on his own 'Dyspepsias and tracheas and heart flutterings and head swimmings – and varicosities and dimness of sight – and a very little Lazar house of my own – a nice epitome of nosology!'
3.   Leith, presumably, the port on the Firth of Forth immediately to the north of Edinburgh. (Jeffrey spells it correctly in his letter of 4 January 1829, below, so he is punning here.)
4.   Home from Loch Lomond, that is, via the waterfalls on the River Clyde, a mile south of Lanark and to the south-west of Edinburgh.
5.   Jeffrey's dog. Jeffrey was renowned for the pets he indulged. David Alec Wilson records an occasion in September 1843 when Carlyle enquired about a parrot of Jeffrey's that had since died: '"Whisht! Whisht!" said Mrs. Jeffrey, too late. Jeffrey's face was flushed and his eyes were moist. Few living things were dearer to him than the pet parrot which had died; and instantly Carlyle divining the truth exclaimed: "Jeffrey, Jeffrey, you're surely not going to cry over that horned beast!" And they talked of Charles Dickens

and others' (D. A. Wilson, *Carlyle*, 6 vols (London: Kegan Paul et al.; New York: E. P. Dutton, 1923–34), vol. 3: *Carlyle on Cromwell and Others (1837–48)* (1925), p. 239). The transition from sentimental abandon over a beloved pet to the novels of Charles Dickens is telling.

TO THOMAS CARLYLE

date 23 September 1828
from Craigcrook

Craigcrook 23 Septr 1828

My Dear C —

I have been working at Glasgow and dawdling in Ayrshire – and only returned and found your letter, and packet last night – I write now, in the midst of some bustle, to assure you that it has come safely – and to set your heart at ease about proofs &c by informing you that as it is too late, and far too large for the present Nº – (which ~~will~~ is finished indeed, and will be out in a few days) I shall be able without any inconvenience to let you have the proofs for the next – Tho' I only arrived last night, and had packets enough to look into I contrived to <u>read through</u> your paper before going to bed – some proof I think that I either liked it – or took an interest in the writer [–] The truth is I do both – But it is distressingly long – you do not know how much I am abused, and by my best friends and coadjutors, about these long articles – and really you are <u>diffuse</u> this time, as well as long – I cannot venture to print 60 pages of such matter (and it would go to that) and it is the more provoking, because the article would be far better – more striking – more indicative of genius, and more effectual for your purpose, if it were condensed to half the size — <u>I</u> cannot reduce it so far – for it would require to be written nearly over again – but I <u>must</u> make some retrenchments[1] – and I will send you the proofs when that is done – The latter part is far the best – the best written and best conceived – I wish there had been less mysticism about it – at least less mystical jargon – less talk and repetition about entireness, and simplicity, and equipments – and such matters [–] There is also much palpable exaggeration – and always the most dogmatism where you are either decidedly wrong or very doubtfully right – But there is a noble strain of sentiment – and kind and lofty feeling – and much beauty and felicity of diction – You will treat me as something worse than an ass I suppose when I say that I am firmly persuaded the great source of your extravagance, and of all that makes your writings intolerable to many – and ridiculous to not a few, is not so much any real peculiarity of opinions as an unlucky ambition to appear more original than you are – or the humbler and still more delusive hope of converting our English intellects to the creed of Germany – and being the apostle of another reformation — I wish to God I could persuade you to fling away these affectations – and be contented to write like your famous countrymen of all ages – as long at least as you write <u>to</u> your countrymen and <u>for</u> them — The <u>nationality</u> for which you commend Burns so highly might teach you I think that there are nobler tasks for a man like you than to vamp up the vulgar dreams of these Dousterswivels[2] you are so anxious to cram down our throats – but which I venture to predict no good judge among us will swallow – and the nation at large speedily reject with loathing — But we will talk of this by and bye – I have no time now for it –

O yes – we are coming – do not expect to escape us – Yet I cannot exactly say when – but I think in less than ten days – I shall write to give fair warning – Must we come first to Dumfries, on our way from Edin^r? – give us an exact route – that we may not wander and be benighted in your desarts — Why does not my little cousin write to me? We think and speak constantly of her, and you — We are all well – except me and my throat occasionally – but it is no worse – if I could find time I should go to London for a proper consultation – and perhaps I may –

God bless you now – for I have much dull work before me – Ever yours
      F. Jeffrey

National Library of Scotland, MS 787, ff. 28–9.

1.   Carlyle's response to Jeffrey's editing and abbreviating his article on Burns for the *Edinburgh Review* is recorded in a letter to his brother John in October 1828: 'Jeffrey had clipt the first portion of it all into shreds (partly by my permission), simple [*for* simply?] because it was too long. My first feeling was indignation, and to demand the whole back again, that it might lie in my drawer and worm-eat, rather than come before the world in that horrid souterkin shape; the body of a quadruped with the head of a bird ... However, I determined to *do nothing for three days*; and now by replacing and readjusting many parts of the first sixteen pages ... I have once more put the thing into a kind of publishable state; and mean to send it back, with a private persuasion that probably I shall not soon write another for that quarter. Nevertheless, I will keep friends with the man; for he really has extraordinary worth, and likes me, at least heartily wishes me well' (*Carlyle Letters*, vol. 4, pp. 413–4). See M. H. Goldberg, 'Jeffrey, Mutilator of Carlyle's "Burns"?', *PMLA*, 56:2 (June 1941), pp. 466–71.

2.   From the character Herman Dousterswivel, the fraudulent magician in Walter Scott's novel *The Antiquary*. 'Dousterswivel' became a common term of abuse which Jeffrey and his circle applied to charlatans, especially those inhabiting that grey area between science and magic and between philosophy and mysticism. See, for example, John Gibson Lockhart: 'Dr Spurzheim (or, as the Northern Reviewers very improperly christened him in the routs of Edinburgh, Dousterswivel)', *Peter's Letters to His Kinsfolk*, 3 vols (Edinburgh: Blackwood, 1819), vol. 2, p. 341.

TO THOMAS (AND JANE WELSH) CARLYLE

date 3 October 1828
from Craigcrook

Craigcrook Friday 3ᵈ Oct

My Dear C –

I think at present that we shall be with you on Tuesday – sleeping on Monday at Thornhill[1] – and eschewing the mail coach, and all that appertains to it – I cannot fix absolutely however – but if I do not write again, you may hold that we are on our pilgrimage – and pray for us accordingly — I should probably have delayed this intimation till I could make it more peremptorily But cannot delay a moment letting you know how much I am gratified by the kindness of your letter – and the reasonableness – (though I am afraid it is rather resignation than docility) of your remarks on my proposed mutilation of your dissertation on Burns – That cruel operation is now over – the M.S. is at press – and I hope to bring the proofs with me – But for your relief I hasten to say that I am not without hope that you will think my proceeding merciful – and that I have not <struck> out much that you were much in earnest about – or would be particularly anxious to retain – In the first place I have left you as much as, I reckon will print to 48 pages or more – then my retrenchments have been chiefly on the first 20 pages – and include most of your long quotations from the poetry – and finally I honestly think <they> are confined, with very little exception, to mere repetitions, having removed scarcely anything that is not still to be found – two or three times over – in the substance of what remains – all your general speculations – tho I think some of them rash and unsound enough – are retained – and tho' I have relieved you of about 10 pages in all, I hope they will not be much missed – even by their author – but we shall see — In the mean time I cannot but thank you again for the frank and goodnatured manner in which you submit to this sad infliction and which, tho' I could not decline it, I had some fear would appear very grievous to one who is so firm in his opinions – and so sincerely impressed with a belief of their importance as I take you to be [–] As for <u>mysticism</u> and Dousterswivels – we shall talk about them when we meet – only I cannot but think that you have no right to refuse that honourable appellation so long as you profess to think lightly of all that can be readily understood – and to measure the depth of any thing by its darkness — As for <u>jargon</u> I shall point out to you what I mean by it – when we have certain works on the table before us – and in the mean time I may intimate that I hold the frequent use of words at once vague and unusual to come fairly within that description – or any use of words by the mere mention of which everybody at once recognises the writer – and smiles at the recollection. It is surely desirable to avoid such badges. I have read your discussion on Goethe in the new Nº of the Foreign[2] – and read it with great pleasure, and pride on your account, as a work of great eloquence, ingenuity and good feeling – It is indeed the only good thing in the N° – the only sunny spot (or region rather) in that dull waste – Unless you write the whole of the next – I do not think it can be long for this world – The rival work is far superior in general – and you ought to transfer yourself to it – if you prefer a better vehicle for your opinions to the glory of upholding a falling state — But tho' I admire the talent of your paper, I am more and more convinced of the utter fallacy of your opinions – and the grossness of your idolatry – I predict too, with full and calm assurance, that your cause is quite hopeless – and that England <u>never will</u> admire – nor indeed endorse your German divinities — It thinks better and more of them indeed at this moment than it ever will again – <u>Your</u> eloquence and ingenuity a little masks their dull extravagance and tiresome presumption – as soon as they appear in their own persons everybody will laugh and yawn, and run out of the room [–] If you really think otherwise bring them to the test by translations – for a kindred dialect like theirs it is a perfectly fair one – and only observe the result — There can never be a better time to introduce them with advantage than after the flourish of trumpets with which you have announced them and yet, if they are not hissed off the stage, I too shall begin to think of worshipping – I am really anxious to save you from this <u>fœda superstitio</u>³ – The only harm it has yet done you is to make you a little verbose and prone to exaggeration – There are strong symptoms of them in your Burns – I have tried to staunch the first but the latter is in the grain – and we must just risk the wonder and the ridicule it may bring on us – I can afford it — God bless you

    Very Affectly Yours

    <u>F. Jeffrey</u>

My dear child and cousin – you see we are coming – I wish a reliance on our love for you could make you happy – for no creature could then be surer of happiness – and I will believe, because I feel, that it helps [–] We are in no fear of anything at Craigenputtach⁴ – but the pain of leaving it again – and do not care even about the trouble to which we may put you – I hope to find you rosy – and fond of roses — There is nobody of whom I think so often – or with so much affection – Heaven bless you

    Fr. J.

National Library of Scotland, MS 787, ff. 30–1.

1.   A Dumfriesshire village on the River Nith, 14 miles north-west of Dumfries.

2.   A reference to Carlyle's article on 'Goethe's Helena', *Foreign Review*, 1 (April 1828), pp. 429–68.

3.   Latin: unseemly or detestable religious awe.

4.   Jeffrey consistently (mis)spelled Craigenputtoch (sometimes also spelled 'Craigenputtock') in this way, with a final '-ach'.

TO THOMAS (AND JANE WELSH) CARLYLE

date [12 October 1828]
from Craigcrook

Craigcrook Sunday Morng

My Dear Carlyle

If we have any true community of feeling, you must be aware that I have a
<u>besoin</u>[1] to write to you today – first that I might say <u>to</u> you what we have all been
continually saying to ourselves since we left you[2] – What will they be doing <u>now</u>
at Craigenputtach? will they miss us a little – or be relieved by our departure?
Will Mrs. C. blame the rough walks we took her for her cold? – will C. himself
be the worse for the late hours and horrid wrangling into which we led him?
You understand all that, without telling – and the sort of flatness that ensues
upon such a parting – and the feeling that we did not make enough of the meeting – and did not comport ourselves in a way to do justice to the kindness and
esteem that are in our hearts? – and it is to say this, which you would understand
without saying – that I cannot rest till I have written to you, and that I leave all
my <u>business</u> neglected, till I have disburdened my soul of it! — There is one thing
more – or rather a part of the same thing – which I feel to be equally urgent –
and that is to ask your pardon again for the little burst of irritability which came
on me by surprise during our last vigil – and also to explain – tho' that I believe
is less necessary – why I spoke with so little softening – perhaps with so much
asperity – of what I conceived to be the error, or at all events the monstrous exaggeration, of some of your cherished opinions – Sincerity required that I should
speak plainly and firmly – but I was anxious to show you also not only some of
the reasons for which sensible people would reject your conclusions – but the
tone and temper in which even the candid and thoughtful part of them must
necessarily regard them – It would have been more polite and agreeable to have
veiled this temper a little — and, as I myself really care less than most people
about theories and speculative whimsies, I do not think I should have displayed
it at all seriously – if you had been confiding yours to me alone – but it seemed to
be a necessary part of my warning ag[ains]t your public apostleship – and I have
only to add that I feel confident you cannot now <mis>understand my motives
– nor doubt for an instant that our verbal and metaphysical differences are perfectly consistent with the greatest respect and affection – I will say further that
I shall think calmly over all you have said to me, and consider, with every possible desire to come to an affirmative conclusion – whether grounds may not be
found upon which those who agree cordially as to fact and feeling and practice
may agree in theory also – tho' after all there is no great harm done – and so God
prosper the right! ——

We had a sad blasty day as we passed by the sweet scenery about Penpont – and came thro' the gorge of Dalveen under the grand gleam of a furious black shower – We slept at Crawford[3] – and got here about dark yesterday — We are very green and tolerably leafy still – and I begin now to prize my rustic leisure the more as I see the end of it so fast approaching – I must be at Glasgow for Jury trials[4] the first week of No[v] – and the end of that spell will bring the beginning of the Session. If I could be sure of my voice I should care little about it – but the distrust of that is uncomfortable —

I cannot bring myself to think that either you [?or *MS torn*] Mrs C. are <u>naturally</u> placed at Craigenputtach – and tho' I <u>know</u> and reverence the feelings which have led you to fix there for the present, I must hope that it will not long be necessary to obey them in that retreat — I dare not advise and do not even know very well what to suggest to a mind so constituted as yours – but I shall be proud to give you my views upon anything that occurs to yourself – and pray understand that few things in this world can give me more gratification than being able to be of any serious use to you —

Take care of that fair creature who has trusted herself so entirely to you – Do not let her ride about in the wet – nor expose herself to the country winds that will by and bye visit your lofty retreat – Think seriously of taking shelter from them in Moray place for a month or two – and in the mean time be gay and playful, and foolish, with her, at least as often as you require her to be wise and heroic with you — You have no mission upon earth – whatever you may fancy – half so important as to be innocently happy – and all that is good for you of poetic feeling, and sympathy with majestic nature, will come of its own accord, without your straining after it – That is my creed – and right or wrong – I am sure it is both a simpler and an <u>humbler</u> one than yours – and so God bless you — tell me again how I am to address the old books I am to send you – Will you write me another review soon? and on what? — Ever Very Affectly Yours,

<u>F. Jeffrey</u>

My Dear Child. The sight of you has refreshed my heart within me – and the kindness and the confidence you showed for me has justified the tender interest I took in you since I first heard the sound of your voice – I would willingly have come twice as far for the pleasure I had in seeing you – Tell me you have forgiven my harshness about that manuscript[5] – and that you can look at it, with all its erasures – without hating me – Take care of yourself – mind and body and write me a kind line sometimes — Ever Yours

Fr. J.

National Library of Scotland, MS 787, ff. 32–3.
1.   French: need.

2. Carlyle celebrated the Jeffreys' visit to Craigenputtoch from 7 to 10 October in a letter to his brother John misdated 10 October 1828 (it was written several days later): 'We had three such days of [Jeffrey] last week! Wife and child and lapdog and maid were here with him; and the storm vainly howled without, and the *glar* [mud] vainly gaped for us ... for we had roaring fires within and the brightest talk, enough and to spare! It was a fairy time' (*Carlyle Letters*, vol. 4, p. 414).

3. Returning to Edinburgh from Craigenputtoch, the Jeffreys journeyed north-east to the parish of Penpont, through Dalveen Pass over the Lowther Hills on the border of Dumfriesshire and Lanarkshire, and then via the Lanarkshire village of Crawford.

4. Jeffrey had to plead before the new 'Jury Court' introduced in 1816 when civil cases were tried by jury for the first time under Scottish law.

5. Carlyle's Burns article.

TO THOMAS CARLYLE

date 22 October [1828]
from Craigcrook

Craigcrook Wedy 22ᵈ Oct

My Dear C.

How can you be so absurd as to talk of cancelling that excellent paper of yours on Burns,[1] after it has given both of us so much trouble – or to imagine that I do not set a due value on it, because I was compelled to make it a little shorter – and induced to vary a few phrases that appeared to me to savour of affectation – or at all events of mannerism? It is really too childish – and I am tempted to give you a sound scolding for your folly – However I shall only say that I do not think I shall let you have any more proof sheets – It only vexes you and – does no good – for you correct them very badly – leaving half the typographical errors unredressed, and exerting yourself only to replace all the words and phrases, which I, for very good reasons, had taken out. I am afraid you are a greater admirer of yourself than becomes a philosopher, if you really think it material to stick to all these odd bits of diction – and to reject any little innocent variation on your inspired text – How could you dream of restoring such a word as <u>fragmentary</u> – or that very simple and well used joke of the ~~tailor~~ <clothes> making the man – and the tailor being a creator? It was condescension enough to employ such ornaments at first but it is inconceivable to me that anybody should stoop to pick them up and stitch them on again, when they had once been stripped off — You really must not take the pet, because I do my duty[2] – He who comes into a crowd must submit to be squeezed – and at all events must not think himself ill treated if his skirts are crumpled or the folds of his drapery a little compressed – You may be assured that I have given you more room than I have given any other person – and I cannot think you have any reason to feel sore because I have scored out 3 or 4 pages of very ordinary quotation – and about as much of the least important of your remarks – You have still a good portly article of 46 pages, on a subject by no means new – not interesting in itself to readers and now treated in a manner of which many, tho' I think unjustly, will disapprove – If you had my office to fill <but> for one year, you would be more indulgent to the apparent errors in my administration of it – In reference to your particular case you should remember that I have 2 duties to perform – one certainly to give you a fair field to display your talents and enforce your opinions – but another, to promote the popularity, circulation and effect of the review – I am afraid the last is the paramount duty – and to you I can only say that I have trenched more upon it already for your sake than I ever did for that of any one besides – If I had altered this last paper purely with a view to that object I would have scored out twice as much — and obliterated the mannerisms far more boldly — But I am quite satisfied with the compromise I have made – Your paper I have no doubt will give great pleasure and do us great credit – tho' it will be called tedious and sprawling, by people of much weight [–] whose mouths I could have stopped – and I think you must own that it affords a very fair and very ample scantling of your doctrines and manner of writing – tho' not quite so full and perfect as you had desired — So pray be a good boy – and do not sulk or make faces again at slight inflictions ——

You would get my Sunday letter the day you [?sent/posted *MS torn*] yours – I am glad I was beforehand with you – and that my modest expressions of kindness could not appear as returns to your magnificent compliments – I wish I were worthy of them – or rather that you would like me without supposing that I am — But you mystics will not be contented with kindness of heart and rea-sonable notions in anybody – but you must have gifts and tasks and duties – and relations with the universe, and strugglings to utter forth the truth — God help you and your vainglorious jargon, which makes angels smile I take it – and sen-sible men laugh outright   You have not told me yet how I am to send you the books – but I really know no Scottish history that is worth anything in com-parison with those you have excluded – There is controversy about Queen Mary and such trash – and Drummonds history of the Stewarts[3] – inaccurate and unwise – and some old Chronicles – full of lies and obscurities – Pinkerton and Lord Hailes[4] are enough for the old past – and Robertson and Laing[5] for what follows – what more would you have? —

I am afraid it is wintry now at Craigenputtach – our leaves are falling fast here – but we are still very green and shady with a respectable show of flowers – I enclose some carnation leaves for my bright child to whom we send all love beside —

You will understand that your article is actually printed, and has the honor of standing in the van – and yet you think yourself shabbily used – O Vanity of

Vanities. — I enclose a draft as an account of it – for which you will get cash at Dumfries – and So God bless you and keep you – Write me soon – and tell me whether you have any good matter in your head for another review — Ever Very Affectly Yours

Fanny[6] desires her respects}

F. Jeffrey

What is this about the Chair of Rhetoric and the death of old Brown?[7] Is he going to die immediately? And have you any hopes or pretensions to that Chair, other than what may be founded on your general merit? Can I be of any use, either in making enquiries or otherwise? In one way I might, indirectly – by correcting and keeping out of sight your mannerisms and affectations in the review – and you will not let me – o cæca mens hominum![8] —

National Library of Scotland, MS 787, ff. 34–5.

1. Carlyle had already decided to go ahead and publish the heavily retrenched version. See note 1 to the letter of 23 September 1828, above.

2. Jeffrey kept a close editorial eye on most of the articles he published, making emendations, omissions, and insertions at will. The following letter, written nearly twenty years earlier to Horace Twiss on 30 March 1810, gives a good indication of his editorial policy:

    in order that we may understand each other I think it best to tell you, that I should wish to be at liberty to add and to suppress a sentence or two in the introduction – to shorten the abstract and extracts from the pamphlett, and to abate something of that tone of implicit confidence in the accuracy of the author in which you appear to me to have exceeded – I rather think also that I should like to add a word or two to develop and illustrate the nature of that process by which we both agree in conceiving that the powers of France would be weakened by taking away the occasions of warlike exertion – There is no alteration which I should wish to make in the strain of your general reasoning, which coincides indeed pretty much with my own impressions – nor is there any other paper or essay which I should think of combining with yours – all I wish is to have your express permission for adding with my own hand a few cautions, illustrations, or additional remarks which appear to me to be important and to fall in with the general tenor of your doctrine –

    If I have your permission to deal thus with your paper I can answer for its appearing – and probably as the leading article – in next No If this is withheld I must beg leave to consider further about inserting it at all – you know how very severely we are watched and scrutinized as to our political opinions – and I do perceive some few things in your paper which I think might embarrass us here after or give the enemy a present advantage – You will excuse me also for adding that it is unusual to make extraordinary concessions to an *unknown* correspondent and that the powers I ask from you are only those which I exercise over the oldest and most respectable of our contributors (NLS, MS 2257, ff. 63–4).

3. William Drummond (of Hawthornden), *The History of Scotland, from the Year 1423 until the Year 1542: Containing the Lives and Reigns of James I. the II. the III. the IV. the V.* (1655).

4.   John Pinkerton, *History of Scotland from the Accession of the House of Stuart to that of Mary* (1792) and Lord Hailes [Sir David Dalrymple], *Annals of Scotland* (1776, 1779).
5.   William Robertson, *The History of Scotland during the Reigns of Queen Mary and King James VI* (1759) and Malcolm Laing, *The History of Scotland from the Union of the Crowns on the Accession of James VI ... to the Union of the Kingdoms in the Reign of Queen Anne* (1800).
6.   Jeffrey's daughter Charlotte's nanny.
7.   Andrew Brown (1763–1834), Professor of Rhetoric and Belles Lettres at the University of Edinburgh from 1801 until his death in 1834, six years after this letter was written. Carlyle had obviously heard he was ill. (See note 1 to the letter of 4 February 1834, below.)
8.   Latin: O blinded is the mind of man.

TO THOMAS CARLYLE

date 11 November 1828
from Edinburgh

Edin[r] 11 Nov[r] 1828

My Dear Carlyle

I have been dreadfully busy – and am just returned from a wearisome campaign of ten days at Glasgow – I intended to have answered your letter there – but found it actually impossible – having literally <u>lived</u>, from rise to set, in courts and consultations – not having even the reasonable refection of a dinner, but once, in all that time – I am busy enough still, you may suppose, as our courts begin again tomorrow – But I <u>must</u> write one line – to say that I admire and approve of your letter in all things. Your candour and sweet blood are indeed admirable and as somebody makes a dying pagan say in a play "If these are Christian virtues, I am Christian"[1] so I am ready to exclaim "If these are mystic virtues, I <u>am mystic</u>" – But it is not so – The virtues are your own – and you possess them not in consequence of your mysticism – but in spite of it — You shall have proof sheets – and anything you like – I really cannot chaffer with such a man – or do anything to vex him – and you shall write mysticism for me too – if it will not be otherwise – and I shall print it too, at all hazard – with few, very few and temperate correction – I think you have a great deal of eloquence and talent – and might do considerable things, if — but no matter – I will not tire of you – and after all there are many more things I believe as to which we agree – than about which we differ – and the difference is not radical, but formal chiefly – and now God bless you — I am not sure that I shall be able to send your books even today – but you can do very well without them – with Don Quixote[2] and the mystics – The kindest love to my fair cousin – let her write a word to me now and then – it is like dew to a thirsty land – in this fever and bustle — I shall write soon again

Ever Very Affectly Yours
F. Jeffrey

National Library of Scotland, MS 787, f. 36.

1. The Peruvian Indian sovereign Zamor, responding to an act of charity on the part of the Spanish governor Don Carlos in the play *Alzira* (1736) – a translation of Voltaire's *Alzire* published in the same year – by dramatist and librettist Aaron Hill (1685–1750).

2. Carlyle wrote to his brother John on 26 November 1828: 'I write hard all day; then Jane and I (both learning Spanish for the last month) read a chapter of Don Quixote between dinner and tea, and are already half thro' the first volume, and eager to persevere' (*Carlyle Letters*, vol. 4, p. 422).

TO THOMAS CARLYLE

date 8 December 1828
from Edinburgh

Edin^r Decr 1828

My Dear Carlyle

I begin to be unhappy about you in these long, dark howling nights – I wrote you – from Glasgow I think – and I have heard nothing from or about you since that time – and a good while before – Pray tell us what you have been doing – or suffering rather in that supramundane retreat – I sometimes fear you are ill – and sometimes that you are so happy with your mysticism – and your Spanish – and your fumigations, that you forget there is anybody to care for you in this lower world – and disdain to spend a thought or a drop of ink upon us – however I should like at all events to know – and I do therefore entreat you, immediately on perusal of this, to indite me a faithful epistle containing a full and true account of your experiences, since you last vouchsafed me any communication —

Oh about your old books – you are yet to learn what a miserable <u>commissionaire</u> I am in such matters – and how little able to help either myself or my friends by exertions that imply any physical effort, or approach to punctuality – I have utterly forgotten what books you wanted – except that I recommended the Judicious Hooker[1] to you – and spoke something in praise of histories which you vilipended I have resolved too, several times every week – to import Hooker from Craigcrook for you – and have always forgotten – But if you will put down the titles of those you really wish for in a corner of your letter, I will take care of the order – that is I will get Mrs J. and Adam Black[2] to take care of it – and the odds are – that the parcel will reach Dumfries about the time your are snowed in for the Christmas holidays — But after all do not you think the better way would be to make yourself independent of the snows – and come and meet the books and the Christmas holidays with us? If you stay much longer the pass of Dalveen will be impassable – and then you will be frozen in till the spring thaw come to release you – So ponder the matter and act promptly – you will find your room ready for you here on an hours warning – and all of us on the alert to give you welcome —

I am tolerably well – rather better I think on the whole than I was this time last year – and rather less busy – I suppose I am going out of fashion – so that I shall have more leisure to mystify myself with you than formerly – which may perchance be [?a *MS torn*] great gain – Mrs J. has had a bad cold – but is well again – Charley[3] is in perfect vigour – and Polly[4] and Fanny I am happy to say in very tolerable condition [–] The review creeps on slowly and steadily – I have more than three fourths printed – and shall be out by Christmas, if I am not embargoed by some one of Broughams orders in council.[5] What of the Foreign?

Kind love to my fair cousin – how does she stand those plashy, blasty moon-less starless nights and dark gusty days? If she have any of my blood in her she should be subject to those skyey influences – and they are not genial at this moment — I long and pant to bathe my eyeballs in a pure sky again – I must not write any more tonight so God bless you – This indeed is but a line of enquiry and I want to send it off, so as to reach Dumfries for your weekly messenger tomorrow – He will have a sweet promenade up to your fastness in the teeth of a blast like this — Ever Very Affectly Yours

F. Jeffrey

National Library of Scotland, MS 787, ff. 37–8.

1.   Richard Hooker (*c.* 1554–1600), author of *Of the Laws of Ecclesiastical Polity* (1594, 1597). Carlyle needed no convincing: 'These men, these Hookers, Bacons, Brownes were *men*; but for our present "men of letters", our song manufacturers, I shall only say: May the Lord pity us and them!', in a letter to Anna Montagu, 25 December 1826 (*Carlyle Letters*, vol. 4, p. 173).
2.   The Edinburgh bookseller and publisher.
3.   Daughter Charlotte.
4.   The parrot.
5.   Jeffrey often complained (not always ingenuously) about the sway that Henry Brougham exercised over his editing of the *Edinburgh Review*, a combined effect of the sheer force-fulness of Brougham's character and the ever-present threat that he might cease his generous contributions. (Brougham was famous for having had the Orders in Council restricting foreign maritime trade, so detrimental to American shipping, revoked in par-liament in 1812, too late to avert the brief war with America that ensued.)

1829

TO THOMAS (AND JANE WELSH) CARLYLE

date 4 January 1829*

from Edinburgh

Edinr 4 Jany 1828̶9

My Dear Carlyle

One never does anything one wishes or intends to do, in this bad world – I have resolved to write to you every morning, for these two months and have gone tired to bed, every night, without having written – I have not even sent you half the books you wanted – God help me – I grow every day more lazy and irregular – and am beginning to tell myself that I must be indulged a little now, as an old fellow – out of whom the best of the work has been taken – Still however I persist in kind thoughts – and good purposes – and firm opinions ag[ains]t all dogmatism and clear views of the desperate darkness of wilful and audacious mystics —— and so we are at another year – so soon – so imperceptibly – It is strange that years should seem shorter and shorter as there are fewer of them remaining – and less done in each – That I suppose is the reason – and therefore it is likely that you have never felt this truth yet – But it will come one day – and it is less distressing than you might imagine – startling a little perhaps as it comes suddenly on you – but prompting at the last a smile rather than a sigh – We have been all living here, you will have seen, in the fear of fever and dissection[1] – and yet not less gaily and carelessly than formerly – We are all predestinarians in our hearts I fancy – and run our risks patiently – simply because we cannot avoid them –In the mean time we have escaped marvellously – and the pestilent and murdering angels have hitherto passed us over – I hope we shall live to see you in Spring and that I may then be the means of weeding out some of those damnable heresies to which I see you are still devoted – one is, that our modern songsters in the minor key, are worthy of bitter hate and indignant reprobation – which is much more like the sentiment of some spiteful disappointed brother of the craft, than the judgment of a philanthropic philosopher – The truth is they are worthy of a good deal of love and gratitude – with some pity no doubt – and some scorn – and many prayers for their improvement — another is that men are less noble – less happy and less deserving of happiness – than they were in the days of Shakespere or Cervantes – which I take to be a notable mistake. Do you really believe that there were not plenty of shabby fellows – whining over petty aches and finding life irksome in palaces, in the age and the country of Cervantes? – or that there are not men stout hearted bright spirited men enough, who bear up ag[ains]t captivity, and worse ills, as cheerily as he did? Do cure yourself of this tendency to exaggeration – which is a propensity too youthful even for you – and brings me in mind of the boyish elation of spirit with which I used to read Rousseau['s] encomiums on Savages – and fancy that I had outlived the true manhood of the world – I do not deny that those are swelling themes for eloquence – but they are rather out of date now – and never convinced anybody – You may talk as long as you like about a false principle of pride or honor – and the necessity of having a right creed as to your relations with the universe – but you will never persuade anybody that the regulation of life is such a mighty laborious business as you would make it, or that it is not better to go lightly thro' it, with the first creed that comes to hand, than to spend the better part of it in an anxious verification of its articles — If you were only amusing yourself with these paradoxes, I should have no objection – but you take them so dreadfully in earnest that it vexes me – for it will neutralise half the fame, and all the use of your talents – and keep aloof from you most of the men who are fittest for your society — and so much for my renewed testimony ag[ains]t mysticism, which I repeat, you see, as Cato did his <u>delenda est Carthago</u>[2] – and I hope with the same chance of ultimate success as attended his damnable iteration –

I will look you out other books – But in the mean time Hooker is enough to stay your stomach – a grand fellow beyond all doubt – thoughtful – learned and vigorous – but intolerably verbose, and with all his intellect occasionally very obscure – That I suppose will be his chief charm in your eyes – However I will allow you to be a stout reader if you get fairly through him by the time ~~you~~ we meet — I have also sent Dr H. More[3] – who is a good specimen of one class of our great Divines – and is something German too, I take it, in his ways – and 3 vol of Fletcher instead of one – because I had just been reading them myself and had delighted in them beyond all measure – I am particularly struck with the Maid's Tragedy – and have doubled down one scene which appears to me as full of terror and the tragic power as anything in English – Indeed the whole play – in spite of the tremendous obscenities – is written with a force and spirit only to be equalled in Shakespere – The Island Princess too – tho' more unequal, is full of fire and genius – and the end of Boadicea[4] is divine – But this is only fit for talking – and I will not write another word on the subject –

I wish you would write me a review – if it be not very irksome to you – But I am not much captivated with either of your subjects – What can there <be> to be said new about Voltaire or Johnson? However if you will have one <of them>, I would rather give you Voltaire – both because being a little older and a little farther off, the subject is rather less trite – and because any mistakes we may make about him will be more likely to escape detection – The new N°, which has lingered sadly in the press is just finished – and I hope will come to you on Wedʸ I do nothing but Bishop Heber – whom I entreat you to love for my sake – and bits upon Bentham⁵ – There is a curious paper on Palimpsests and some others you may think worth reading – after you have sufficiently mooned over the shortness and mutilations of your own – But we shall see –

We have had lovely weather all last month – more like April than Decʳ* – I rode out the other day to Craigcrook and found everything as green as July – and we have great bunches of China roses – stocks – wallflowers, mignonettes and anemones, twice a week – It is a pity it is so unhealthy But even the fever can scarcely make me wish for the past [–] Thank you for your chafer of charcoal – tho' it is scarcely a new invention – we used to boil our tea kettles on such machines at Oxford⁶ when the weather was too warm for a fire – only we stuck them out of the window, and believed we should all have been choked in half an hour, if we had sate by them with closed windows – seriously I believe the risk is greater than you seem aware of – your drying vapour being neither more nor less than carbine acid gas in its purest and most fatal form – But with precaution I daresay it may be useful —— Now a word to the Cougina⁷ – and good night –

A good new Year to you my good child – I am glad you have got a pony to tempt you down sometimes to the lower world – and also that you are getting bits of ground to tempt you to walk a little when the sun gets as high as Craigen- puttach – which is seldom the case I fancy in Decʳ – and so you are learning Spanish prosperously and pleasantly – and doing your lessons, like a good girl, without murmuring — You are quite right – and I am persuaded you envy less than many a fine lady in the midst of crowds and amusements – Still I fear you are too lonely – and wish you could have come to us in those long nights – But we have your ideal presence at least – and I hope you do not quite despise the resource of ours – we are all very well, and constant as truth to our absent friends. We have been very domestic these holidays – and have walked about at a great rate – I mean the two Charlottes and Fanny and I – to Leith and Newhaven – and Duddingstone⁸ and Craigcrook – without minding dirt or contagion – My work begins again tomorrow – and then I shall bustle on and on, till you come to cheer me in March – I have been reading a book lately which I think you would like – tho' it has an affected enough title – being called "our Village"⁹ [–] It is written by a lady, and gives a very sweet and cheerful; picture of rustic life and retirement – If you have not read it I will send it to you, as a new Year's gift – or would you rather wait till you come for it? I am not quite sure that you will like it as much as I do – for you are much more difficult about books – and more apt to despise and laugh at innocent defects – which is a misfortune.

I hope you keep down your husband's mysticism – and persuade him that so great a philosopher should be [?above] the sensuality of intoxicating himself with that vile tobacco – twelve pipes a day, I take to be on a par with a bottle of brandy – or 4 gallons of beer O monstrous — We were very much shocked to hear of the fate of poor Anderson[10] – I think you must feel the loss of a cheerful and obliging neighbour – where neighbours are so scanty –

Write me – a whole letter or a bit as you like best – The Curl[11] sends his love to you – he has lately learned to shake hands – and is hourly growing in wisdom, and amiableness – and so God bless you and good night   Ever Very Affectly Your's

     F. Jeffrey

---

* This letter was obviously begun at the end of December.

National Library of Scotland, MS 787, ff. 40–3.

1. Jeffrey was probably referring to the dysentry epidemic that appeared in the autumn of 1828 (M. Cosh, *Edinburgh: The Golden Age* (Edinburgh: John Donald, 2003), pp. 823–4). The typhus scare of 1827–8 had passed and the cholera epidemic of 1831 was yet to threaten.

2. Latin: 'Carthage must be destroyed' – Cato's 'damnable iteration' before the Roman Senate. A despondent Carlyle wrote to his brother John on 13 January 1829 that Jeffrey 'chatters unprofitably about *Mysticism* and so forth. I am very much alone in this world' (*Carlyle Letters*, vol. 5, p. 6).

3. Henry More (1614–1687), scholar and bishop and one of the Cambridge Platonists whose extensive philosophical and theological writings include *Divine Dialogues* (1668).

4. Jeffrey refers here to the Elizabethan and Jacobean playwright John Fletcher's *The Maid's Tragedy* (written with Francis Beaumont, 1611), the romantic comedy *The Island Princess* (1621), and the 1614 tragedy *Bonduca* (an alternative name for the ancient British queen 'Boadicea' or 'Boudicca').

5. Jeffrey, in other words, reviewed Bishop Heber's journal and contributed to William Empson's review of Bentham's *Rationale of Evidence*, *ER*, 48 (December 1828), pp. 312–35, 457–520 (the latter not registered in the attributions in the *Wellesley Index to Victorian Periodicals*).

6. Jeffrey went to Queen's College, Oxford, from the University of Glasgow in September 1791 and left again half-way through the following year. See the letter to Jane of 6 February 1832, below, for his reflections on a recent visit.

7. Italian: cousin.

8. Towns and villages within three miles of the centre of Edinburgh (north, north-west and south-east respectively), all now suburbs of the city.

9. A collection of essays by Mary Russell Mitford entitled *Our Village, Sketches of Rural Life, Character, and Scenery*, begun in *The Ladies' Magazine* in 1819 and published separately between 1824 and 1832.

10. The Andersons owned Stroquhan, a farm between the Carlyles' Craigenputtoch and Dunscore, and the old man had recently died (see *Carlyle Letters*, vol. 5, p. 7 and n.).

11. The dog.

TO THOMAS (AND JANE WELSH) CARLYLE

date 17 April 1829
from Glasgow

Glasgow 17 April 1829

My Dear Carlyle

Why have you not written to me? That is my first question – and it is for you to answer it – But why have I not written before to you? is my second – and tho' it is one for me to answer, I declare I do not really know what answer to give to it – I have been busy of course – and I have expected you to write – and you <u>ought</u> to have written – but still I cannot satisfy myself why I have not written before, to tell you even this – if for nothing else – It must rest there I suppose – and there I shall let it rest – after I have merely said that it was not because I thought less, or less kindly of you – or cared less to give you pleasure or do you service – Believe <u>this</u>, – and neither of us need care much about our answers — You may have gathered perhaps from public manifestations that I was alone, and in my vacation – But I have not heard once about you – and am not altogether without suspicion that you have been frozen to death – or swallowed up in a morass – or suffocated with charcoal in the course of this dreary winter — If it be not so pray let us know – and give us some notion of the sort of existence you have had since July — For us, we have been making a duplicate of the preceding year – or any of our late years – and, however shameful it may appear to you, without any remorse, or self disdain for the poor copymaking – I have longed a little more I believe for the late coming spring – and the never coming leisure – but without any purpose of using them for anything better than that enjoyment which you hold in such horror — We are all pretty well – and very much as when you saw us, except that Fanny has a cough – and little Charly has made some acquisitions of French and drawing – and has grown a little taller —— But the main thing is this, when are you coming to see us? – I once feared that I should have been obliged to go to London about this time – and one of my <u>bad</u> reasons for not writing I believe was that I hated to say this to you – lest it might be the means of interfering with your visit – But now that the danger is over – for it is scarcely possible now that I shall be called for, we are anxious to have you as soon as possible —— We return to Craigcrook to-morrow – and shall be there till the 9th or 10th of May – and shall be most happy to have you with us all that time – and as much longer after as you can afford also – your old apartment in Moray Place being entirely at your service – So say you are coming im[m]ed[iate]ly – and let us have some talk in any easier way than this slow long obscure one of writing for which I have every day less patience –

And you my little cousin – send me a line of promise and kindness – I will excuse you your heresies – which are not so much to my fancy – But tell me what you have been doing – and how much wiser you are since last autumn – and consequently how much more indulgent to people who do not think exactly as you do – and yet are very good peop[?le *MS torn*] God bless you – my Dear Child – I wish we had [?you *MS torn*] more in our reach – But you cannot be much more in our thoughts and affections – Pray for me, in your own way – as I do for you in mine – I am obliged to go out – and to end here

Ever Very Affectly Yours
F. Jeffrey

National Library of Scotland, MS 787, ff. 44–5.

TO THOMAS (AND JANE WELSH) CARLYLE

date 3 November 1829
from Craigcrook

Craigcrook Tuesday 3ᵈ Novʳ 1829

My Dear C.

You should have written first – Those who go away should always write – for they have all the adventures and the novelties – and nothing ever happens you know to those who stay at home – but being left to regret those who leave them – However since you will not write, I must – especially as the Session[1] is coming fast on me, when no man can write anything but law arguments and opinions – One thing I want to say too which, though hinted at, was not properly said when you were here – I mean about your continuing your contributions to the E. Review[2] — Napier – though his nose may have a tyrannical expression – has a high opinion of your talents, and is anxious to avail himself of them – But he is more alarmed at your mystical propensities even than I am – and would naturally feel more shy and awkward in remonstrating ag[ains]t them — What I have to suggest therefore is, that you should indulge these propensities as little as possible, in the beginning at least of your intercourse with him – and then that you should apply to me, whenever you are in any perplexity, as freely as if I were still in the chair of the Editor – To you, and for your sake I will be Editor always – I think too that you should mention to N. or me any subjects that you contemplate, and come to some resolution about them <with us>, before giving yourself much trouble in the preparing for them — My chief object however is to offer my services, to facilitate your communication with my successor till you get over your fear of his nose, and become better acquainted —— —

And so you are back again at Craigenputtach – in full enjoyment of solitude and tobacco – unmolested by those idle socialities you hold in such contempt – and those audacious contradictions which wear out your spirit still more – Well – if you are happier there, I am sure we ought not to repine – But it is impossible not to wish that you were a little more tolerant of this lower world – and difficult to believe that it is really good for you to be so alone — I do not care a farthing for your opinions – and never imagine that either your speculative errors or mine are much worth enquiring into – But the unsocial dispositions which yours lead you to indulge are a matter of regret to me, and I cannot but suspect, a source of discomfort to yourself – My main practical quarrel with you is for the unreasonable and really absurd contempt you foster, first for the genius of your country – and next for multitudes of men in all countries, whom it would suit you far better to admire – There are so few high intellects in the world that it is pitiful to see them grudging and carping at each other – and then it is so much more agreeable and amiable and useful to admire – But I will not preach any more to you — forgive this — and believe that nothing could give me more pleasure than to see you happy and famous in your own way—

One other word of what I think I forgot while you were with me – I mentioned to you confidentially more than I ever mentioned to anyone else, of my alienation from Wilson[3] – and what led to it – I wish that to be confidential – Perhaps it was not right to speak of it at all to a third person – But I should hate above all things to have any going back upon such matters – and beg that you would not mention them, as from me — and so God bless you – I have a word to say to my fair cousin

—— —

And so the Peas[4] were not sent you – It was not my fault – but I begin now to think it was right – They are happier here, under the wing of their mother – and you will remember us without them – and I never see them pacing elegantly about the green without thinking of you and Craigenputtach and the places where they should have been – It is as if you had given them to us – and that is as good as the other way — I hope you were not too much chilled on your journey – and not <u>too glad</u> to find yourself on your own lofty perch again – Thursday was but a gloomy day for your reascending to your clouds – but we have had bright hours since – and I hope your roses have taken kindly to their new beds – These partings are sad things – but they are tests of strong affections and it is a pride to set them at defiance – We miss you still very much – and think of you as much as if you were here – I walk every night in the garden, at the old hour – tho' without the protection of a cigar – and say a little evening prayer for you – I shall have a moon in a night or two – but even stars have been scarce lately – I enclose two leaves of carnation for you — I called on Moir[5] yesterday in hopes of learning something about you – but did not find him – I think you should have given him some little note or message for us – or at least a little drawing of Craigenputtach – and so Heaven bless you – Write soon and let us know what you are doing and meditating – With kindest love from all the house – Molly[6] included Ever Most Affectly Yours

   F. Jeffrey

National Library of Scotland, MS 787, ff. 46–7.

1. The legal term in Scotland.

2. Jeffrey had resigned his editorship of the *Edinburgh Review* in June of 1829 on being elected to the non-partisan position of Dean of the Faculty of Advocates. The new editor was Macvey Napier (1776–1847) – a Scottish Whig lawyer, like Jeffrey, and the editor of the *Encyclopaedia Britannica* – with whom Carlyle felt less comfortable, though he continued his contributions intermittently over the next four years.

3. John Wilson (1785–1854), a poet and (as 'Christopher North') a leading figure in a group of talented, often aggressive Tory satirists writing for *Blackwood's Edinburgh Magazine*, who later became Professor of Moral Philosophy at Edinburgh University. Jeffrey and Wilson had fallen out over an attack in *Blackwood's* on the implied atheism of Jeffrey's friend and fellow reviewer, the mathematician and scientist John Playfair (1748–1819), once a Presbyterian minister and, until his death, Professor of Natural Philosophy at the University of Edinburgh. Jeffrey wrote at the time (13 October 1818) to Wilson in his capacity as 'a principal writer in, and a great director and active supporter' of *Blackwood's*: 'In the last number of that work there is an attack upon my excellent friend Mr Playfair, in my judgment so unhandsome and uncandid, that I really cannot consent either to ask or accept of favours from any one who is aiding or assisting in such a publication' (as quoted in Mrs Gordon, '*Christopher North': A Memoir of John Wilson* (Edinburgh: Thomas C. Jack, 1879), pp. 211–13).

4. Peacock and peahen chicks.

5. George Moir (1800–1870), lawyer, German translator and for a time a friend of Carlyle's, who became Professor of Rhetoric at the University of Edinburgh in 1835 and was later Sheriff of Ross-shire.

6. Unidentified.

TO THOMAS (AND JANE WELSH) CARLYLE

date 9 December 1829
from Edinburgh

Edin^r 9 Decr 1829

My Dear Carlyle

. I am glad to hear you are busy – for your's is all willing work – and you are best pleased with yourself when you work it – and we may all profit by it in season – and the more you work now the less you will grudge being idle hereafter with your friends – I have been busy enough too – tho' not very willingly or proudly – and for no great pride or profit hereafter – but it is the task appointed me – and I try to do it cheerfully – of late however I have been less cheerful than usual – for I have been unwell – I have had a feverish cold, which confined me for days to bed – and still hangs on my voice and lungs in the form of a restless cough – But what is still worse – an enlarged vein in one of my legs has become more enlarged, and something painful – and alarms me with fears of confinement – and vistas of bloody operations – alas – alas – for our poor fleshly nature – and without some aid from the spirit it would quickly weigh us down – but I will not sink under it, if I can help it — I hope to set a good example in suffering – if that should fall on me in the end – But I hope to weather this gloom yet – and to continue still a while in my vocation —

You have got the review I find – and I hope you still take some interest in it – as the field of our first alliance – for my part, my heart warms to the old blue and yellow as Jeannie Deans Duke of Argyll's did to the tartan[1] – and I shall ever care more about it I fear than about my law – one article I think must have given you particular pleasure – being genuine German and mystical. – and altogether unintelligible to ordinary mortals. – I venture to pronounce it without any exception the most <u>unreadable</u> thing that ever was printed in Great Britain and moreover downright sheer gibberish and nonsense – It is the <u>opus majus</u> of our friend Sir Wm Hamilton[2] – who tho' never very clear headed, was a man of sense and vigour till he fell into that bad company – Do take warning in time by his fate – and repent while there is yet acceptance – you see to what likeness you will come at the last, if you go on in the course you are following – I hope you have indulgence for Felicia – and me – and also for my Lady Fanshawe[3] – I cannot reason and will not be importunate with you about reviewing — But if you <u>do</u> review, pray do not give all your custom to the Foreigner[4] – but let some of your lights shine before those of your own kindred – I have no news for you – we are all well — C[harlotte]. has got another Polly – rather ag[ains]t my inclination. – I was willing to be faithful to the memory of my buried love – and really do not see a stranger in his poor old cage – without a pang – But as he is of the same breed and complexion I may in time come to love him too – We have also another puppy – a very sweet, fat curly thing as meek as a lamb – and as playful as a kitten – I wish we had had it to give to my sweet coz – It would have invited and repaid fondling – and been a far better emblem of love than peabirds, and rose twigs – perhaps she will have it when she next comes to see us —— I am going to write the rest of this paper up to her – So good night to you –

Pity me my dear child – for I am sick and sorry and obliged to work thro' it all, like an old pauper – I am allowed to take no exercise, and that has made my little sleep less than ever – and if it were not for some kind friends – and loving hearts, that are with me in the lonely watches of the night, I should often be low enough – But true affection sustains me – and the entire reliance I have on those to whom it is directed – O I assure you it is worth while to have a few sleepless nights now and then for the sake of the communion into which they bring you with absent friends – and the high and deep feelings they cherish – which your snorers and snorters know nothing about – But yet I do not wish you to be sleepless – tell me what you are doing – I have had many visions about Craigenputtach of late – especially since this mild Decr moon has risen upon your desarts – I hate dark nights – and am inexpressibly soothed with the calm light which now gleams thro' my shutters – Pray write me a letter – or a little bit of a letter, direct to myself. – and do not always put me in the third person — Why do you say nothing to my humble request that you would translate a bit of Electric Affinities[5] for me? Is it too much trouble – or do you think my darkness incapable of any illumination? I wish you would put me on doing some good or kind action – I have a great besoin[6] of that sort upon me at present – a sort of deadness of the heart, for which I feel instinctively that that would be the best relief — My Charlottes send their love to you – they are very busy too – very innocent – and I hope very happy — Do not envy Felicia – or me – that was a sort of breaking out of the besoin I have mentioned – a kind of rage to confer happiness – to catch it I suppose in the reflection – I cannot tell how often I wish to have you near me — but let me know that you are happy – and the reflection will reach even thus far — are you busy still with your Spanish? or have you actually advanced into Greek? What is C. working upon? That view of German Literature?[7] – or only things for his Foreign Quarterly? – Does he get books enough from the libraries near – or does he still indulge in illiberal murmurs at their illiberality? – and now good night and God bless you – I shall have some private talk with you yet before morning – but you have nothing to do with that — a prayer and a kind thought for me now & then will not be missed.   Ever yours
     F. Jeffrey

National Library of Scotland, MS 787, ff. 48–9.

1.   Two characters (the second historical) who share a sentimental allegiance to their Scottish homeland in the novel *The Heart of Midlothian* (1819) by Walter Scott. ('Blue and yellow' were the colours both of the *Edinburgh Review* and of the Whig party.)

2.   The review of Victor Cousin's *Cours de Philosophie* in the *Edinburgh Review* by William Hamilton, *ER*, 50 (October 1829), pp. 194–221. Hamilton (1788–1856) would become the Professor of Logic and Metaphysics at Edinburgh University in 1836 and his review did indeed give his friend Carlyle pleasure. 'Sir W. Hamilton's Paper gave proof of much metaphysical reading and meditation', Carlyle wrote to Napier in response both to the article and to this letter of Jeffrey's, 'but I daresay your readers would complain of unintelligibility and so forth; indeed it is full of subtle schoolman logic, and on a subject difficult above all others to discuss for English minds' (*Carlyle Letters*, vol. 5, p. 64).

3.   Jeffrey had reviewed Felicia Hemans's *Records of Women* and *The Forest Sanctuary* in one article and the *Memoirs of Lady Fanshawe* in another, *ER*, 50 (October 1829), pp. 32–47, 75–85.

4.   The *Foreign Review*.

5.   The controversial novel of marriage and passion *Die Wahlverwandtschaften* by Goethe, first published in 1809 and usually translated as *Elective Affinities* (Jeffrey is mocking).

6.   French: need.

7.   In late 1829 and over the early months of 1830 Carlyle was working on a major (four-volume) history of German literature from the middle ages, which he would later abandon. (Jeffrey's harsh comments in his letter of 28 October 1830, below, on Carlyle's method and introductory discussion could not have helped.)

1830

TO THOMAS (AND JANE WELSH) CARLYLE

date 17 January 1830
from Edinburgh

17 Jany 1830

My Dear Carlyle

It is not want of will or of kindness that has delayed my answer to your letter – and I know you will not suppose it is – But I live the life of a cart horse
– and am not long enough out of harness to eat and sleep – You Eremites have
no notion of such a life – and well for you – But you must pity and make allow-
ances ~~with~~ <for> those who have no other — I have had some talk with Napier
about your projects – He is not averse to Napoleon – But he has somebody at
work on some subject which he suspects may include that – and must enquire
before he can be safe with you – In the mean time he has suggested that he would
like still better if you would do him a paper on Wycliffe or Luther – and the
history and philosophy of the Reformation[1] – which were favourite subjects I
think with you when we feasted — You cannot be ready in any event for the next
No – which is half printed and will be out in three weeks or sooner – so that
you will have reasonable time for either of the others – or anything else you may
resolve on — N[apier] thought that you might make a striking article on some
Practical subject – But when I let him a little into your scornful, and I do think
utterly unjust and erroneous, estimate of all our late and living poets, he shud-
dered at the massacre of the innocents to which he had dreamed of inciting you.
However if you should be falling into a relenting mood – as I foresee and foretell
~~that~~ you will one day – and wish to exalt and mystify us by a fine rhapsody on
the divine art, I should rather encourage you to the task – only spare us, if you
possibly can for once – the laud and exaltation of your Germans – which doth
somewhat nauseate our insular taste – even in moderate doses

For my health, I am I suppose better – at least I am more used to my maladies – and think less of them I have got my great veins laced up in a fine soft leather boot or stocking, tightened with a handsome silk lace which is expected to brace and support them, and is not very troublesome and I practise my philosophies – and turn away my thoughts all I can from disagreeable consummations, that must come but need not be anticipated – I am much touched and gratified by your kind and genuine sympathy – and feel almost that it was but selfish in me to make such a call on it – But no exercise of kindness can be purely painful – and I will do as much for you perhaps some other day. The rest of my household is well – and talk and think, I will bet you any wager, as much of you and yours, in their stirring and half racketty existence, as you can do of us, in the tranquillity of your lonely upland — Tell us a little more of your occupations – How do you come on with the Spanish? – to how many score of pipes do you restrict yourself? What practical futurity do you look forward to, in this life? What do you most wish for, that can be procured by your own efforts, or those of your friends? What portion of your time do you pass in talking idly – or do you ever at all indulge that gentle and fair spouse of yours with a measure of gossip? – I will give her a little taste of it myself – and this very moment – so goodnight to you my most magnificent of mystics –

I am very sorry for your sore throat my very dear child and do not half like the thought of your being confined for weeks to bed, up in that icy desart, without medical aid – and the tender tendance of women – I wish we had you here – where we should give you plenty of nursing and cheering – and <u>force</u> you to think of us now and then, in spite of huskiness and difficult swallowing — But you are better now? – and able I hope to govern your thoughts – and willing to turn them <again> into kind channels – I cannot tell how often I wish to have you by me – and yet it would be to little purpose, as long as I have this busy life – only a little squeeze of the hand in the morning – and half an hour's chat at dinner and a kind word or two at tea, and a compassionate good night when you go to bed, and I to the last act of my drudgery – late, lonely and cheerless – not much certainly – but yet something – and something worth wishing for too – But we shall have days of greater leisure – and the pleasure of them will be enhanced by the recollection of these wearyings – I am not unhappy – and am not altogether sure that I should be happier for <u>much</u> more leisure – or the necessity of finding tasks for myself – and I have no reason to murmur on the whole and I do not – and no occupations are irksome which exercise the understanding – and leave room for the deeper reflections which make all occupation seem frivolous – and the still deeper affections to which they are but interludes and disguises — Write to me my dear child – and soothe my heart with some words of potency and truth – I am afraid you are right about Mrs Jeffrey and the pup – she insists upon fondling it as her own – but if you will but come and

fall in love with it on the spot, I think you could not be resisted – Take care of your health – That desart is too cold for you – and I fear those cold night walks did you no good – your backaches are mostly rheumatic – with perhaps a little ague – try a little cold infusion of Bark – or rather the quinine – bathe your head and neck with cold water – and do not rise till 2 hours after the sun – God bless you   Very Affectly Yours
    F. Jeffrey

National Library of Scotland, MS 787, ff. 50–1.

1.   *Wycliffe or Luther* – and the *History and Philosophy of the Reformation* – nothing came of this project, or of Carlyle's plans to write a major biography of Luther, though in the previous year William Fraser had also urged Carlyle to write on Luther for the *Foreign Review*. See *Carlyle Letters*, vol. 5, p. 21 and n. Carlyle's fascination with Luther would have to wait for his discussion of 'The Hero as Priest' in his lectures on heroes and hero-worship. See T. Carlyle, *On Heroes, Hero-Worship, and the Heroic in History*, ed. M. Engel, M. K. Goldberg and J. J. Brattin, The Norman and Charlotte Strouse Edition of the Writings of Thomas Carlyle, 1 (Berkeley, CA: University of California Press, 1993).

TO THOMAS (AND JANE WELSH) CARLYLE

date 13 February 1830
from Edinburgh

Edin^r 13 Feby 1830

My Dear Carlyle

    I am glad you think my regard for you a Mystery – as I am aware that must be its highest recommendation – I take it in an humbler sense – and am content to think it natural that one man of a kind heart should feel attracted towards another – and that a signal purity and loftiness of character, joined to great talents and something of a romantic history, should excite interest and respect – You hermits really must not think all who live in the world mere worldlings – when the truth perhaps is, that there is as much morbid feeling in your distaste for ordinary pursuits, as there is of corruption in our too great devotion to them — It is a great triumph for me to find that your wishes at least, are turned towards a more social existence – But you must begin by tolerating the ordinary specimens of our common nature a little more than you now do – which you would certainly do if you were only forced to mix long and intimately with a large assortment of them – It is for this reason I have wished so earnestly that you had betaken yourself to some profession which is the great ease for ennui and all the fantastical miseries it leads to – I have not time however to lecture you to-day – and indeed write only to confirm you in your purpose of stepping down from your cloud throne in the desert, and mingling a little with us of the vallies

– Come straight to us here – where you shall have a warm room, and a warmer welcome – and where the sight of your quiet smile and thoughtful eyes will diffuse general satisfaction – But the satisfaction will not be complete if you come alone – <u>You</u> too must come (tho' not on the outside) my fair, forgetful cousin – We are all resolute as to that – and shall be vexed and mortified if you prefer your solitude to our fireside [–] It is spring now – and feels balmy and reviving – and we have got two beautiful little <u>love birds</u> – which you may perhaps be allowed to carry away with you – and there are two Exhibitions open – and tho' I am as busy as a waiter at an ordinary, we may have little walks before dinner, – and see the sun go down among golden clouds and dim clustering hills — My swelling veins are rather in better order, and I venture to walk nearly as usual – I [*over* and] have no pain now – and but little fear – The worst thing is the perpetual hurry of my Session life – and I foresee that I shall be tantalised by seeing little of either of you – But my Charlottes will be kind to you and it will be a [? *tear*] delight to think that you are comfortable under my roof and so come and God bless you — Ever Most Affectly Yours

    F. Jeffrey

O I must tell you that Sir W. Hamilton's review of Cousin has been prodigiously admired at Paris[1]– and has exalted the Scottish name in all the mystical circles of the continent — So you see there is encouragement for you yet and I hope you admire the magnanimous candour with which I impart it. Why have you not put on your name, with a remembrance my kind coz? I repeat mine here for you — Ever Yours

    F. Jeffrey

National Library of Scotland, MS 787, ff. 52–3.
1.   See Jeffrey's letter to Carlyle of 9 December 1829, above.

TO THOMAS CARLYLE

date 1 March 1830
from Edinburgh

Edin[r] 1 March 1830

My Dear C.

    I wrote you, I think the very day after I received your last letter – pressing you to fulfill your threat of coming here – and desiring you to set up your rest at once with us — From your neither answering, nor appearing, I begin to fear either that you have not received my letter, or that something has befallen you which I ought to know — I think it right also to apprise you that I live in fear of being called up to London – on some foolish appeals, soon after the 23^d, and shall probably be absent near a month and I should not like to miss your visit here – I am making interest to have the cases put off till after Easter – which will be about the 10th April – which would suit me better – but I shall not know the result for a little while yet —We are all well – except my trachea – and my varicosity – both which are less troublesome than before — But I am still miserably lazy — — Sir Walter has had a little attack of speechlessness – for ten minutes – which has alarmed his friends, something – but he has had no return of it for a week – or of any other illness – and is not only going about as usual – but is to assist at a great dinner, which the members of the new club are to give him next Friday – when all his admirers are to attend –

There is a sweet vernal delight in the air these three last days – and this young moon looks beamingly on us once more — There is a new review too – with some good articles – but no mysticism, that I have fallen on yet – My friend Macaulay has come into Parl[iamen]t for the Burgh which was held by Abercromby[1] – who, you know, is our new Chief Baron —

I have not time to say one word more – and you will observe that this is not a letter – but an enquiry – and a notice — Pray do not despise your fellow creatures – and especially your fellow scribblers – who are among the best of them – and at all events as much above your hedgers and ditchers, as <u>they</u> are above their <u>collies</u>. Your intellect will never be in its right plane until you have a reasonable respect and <u>admiration</u> for <u>many</u> of your modern English poets – and the best way I take it to teach you that, would be to make you try to do anything as good as the better part of them – If you succeeded you would only be on their level – if you failed, it would be rather ridiculous <still> to hold yourself their superior – I have known diverse ingenuous youths [?cu *MS torn*]red of misplaced contempt by an experiment of this [?kind *MS torn*] – but the disease with you is more inveterate –

God bless you – and mend us all –

Ever Affectly Yours,

F. Jeffrey

National Library of Scotland, MS 787, ff. 54–5.

1. Thomas Babington Macaulay (1800–59), the historian, Whig ideologue, *Edinburgh* reviewer and MP, took over the seat of Calne when James Abercromby (1776–1858) was made Chief Baron of the Exchequer for Scotland. (Abercromby would share the liberal ticket with Jeffrey in the elections held in late 1832 for the seat of Edinburgh in the reformed parliament.) Jeffrey followed Macaulay's career with admiration and anticipation, while on his side Macaulay looked upon Jeffrey's writings and career as exemplary. Jeffrey's allusions to Macaulay as the man of the moment, here and elsewhere, may have been designed to provoke Carlyle, who was patently annoyed by them.

TO THOMAS CARLYLE

date 9 and 10 March 1830
from Edinburgh

Edin^r 9 March 1830

My dear Carlyle

Why should there be any ceremony or any awkwardness between people who have an affection and respect for each other? – You would be more comfortable if you had more money – and I would be <u>much</u> more comfortable, and more happy, if you would take a little of mine – Why then should you not? You wrote me lately that one of your objects in life was – for the present, to earn, by work, not always suitable or grateful to you – something about £100 a year – Now that is a sum, which would not be felt out of my income:[1] and I cannot but feel <u>ashamed</u> that I should either hoard it up, or squander it in useless vanities, when such a man as you might be spared some irksome and anxious hours – by merely consenting to let me apply it more worthily –

Now nobody knows – or shall know, of this project of mine – but you and me – not even my wife – so answer me in the simplicity of your heart – and as one man would have done to another before coins and dignities were invented – Remember that you would have been richer at this moment if you too had not been a giver[2] – and where there was less call – and I suppose you will not insist on monopolising that practice – If you have really a religious heart, you must have done only as you would be done to – and I can only add that I would not have made you this offer if I did not feel that in similar circumstances I should have freely accepted it from you –

And now God bless you – I feel assured that you will not at all events <u>resent</u> this proposal – nor misjudge the spirit in which it is made – To show you how much I trust you, I at once enclose £50 – and <u>expect</u> you to keep it – and to tell me quietly that we have both done right – and no more about it –

Ever affectly Yours,
<u>F. Jeffrey</u>

I do not like Cousin being sick – or out of spirits – and I long much to see her – I do not move now till Easter – about a month hence –

P.S. 10th — I wrote this last night – and have been so wretchedly hurried all day, that I quite forgot to provide myself with the means of making the enclosure with which I threaten you, while the banks were accessible[3] — But as you only get your letters on Wednesday, I cannot on that account consent to leave this scheme of mine withheld for a whole week – and therefore send it empty

– knowing you will take the will for the deed and answer, all the same as if it had been done — F. J.

National Library of Scotland, MS 787, ff. 56–7.

1. 'I have just sent the meekest, friendliest, but most emphatic refusal', wrote Carlyle to his brother John ten days later on 19 March, 'for this and all coming times' (*Carlyle Letters*, vol. 5, p. 81). Jeffrey actually had begun pressing financial assistance upon Carlyle very early in their relationship. 'That wonderful little man is expected here very soon', Carlyle wrote to John from Craigenputtoch on 25 August 1828, 'he even offers me in the coolest lightest manner the use of his purse, and evidently rather wishes I would use it ... And this from a Scotchman and a Lawyer!' (*Carlyle Letters*, vol. 4, p. 399). This offer of regular assistance – effectively, of patronage – is of a different order, however, and one which disturbed Carlyle (according to his notebooks, at least). 'What a state of society is this', he wrote analysing his refusal of Jeffrey's offer, 'in which a man would rather be shot thro' the heart, twenty-times, than do both himself and his neighbour a *real ease*! How separate Pride from the natural necessary feeling of Self?' (*Two Note Books of Thomas Carlyle, from 23d March 1822 to 16th May 1832*, ed. C. E. Norton (1898; Mamaroneck, NY: Paul A. Appel, 1972), p. 155).

2. Jeffrey is probably referring to Carlyle's supporting his brother John while John was a medical student at the University of Edinburgh (see note 3 to the letter of 13 or 14 April 1830, below), and/or to Jane's signing over the rent of £200-a-year from Craigenputtoch to her mother, Grace Welsh (née Welsh; 1782–1842).

3. Two months later, Jeffrey was able to make up for his failure to deliver this well intentioned foretaste of the £100 per annum he was urging on Carlyle. Having knocked back Jeffrey's offer of patronage, Carlyle applied to him for a loan of £50, and Jeffrey sent a draft of £60 with his letter of 22 May 1830 (see below). Carlyle had occasion to chafe under this debt and was greatly relieved when it was finally discharged in September 1832.

TO THOMAS (AND JANE WELSH) CARLYLE

date 25 March 1830
from Edinburgh

Edin^r 25 March 1830

My dear C.

I am rather disappointed, tho' not absolutely surprised at your decision — I respect your feelings far too much to think of <u>doing</u> anything in opposition to them – and do not care even to <u>say</u> a great deal – I think it right however to state that, agreeing as I do, in your <u>premises</u> I humbly conceive that you err in your <u>conclusion</u> – I admit the general rule to be as you put it – and that a man must be either above or below the average, to depart from it with safety – But I did venture to suppose that <u>we</u> were <u>above</u> it – and I assumed this, with the less hesitation, on the understanding that as the transaction was to be entirely private we had to answer only to each other – I am foolish enough to fancy that this makes a great difference, and almost <u>excludes</u> the operation of all rules that depend on common opinion – Whatever <u>would</u> be right, if all the world were above low suspicions and misconstructions – <u>is right</u>, I take it, as to anything that passes exclusively between those who <u>are</u> above them – and have no distrust of each other — I say this merely for my own justification, and your farther reflection – and beg you would not imagine that I am capable of importuning or urging you on such a matter – If we once understand each other – all the rest must come of free will – and <u>will</u> come, if it ought — In the mean time, believe that I am gratified, as I ought to be, by your promise of applying to me if you have occasion – tho' I cannot but say that I am mortified by your expressions of surprise at the very simple and natural course I have followed –

I wrote to Moir[1] the day after I received your letter – but I do not know what he has been able to do for you — This is the first day of my actual vacation – or rather the first evening – for I have been the whole morning in the Jury court – and have since been dining with our new Chief Baron[2] – I am now setting out (at 11 o'clock) for Craigcrook – where my Charlottes went this morning – and where we hope to have a quiet fortnight, before we start for London — Why should you not come to us – <u>both</u> of you, for a short pass? And see the wonderful work of transplanting to which I mean to devote the greater part of that time? – at all events let me hear from you – There is a sweet spring feeling in the air now – and the blackbirds and thrushes chuckle delightfully at sunset – even in these smoky regions – I hope to sleep more softly now, and am sure at any rate with a fresher and blander feeling of union with nature — God bless you – my fair cousin – I think nothing but what is kind and just of you – our poor curly pup is dead of the distemper and has cost us some tears – I ~~am in~~ half resolved to have no more pets – but the thirst for having cherished and loving beings around one is too strong — Good night – now and all happiness

      Ever affectly Yours

      F. Jeffrey

National Library of Scotland, MS 787, ff. 58–9.
1.   See note 5 to the letter of 3 November 1829, above.
2.   James Abercromby, see note 1 to the letter of 1 March 1830, above.

TO THOMAS CARLYLE

date 13 or 14 April 1830
from Craigcrook

Craigcrook Tuesday Evg

My Dear Carlyle

I have got a respite from the Chancellor[1] – and we do not start till Saturday – else we should have gone without hearing from you – and heaven knows what might have happened! – I am sorry that we shall not see each other first – but I am too deep in arrears of all work, to make any detours – and must rush up and down, in the dullest of straight lines – while you are too lazy to move till you are sure that I am clear out of your way — I do not quite know yet where we shall be in London – but a letter addressed to the care of Jo. Richardson[2] Esq <21> Fludyer Street Westminster will be sure to reach me. — Nothing will give us greater pleasure than to see your brother[3] — I only wish that you would make yourself visible at the same time — I start a little at your project of hibernating at Weimar – and feel as if you were in danger of forgetting to come back to us – otherwise I am sure I ought not to start at anything which is so likely to give you pleasure – Suppose, as a pledge of your due return, you leave hostages with us – and impawn your wife in our hands, till you come to redeem her? – I am rather inclined to be jealous of the personal presence of that old ass[4] – who has half bewitched her at a distance – but still I think better of her judg[men]t – and half hope that the spell will be broken by the visible presence of the wizard – I have been reading Moore's Byron – or rather Byron's own Byron[5] – for the charm is almost entirely in his own letters and fragments – with intense, interest, pity and delight – I feel sure we should have been such friends, if we had met! – and can scarcely help gnashing my teeth with spite that we never did – and alas never can – There are some traits of <u>mysticism</u> about him, for which you should like him all the better – and I believe I do not like him less – It is miserable that he should have perished in the golden prime of his days —

I am glad the spring has visited you at last – It's earliest visits I take it are not to your heights – here we are as [? *MS torn*] as velvet – and full of ewes with red backs[6] and lambs, very white – moreover I have been transplanting trees, after an astonishing fashion – I have moved 14 of 50 years old – and 30 of more tender growth – If they grow I shall have quite a silvan lodge here – and the work has been succeeded by delicious rains, and very respectable thunder showers – for April — Can I do anything for you – or little coz. in London? – I hope we shall be down again before or about the 12th May – otherwise it will go hard with me and some of my clients – You see they are going to take a whole month more from our vacation which afflicts me more than the abridgment in the number of Judges – tho' that is ag[ains]t the chances of aspirants [?   ] of 50 – and takes a lamentable proportion of prizes out of the wheel for younger men – but if it be for the <u>salus populi</u>[7] – fiat – I care mighty little about the matter – To be sure, anybody, having an interest – that is anybody nearly connected with the slain – or having an interest in his life – may indict and hang the murderer – at his own instance – the Lord Advocate being <u>obliged</u> to grant his nominal concurrence – The only difference in such private prosecutions being that the whole expense must be defrayed by the private party – and that he may be made liable in damages if it turns out that he prosecutes without sufficient grounds – If it be a strong case however – and properly represented to the Lord Ad[voca]te I have <u>never</u> known him refuse to bring it to trial at the expense of the crown – God bless you my very dear little cousin Why do you not send me a kind word?

     Ever Yours

     F. Jeffrey —

National Library of Scotland, MS 787, ff. 60–1.

1.   The Lord Chancellor, in London, before whom Jeffrey was due to plead in Scottish cases referred to Westminster.

2.   John Richardson (1780–1864), lawyer, was a relative of Henry Brougham's and a friend of Jeffrey's from their student days who in 1806 had set up a legal practice in London handling Scottish cases.

3.   Carlyle's younger brother, the medical doctor John Aitken Carlyle (1801–79), Carlyle's letters to whom have been quoted extensively throughout these notes. As subsequent letters show, John Carlyle became familiar with Jeffrey, who was able to help with his career.

4.   Goethe, whom the Carlyles were planning to visit ('your project of hibernating at Weimar'), but they decided against it.

5.   Thomas Moore's *Life, Letters and Journals of Lord Byron*, just published by John Murray.

6.   From the dye used to mark them.

7.   Latin: the health or welfare of the people.

TO THOMAS (AND JANE WELSH) CARLYLE

date 17 May 1830
from Edinburgh

Edin[r] 17 May 1830

My Dear Carlyle

    Here we are, safe back again from London – in our old places, and at our old employments, among our old friends — We had the pleasure of seeing your brother in town – and wish we could have seen more of him – He has a very pleasing countenance – with an expression of mixed good sense and good nature, which becomes him very well – and with less of that sublime sadness, which so often testifies, upon <u>your</u> brow and life, in what contempt you hold happiness. I think he is very likely to prosper in the world – if one may venture to maintain such a thing to you – and few things would give me more pleasure (your pardon once more!) than to learn how I could do him any service[1] — We had a delicious foretaste of <u>Summer</u> during our last ten days in London – and nothing could be more lovely than the whole surrounding country – with its fresh woods, violet lawns – flowering horse ches[t]nuts, lilies, laburnums and apples, and its soaring skylarks, and chuckling nightingales — But then we had a revengeful nip of <u>winter</u> on our way down – and are but new emerging, with torn branches and scattered blossoms, from its tyranny — Craigcrook however is very green – and more than a half of my transplants I think will survive – I still have but Saturday glimpses of them till the Session is over – But I hope to see you – I mean <u>both</u> of you – here before that time. – I am anxious to know what you have been doing – and what is now the state of your Weimar project? – and the time of its beginning and ending?

I have a beautiful proof copy of my print[2] laid aside for you – shall I send it to Craigenputtach? or keep it till you come here, to compare it with the original? – If you wish it sent, tell me how I should* address it – and by what conveyance it should go — The said original is in tolerable condition – the London Doctors made but light of his many maladies – but they know little about it – and the old carcase will assuredly fall to pieces in no long time – so you should lose no time in coming to see it, while life yet lingers in it – The rest of my household is well – all glad enough to be in a quiet home again, after the racket and fever of London. <u>You</u> would not perhaps think our home here very quiet – But compared with the other, it is loneliness and stagnation – yet I was very [?well *MS torn*] immersed with the whirlpool – tho' it made me rather giddy – and I found – as I always expect to find – much more real kindness and noble <pr>inciples among persons who appear frivolous and dissipated – than selfishness and baseness among those who seem polished and good natured – I saw your friend Procter – and his wife, for the first time – I do not like her so well as <u>yours</u> – but she seems a nice, sensible and agreeable woman – I gave them a <u>flattering</u> account of Craigenputtach – and I think they will come down one day to see that Eden in the wilderness – so you must beautify and adorn it, to save my credit — Now I have no time to say a word or more – and write this in a great hurry to make sure of your foolish sulky Wedy post[3] – Ever Affectly Yours

    <u>F Jeffrey</u>

God bless you – my fair, pensive high minded coz – I rejoice in the return of Spring, for your sake – and like to think of you among larks and buds – tell me you are quite well – and blooming like all around you – Do pray come to see us – and do not go to that dull region of tobacco and mysticism till I have fortified you with certain holy spells – to keep off all demonical influences [–] We have lost a lovebird – but got another – with whom the <u>widow</u> is well comforted – Polly has[4] his compliments – and all the <u>unfeathered</u> bipeds their <u>love</u> to you – Write me a word – and a spell for my protection   Ever Yours

      Fr J –/

---

* Jeffrey actually subscribes 'shall' at the end of one page before beginning the next 'should'. National Library of Scotland, Acc. 8964, no. 32.

1.   John Carlyle, who wrote to Carlyle on the same day: 'Jeffrey ... received me very kindly and courteously. Before your letter came' – Carlyle had written on 1 May suggesting John look Jeffrey up – 'Jeffrey had got my address from Proctor and written to me to breakfast with them, or if I could not, to tell him when he might find me at home! I liked him very well, and also Mrs Jeffrey tho' I had less conversation with her. He gave me a letter to Charles Bell one of the professors of the University here' (*Carlyle Letters*, vol. 5, p. 101, n.).

2.   A mezzotint portrait of Jeffrey by William Walker, first published in May 1830.

3.   The mail was delivered to Craigenputtoch only once a week on a Wednesday (see the postscript to the letter of 9 March 1830).

4.   For *sends*?

TO THOMAS CARLYLE

date 22 May 1830*
from [Edinburgh]

My Dear Carlyle

I feel very sensibly the kindness of your application[1] – and am – not <u>flattered</u> I hope – but in some better way, gratified by it – I did not receive your letter till last night – so I could not send this sooner – I have made it for £60 instead of £50, knowing that a man who supposes he wants the latter sum, is sure really to want at least £10 more – You shall pay it back – when you please – but not for any convenience of mine – I could do without ten times the amount for ten years – or for ever [–] without being aware of it – But you shall be lord and master of the arrangement, as may seem best for you [–] You will get cash for this upper slip at any bank, by merely writing your name on it, below mine.

You will have a letter of mine before this time – telling you that we are all safe home – and that we saw your brother several times in London – I have not had time to enquire anything about your Foreign Quarterlies[2] – But I do not think it <u>likely</u> that they will come here – or into the hands of Allan[3] – I shall ask however and let you know – The junction I should conceive a very wise and politic thing but not the more probable for that – Into what ever form it goes I have no doubt that <u>your</u> contributions will always be acceptable —

I am glad you are so far on with your <u>opus majus</u>[4] – the first labour is always the most irksome – and by and bye you will be carried along without effort by the impulse it has created — I wish tho' you would come here now that the days are long – and distances consequently short — If you should give a week, and a few pounds to mere idleness and friendship, I think neither God nor Mammon would be offended – but you might get help in your work too – which it is not perhaps perfectly wise to despise —— I have been oppressively busy ever since my return – and with little prospect of respite for a while to come – and now we have the Venerable Assembly[5] over and above our daily work —

I dare not write any more – The king has got a respite [?during] pleasure – but cannot live long – Do make that female woman write to me – and tell me what to do with my print

> Ever Affectly Yours
> F. Jeffrey

---

* Postmarked 22 May 1830.
National Library of Scotland, Acc. 8964, no. 33.

1. This is the loan that Carlyle would repay in September 1832 (see note 3 to the letter of 9 and 10 March 1830, above, and note 2 to the letter of 22 September 1832, below).
2. Jeffrey is referring to speculation about the merging of the *Foreign Quarterly Review* and the *Foreign Review*, which had in fact taken place in April (see note 2 to the letter of 24 or 25 August 1827, above), and about the possibility of their being managed from Edinburgh.
3. Probably Thomas Allan (1777–1833), banker and proprietor of the *Caledonian Mercury*.
4. Referring to Carlyle's projected history of German literature, which remained incomplete (see note 7 to the letter of 9 December 1829, above).
5. When the General Assembly of the Church of Scotland met in Edinburgh in May, it conducted special tribunals on cases relating to the conduct and administration of the ministry, and thus required advocates from the secular legal system. (There had been times around the turn of the century when it had been the only work available for Jeffrey as a young Whig advocate in a Tory-dominated profession.)

TO JANE WELSH CARLYLE

date 5 June 1830
from Edinburgh

Edin[r] 5 June 1830

My dear Cous – Here is a whole letter to yourself – for it is to tell you that the Print, which is to be all your own, was sent two days ago, according to Carlyle's direction – and is now probably on its way to you — You must make that shadow welcome – for the sake of the substance – which would like nothing so well as to invert the order of nature, and follow it, and abide with it, in the quietness of your dwelling, and the light of your love forever — Do not doubt then that we shall come to you before the falling leaves – if you do not give us all the slip, and run off to that region of demonology – where you may be spirited away in an instant from all human help – and lost beyond the redeeming power of any human affection – There is a better alternative to be sure – which is that you should come here – and stay longer with us than I am ever likely I fear to be able to stay with you — I never can understand why you seem averse to this – or what serious difficulties there can be in the way, if you are not – But I, who never make difficulties, will come to you, if no better can be made of it – and we shall see one another again under smiling skies – whatever happens to the rest of the universe — I am shamefully busy – and forced to neglect, for the poor drudgery of this worlds business, the things that belong to my peace – and things still better – This by good luck is Saturday – and everybody is gone hours ago to Craigcrook and here am I, just escaped from the court – refreshing myself before I ascend my steed to follow them, with this little passing benediction to you — We are very green and leafy now at C. and I shall awake tomorrow to the sound of rustling leaves and piping blackbirds – and I shall pace at night round the garden, where I used to pace with you – and regret that you are not there to breathe the breath of dewy honeysuckles and waving briars – and to look up to the pure stars, that are still present to both of us – and may perhaps carry a gentle message between us, if it be whispered in a right tone for the heavens —— I am sorry for your roses – it has been a bad season for them – tho' the parent plants are thriving enough with us – and several of them already in flower – Indeed we are very <u>florid</u> all over the garden and shrubbery already – I wish you would come and see –

Nobody offered to present me to Mrs Montagu[1] – and it did not become me to ask – Mrs Procter[2] looks amiable and is, I do not doubt – but she is decidedly <u>blue</u>[3] – and talks too much of books and the arts – to be thoroughly agreeable to me – She said she had heard you were so excessively <u>refined</u> that she was afraid of you – upon which I undeceived her – and told her you were nothing but a little flirt, that cared for nothing but your own amusement – and altogether a very frivolous person – But she would not believe me – so you must convince her yourself – It was my brother I think who <u>first found you out</u> – and a merciful warning it has been to us all! – It is dreadful to think what impostures are passed on good people in this world – and how much, but for his discovery, we might have been misled — I do not know very well why I write this nonsense – for I am not particularly gay – having passed a night nearly without sleep – and having a very formidable threatening of lumbago to keep me in order —

Well then God bless you – my very dear pure highminded child – be happy – and give me the happiness of knowing that you think often and kindly of me – after all there is no other balm in Gilead but that – and I am almost ready to go so far into Carlyles creed, as to despise all other happiness – but not an inch further – Make him temperate in tobacco – and more indulgent to ordinary people – If God endures them, and cares for them and has made them, such as they are – he has no right either to despise, or to draw back from them – It is all sheer vanity 'and presumption – and he should be chidden out of it — But it is five o'clock – and Cockburn is raging for me by this time on the bowling green – and so, with kindest love from all the house once more God bless You and farewell – You must write me when you get the print – and tell me whether you think it like – It seems to me rather sad – but at least it is not distorted and affected, like the other portraits —

 Very Affectly Yours
 F. Jeffrey

National Library of Scotland, Acc. 8964, no. 34.

1. Anna Montagu (née Benson; *c.* 1773–1856) was an attractive and eccentric London hostess, the third wife of Basil Montagu, a lawyer and friend of Wordsworth and Coleridge, and an admirer of (and admired by) the Carlyles' friend Edward Irving (see note 6 to the letter of 24 [December 1827], above). Mrs Montagu took a proprietorial interest in the Carlyles on first meeting Carlyle in 1824 and during their engagement, and remained an occasional friend and correspondent, though a cooling off occurred in 1831.
2. Anne Procter (née Skepper), daughter of Anna Montagu by her first marriage and wife of Bryan Waller Procter (1787–1874), the lawyer, poet and dramatist who published under the pseudonym 'Barry Cornwall'. It was Procter who had originally given Carlyle the letter of introduction to Jeffrey that he had presented in February 1827 as the beginning of their relationship (*Reminiscences*, p. 359).
3. A bluestocking. Jeffrey's ambivalence towards educated and intelligent women is apparent in his correspondence, for though he was an occasional propagandist for women writers, he could be personally patronizing to and about them – witness the tone of his address to Jane. His favourite saying on the issue was recorded by (amongst others) Henry Cockburn: 'I think it was to Mrs. Hamilton that Jeffrey said, in allusion to the good taste of never losing the feminine in the literary character, that there was no objection to the blue stocking, provided the petticoat came low enough down' (Cockburn, *Memorials of His Time*, p. 267).

TO THOMAS (AND JANE WELSH) CARLYLE

date 19 July 1830
from Edinburgh

Edin.ʳ 19 July 1830

My Dear Carlyle
 Still toiling and bustling on – still wasting the sweet Summer in hot courts – and the glowing nights in poring over bundles of chicanery! – and I ought to have written to you too – though I felt that I could say nothing to comfort

you[1] – and that it was not necessary to say that I would if I could — I feel that an affliction of this sort – with all your philosophy and proud aspirations after death – must fall more heavily on you than on most people – There are so few you will let yourself love – and one young and under your protection and tuition must be parted from with deeper pangs than common — But it is over now –, and your grief I hope is settled only into a more solemn affection with the soothing of having done all that was kind and dutiful – and having ministered to the brief enjoyments of one snatched so early from both sorrow and joy — We must live for those that live – Tell me what you are doing – and how the days and weeks glide away with you, in strenuous labour – or high meditation – Are you not coming to see us? – or must we come first again to see you? However it is, we must meet – It does my heart good to think of your <u>unworldly</u> and pure course of life – even while I condemn something of it in my reason – and mourn over some of its consequences in my heart — We shall go to Lochlomond I think about the 2ᵈ or 3ᵈ of Augᵗ – but must be back here about the 21ˢᵗ, to receive some English friends who promised us a visit at that time – I once thought of running round by Dumfrieshire on our return from the Loch – but grudge now to make what must be so hurried a visit — So if you will not come here about the end of August, I think we must go then to you – But it would be better at Craigcrook — All the Summer I hope is to come yet – for we have hitherto had little but cold and wet [–] We are all well – except poor me – who am never quite well you know — But I have got thro' the Session, without absolute failure – and tho' the state of my <u>veins</u> makes me less fit for my robustious rambles – and my <u>trachea</u> deters me from manly exposure to cold and wet, I am not yet absolutely settled in a chimney corner – and mean to move about worshipping nature [in *MS torn*] her recesses, with some activity of devotion – I have got a beautiful bow and bright arrows, and go about like another god of love in a very dangerous fashion – Charly has got a smaller set – and if my sweet cousin will only come she shall learn to shoot like a heathen Diana – and be painted in that character — have you got my print yet – and do you care about it or think it like? And your German Literature book, is it near done yet? And is there any hope that the closer acquaintance into which it must have forced you with those muddyheaded, half crazy[,] half affected, and uniformly vulgar scribblers, will open your eyes to their true character – or disabuse you at least of your idolatrous admiration — I had some talk with Macintosh[2] about them when I was in London which I shall tell you about when we meet — He knows them and their lingo perfectly – and knows more of those they should be compared to than any other man, who knows <u>them</u> in this country. He places them higher than I think reasonable, but immeasurably below where you do – and now good bye – We are settled in a manner at Craigcrook – tho' I am able to do little more than sleep there – But we are drawing to a close soon – and I shall have idle days before we move to the

West. and this is all for your M^r – here followeth a word for M^{rs} – God bless you, my sweet bright child – Do love me always – and think of me often – and believe that I have no greater pleasure than in thinking fondly of you – and no greater pride than in believing in your affection – your pure – generous, and unchangeable affection [–] What is there else worth saying? Why will you not come to see us? or why do you <u>most</u> wish that we should come to you? Why do you not say you have got my print? Write at any rate – I love to see the letters you have traced – Ever yours

      F. Jeffrey

National Library of Scotland, Acc. 8964, no. 35.

1.   Carlyle's sister Margaret had died on 22 June 1830, aged only twenty-six.

2.   Sir James Mackintosh (1765–1832), educated at Aberdeen and Edinburgh, began a medical career but later took up law and went to the English bar (becoming a judge in India). He wrote a well-known defence of the French Revolution, *Vindiciæ Gallicæ*, in 1791, and was an MP, a regular reviewer with the *Edinburgh Review* and a Whig ideologue whom Jeffrey had hoped might temporarily take over the editing of the *Edinburgh* during his absence in the US in 1813–14.

TO THOMAS (AND JANE WELSH) CARLYLE

date 1 August 1830
from Craigcrook

Craigcrook Sunday Night
1st Augt 1830

My Dear Carlyle

Why do you not write to me? I cannot help being uneasy at your silence – and fancy that you must be ill – or strangely occupied – I have not heard anything from you since you sent me that melancholy letter from Dumfries, on your sister's death – and I told you since that we were going about this time to Lochlomond – and was anxious to hear from you before we went – We go tomorrow morning – and I feel mortified that I have no letters today [–] Pray write to me there – addressed <u>at Stuckgown cottage by Arrochar</u>[1] — We shall not remain more than ten days, and shall be back here most probably before the 17th — Pray let me hear from you —— I have been but a few days free of the courts – and these have not been idle – However, we have slept here for more than a week – and that is asoothing — We had a hot fit for 4 days – but it melted into rain and lightning on Friday in a very grand style — I do not remember a more tropical looking evening – with the heavy still rain hissing in the grass and among the leaves, and the bright blue lightning opening up the glittering landscape every two minutes – from six o'clock till near 12. Yesterday and today have been cool and breezy – and I have been walking with the moon, among the trees on my hill – thinking – not so comfortably as usual – of you in your wilderness – and taking a calm farewell of my shades – I hope there is some summer coming – and that we are to meet somewhere before it is over – It will be an eventful summer for France[2] – and for more than France — It stirs my blood at once and sickens my heart, to see another scene of blood and misery opening on that fair land – and so wantonly and absurdly opened – and you profess to take no interest in politics! – and to think it a fit thing for a man with a head and heart, to occupy them about the conditioned and the "unconditioned" and such gibberish – O fie! – Your brothers blood cries up from the earth ag[ains]t such idleness — But heaven knows I am in no mood for scolding you tonight – I write only because I feel something heavy about my heart when I think of you – and am anxious to be assured that you are well – If _he_ is sick, or called to a distance, or otherwise troubled, why do _you_ not write my forgetful cousin?[3] Am I not fit to be thought of, at such a season? or is this all nonsense, and some working of bad bile and heat oppressed brains? That is the best solution – and I believe the most likely

We are all very well – and I hope you are too and so good night and God bless you – I have many little things to do before I sleep – but I shall sleep better for having given you my blessing.

Ever Affectly. Yours,

F. Jeffrey

National Library of Scotland, Acc. 8964, no. 37.

1. 'Stuckgown – is a beautiful little place on Lochlomond belonging to a Mr Macmurrick, where [Jeffrey] retired for about a week yearly', according to Henry Cockburn (NLS, Adv. MSS 9.1.10, f. 106); Arrochar is a village in Dunbartonshire, at the head of Loch Long, 42 miles north-west of Glasgow.

2. After the defeat of Napoleon in 1814, Louis XVIII had become king of France and a Royalist reaction had set in. However, so reactionary were some of the measures of the new king and of his successor, Charles X, that they precipitated another revolution in July 1830 and the establishment of a (short-lived) liberal monarchy.

3. Jeffrey switches his address to Jane in this sentence.

TO THOMAS CARLYLE

date 22 August 1830
from Craigcrook

Craigcrook Sunday 22^d Augt
1830

My Dear Carlyle

Thank you for being well – and for writing <u>at last</u> – We got home on Thursday – and are beginning to settle into our home habits – We came a long round on our return, by Inverary, Killin and Dunkeld – a very beautiful circuit[1] – some parts of which I had not seen for 25 years [–] Your Arrochar letter came to my abode there, after we had left it – and was dutifully awaiting my arrival here – But the urgent thing, to a man of business, is your business[2] – which came last – I have sent to the Solicitor General about it – and shall let you know his answer – If the matter be at all as you represent it, I am clearly of opinion that there should have been a trial – tho' from what you let out, incidentally and as of no importance, in your letter, I think the man would be acquitted — The person who perished was actually seen it seems, forcing his way thro' a barred window in the night – and when called to, and challenged refused to make an answer, and fled — But for the peculiarities of your rustic courtships, I should say this was quite evidence enough of an act of felony, or housebreaking, to justify the owner, or his servants, in firing – and if the butler was a stranger in the country, I cannot say that I should much blame him – Even if he is not, the man's silence and flight, are very suspicious and unaccountable – If notice was given that he would be fired on, if he did not answer or stop, I think the blame was all his own – but such notice should have been given [–] If there were any doubts or misconceptions as to the state of the facts however, that is only a stronger reason for a public trial – The actual slaughter of an innocent man is ground enough for a public investigation – and I do not understand how it was here dispensed with – We shall see what the Solicitor says to it — We have often considered the question of a Coroner – and I think it now of no consequence. In point of fact there is now no suspicious death that is not enquired into and talked about sufficiently – All the facts about this unhappy case for instance, seem public enough and a coroner should never do more <than make those public.> – I look upon it as a great abuse that in England he often prejudges and decides on guilt or innocence – If he had sate on this body, he ought only to have found – killed by a shot fired at him when coming out of a window at night – or some such thing [–] and what the better would any body have been for this? – if he had found either <u>accidental death</u> – or <u>murder</u> – it would have been equally improper as prejudging what must have been left to a Jury – and should be left quite free and open – But enough of law for this present – We <u>are</u> coming – as certainly as death or winter

– But alas we cannot yet say <u>when</u> – We are expecting some English visitors – who may detain us till the end of this month – and when we do set out, I suspect we must take yours, after two other visits – I do not well see that we can make it before the middle of Septr – having a certain dim prospect of being arrested at Glasgow for some Jury cases ab[ou]t the 10th or 12th – But we shall know better by and bye and shall not fail to let you know in time — I am much concerned at the <u>emba[r]ras</u>[3] of your publishing people[4] – Is there anything I can do, directly or indirectly to assist you? I am anxious that your work – now so far advanced, should come forth – and I cannot but think that a publisher might be found to take up the contract of the defaulter – If you will send me a brief abstract of that contract and some little description of the sort of book it is to be – I rather think I could get an active and judicious friend in London to enquire at least and negotiate – as to make it certain whether such a thing is feasible or not – might not our friend <u>Procter</u> be of use in that way? You will see from the newspapers that we have had a prosperous meeting about France here – The Courant[5] is the only paper which has given any account of my speech, that is intelligible – and that is bad enough – I am still uneasy about the state of affairs – and cannot but fear that our cabinet has a hankering after desolate tyrannies and may have been courteous to that old wretch Charles[6] – whose landing is to be lamented –

I will not say one word to coz today – since she scorns to throw one away upon me – I even puffed away her rose leaf in a pet – tho' I afterwards picked it up, and swallowed it! — We are all well – and we have lovely weather – with crowds of blackbirds – and some remnants of gooseberries – God bless you – I shall write soon again I am scarcely my own man yet – with these heaps of things to read and answer Ever Affectly. Yours

     F Jeffrey

National Library of Scotland, Acc. 8964, no. 38.

1.   Through Argyllshire and Perthshire.

2.   Carlyle had taken an interest in the shooting by the Englishman Edward Lane of a young local, Thomas Bell (whom Carlyle may have known), from its occurrence in September 1829, writing a long letter to the Dumfries and Galloway *Courier* on 12 April 1830 (published 20 April) protesting that the case had never come to trial. When four months after the event there was still no action on the matter, he had obviously consulted Jeffrey as an experienced advocate and Dean of the Faculty of Advocates. See Jeffrey's letter to Carlyle of 26 August 1830, below, and *Carlyle Letters*, vol. 5, pp. 93–5 and nn.

3.   French: financial embarrassments or difficulties.

4.   Carlyle could not interest the publisher William Tait in his history of German literature: 'Tait, to whom I wrote, "declines"', Carlyle told John on 6 August 1830, by which date he had 'got as far as *Luther*' (*Carlyle Letters*, vol. 5, pp. 131–2). Tait (who had published Carlyle's *Life of Schiller* in 1825) had written on 29 July 1829: 'In that department [i.e., German literature] I know you are very superior to any other author of the day; but the subject is one seemingly not calculated to interest the British public. Every one of the

Books on German literature has been a failure; most of them ruinously losing concerns. The feeling in the public mind is that any thing German is most especially to be avoided ... / Your Literary History of Germany, I doubt not, is an excellent book' (NLS, Acc. 8964, no. 36).

5.   A newspaper published every third week out of Edinburgh.
6.   Charles X of France, in exile after the July revolution.

TO THOMAS (AND JANE WELSH) CARLYLE

date 26 August 1830
from Craigcrook

Craigcrook Thursday Evg
26 Augt 1830

My Dear Carlyle

Your homicide is to be tried – so let your bloodthirstiness be satisfied – But pray understand that this is not any consequence of your interference, or of mine, But was determined and in preparation months ago – I have had a very satisfactory explanation of the delay – into the details of which however I am not at liberty to write at present – There were some mistakes and neglects – But never any purpose of hushing up – and those mistakes were neither imputable to the local authorities, nor to the King's counsel – but to certain intermediate persons, who are free at the same time of all suspicion of corruption or partiality [–] The end is however, that the man is to be tried for Murder – and will most probably be acquitted – tho' he <u>may</u> be convicted of culpable homicide – In the mean time the less that is said about it the better – and I have to beg that you would stir no more in it, till the result is seen – This is fair to all parties – and I have indeed pledged myself that, in return for the open and ready communication made to me – my informer would move no farther in the matter –

I am afraid I must be at the Jury court circuit at Glasgow – and probably shall be detained there till the 16th or 17 of Septr – after which I must visit my sister in Ayrshire,[1] before I can come to you – I grudge this very much – <u>and, if I were you</u>, I would have a joyous meeting <u>immediately</u>, here, under the good green woods of Craigcrook! You are living, as you confess, a very idle and good for nothing life at this present – and could do nothing so wise, as to wander down, from your blasted paradise, hand in hand with your blooming Eve, to seek a peaceful shelter in our lower world — But if you are so capable of so kind a resolution, you should not dally about putting it in execution – We shall stay here – if you will come, till about the 8th or 9th at all events of Septr and will return the visit before the end of the month – Our English friends do not come this year – so we have plenty of room for you – except one day next week – which I must give to the Duke of Hamilton[2] – I could easily stay here till the time I have mentioned – and perhaps longer – But if you will not come, I may be tempted to move my tabernacle sooner – So resolve [?it *MS torn*] and say — and you know what I most wish you to [?say *MS torn*]

This leisure softens my heart I think, sweet coz! and I feel now that I must forgive all your neglect of me – Here are five rose leaves for your one – and if you will come here, you shall have a bunch every day for your head – and another for your bosom – It is lovely Autumn weather – with something of the fitfulness of Spring – soft melting showers – attending with splendid sunshine – and clear North winds bearing vast white clouds over mountain and sky – such a deep blue sea as it is worth leaving your inlands to look at – and woods of all colours, still stretching broad shadows over the fields – We are all well – and all join heartily in this invitation – I think it would do me an infinite deal of good only to look on your eyes again – I am not pleased now with the <u>fierce</u> edition of them in my [?Jewess][3] – I hope nev[er] to see your's fierce – You are difficult about my print – It is generally thought not only like, but flattering – however I am glad that it does not take away your desire to see the original – God bless you my Dear Child – Will you cheer me, and be indulgent when I fall into dotage and feebleness? I feel as if I were destined to owe you some such service — I wish I had more clear life before me [–] But those thoughts do not weigh heavy on me – Tell me that you are well and blooming – Give my love to your poney, and all the things you love – Ever Very Affectly Your's

    F. Jeffrey

National Library of Scotland, Acc. 8964, no. 39.
1.   Jeffrey's second sister, Marion Brown, married to a Dr Thomas Brown in 1800. (Jeffrey's elder sister, Mary, had died in 1804.)
2.   Alexander Hamilton Douglas, tenth Duke of Hamilton (1767–1852), a Whig grandee and art collector whose offices included a trusteeship of the British Museum and the vice presidency of the Royal Institution for the Encouragement of the Fine Arts in Scotland.
3.   Jeffrey may be referring here to a sketch or painting.

TO JANE WELSH (AND THOMAS) CARLYLE

date 19 September 1830
from Craigcrook

Craigcrook Sunday Night
19 Septr 1830

My Dear Child – Here is a whole letter for yourself – with only a postscript (perhaps) for your husband – For I have nothing to say tonight worthy of his grave ear – and shall need even <u>your</u> indulgence, I fear, for writing so idly and so soon – No. I do not fear any such thing – but the very contrary, for I would not have written at all, if I were not assured that you too would feel it <u>unnatural</u> if I could let four days of intimate talking[1] pass at once into <u>avoidable</u> silence – or sit down again in my empty home, without trying to prolong their echo – or repeating at least my distant farewell – So I not only write by the very first post you will allow to approach you – but I confidently expect you to write in return – and am sure I shall not be disappointed – O yes – those visits, to persons one really cares for, are precious things, after all – in spite of all the trouble they may occasion – and the tantalising circumstances which always attend them – They are Pilgrimages which confirm the faith that enjoins them – and they awaken kindnesses, which might slumber, tho' they could not die – and minister fresh variations of food to recollections which might languish on their antient stores — Besides they give those who pay them the right to be paid back – and to be importunate with the friends to whom they have given trouble – Why are you not more anxious to acquire all these privileges? ——

We had but a slow journey on Friday – We were unfortunate about horses at almost all the stages, and did not get home till <u>Eleven</u> o'clock – under a glorious canopy of Northern lights – and soft beaming stars – Yet the journey was not altogether unpleasing – we were not impatient – but rather in a pensive and soothing mood – and the air was soft and balmy – and a great bunch of lavender which Mrs Welsh[2] had left for us at Thornhill, filled the carriage with a redolence of friendship and quiet – We talked most of the way of your unwearied kindness – and of our hopes of seeing you here yet – before the end of the season – By the way you were quite mistaken about Charley's being in the pet with you – There was a little pet to be sure – but I, and not you – was the object of it – as I shall explain to you, if you care about it, when we meet – and let it rest till then – She and her mother will write you in a day or two – But they are both now in bed, and I shall leave this to be taken into town in the morning before they are up – How the wind howls! – tho' the stars are bright and steady, and the air mild – It makes me tremble for my transplants – and if it sweep with the same fury over Your uplands your walls I think must now be rocking you to deeper rest – be it so! – We are still very green and shady here – and there is a long lingering of Autumn still to be looked for – if you would only take courage to make use of it — I found I had been quite long enough away, when I got home – and have scarcely had a moment to myself since – with foolish consultations and letters of apology – <u>This</u> is about the first thing I have done to please myself, since I came to what people call a quiet home — I am often tempted to repent of my virtue in not bringing that miniature[3] with me – tho' I am sensible it would have been impolite and improper to Mrs W[elsh]. If it is ever sent to town however – to be fastened, or any thing else – pray let it be sent <u>to me</u> – and if you come, do bring it with you – I think I might have <u>a copy</u> of it without offending anybody – but we will talk of that hereafter —

I hope you had a ride together that fine Friday – and abused us as little as possible – <u>Harry</u>[4] too I hope has profited by the lesson of politeness and sociality I gave him and sticks by your side, in spite of the impatience of his more vehement rider — to whom however I must now say a word – and so my dear pensive and gentle Coz good night – and all happiness – Ever Affectly Your's F. J. —

For you My Dear C – I have room only to say that I have put your parcel in the way of being forwarded by Black – who has also engaged to write your brother by post as soon as it is actually despatched – I have likewise given him instructions about that poor castaway Hazzlitt[5] – and trust that he will not be offended by the liberty I have taken – I have excused myself by throwing it upon your instigation — I shall be able I hope next week to give you some opinion of your <u>opus majus</u>[6] – as yet I have only read a few pages – which certainly struck me as being both too quaint and sarcastic and too faultfinding – for an instructive and impartial history – but we shall see how you get on –

    Ever Yours

    F. Jeffrey

National Library of Scotland, Acc. 8964, no. 40.

1.   The Jeffreys had visited the Carlyles at Craigenputtoch from 14 to 17 September: 'Jeffrey was more than usually friendly and interesting', Carlyle wrote to his mother on 28 September 1830, 'and we were left, with real regret'; and to Anna Montagu, 'a more interesting and better man; a sadder and wiser; than I had ever seen him' (*Carlyle Letters*, vol. 5, pp. 167, 185).

2.   Jane's mother, Grace.

3.   A portrait of Jane, probably the 1826 miniature by Kenneth Macleay currently in the Scottish National Portrait Gallery.

4.   The Carlyles' horse (see *Reminiscences*, p. 130 and ff.).

5.   William Hazlitt (1778–1830), the philosopher, painter and famous periodical essayist who reviewed occasionally for the *Edinburgh Review*. Jeffrey 'has got a Letter from Hazzlitt, strangely requesting £100 from him', wrote Carlyle to his brother John, 18 September 1830, 'and determines to consult you on the subject, and in the mean time to send £50 through your hands' (*Carlyle Letters*, vol. 5, p. 163). The letter and money never reached Hazlitt. Charlotte (Mrs) Jeffrey wrote to Jane on 23 September 1830: 'We were very much shocked to see poor Hazzlitts death in the newspapers – I wish he had [?waited] a few days longer to have got Jeffrey's letter – that he might have seen there was still somebody who had a feeling of kindness for him & that he was not quite so neglected and forlorn as he thought himself' (NLS, Acc. 8964, no. 41).

6.   At the end of his visit to Craigenputtoch of mid-September, Jeffrey had 'insisted on taking my unfortunate Manuscript (of German Literary History) with him to Edin*r*', Carlyle wrote to his mother on 28 September 1830, 'that he might read it, and see whether *he* could not find a Publisher for it' (*Carlyle Letters*, vol. 5, pp. 167–8). Jeffrey's comments can be found below, in his letter of 28 October 1830.

TO THOMAS CARLYLE

date 26 September 1830
from Craigcrook

Craigcrook Sunday 26th
Sepr 1830

My Dear Carlyle

I cannot tell you how much I am touched by the deep kindness and <u>truth</u> of your letter – I do not mean the truth of my secret mysticism – but of the value I put on your Friendship – and the gratification it is likely to afford me – I <u>am</u> rich enough – and known enough and, at least, occupied enough – I have pursued these things – partly from the impulse of my natural activity – and partly as tests, to myself and to others, of the force of my character, and of the place I was entitled to, ~~assign myself~~ among those who pursued them around me – but I never rated them, I think, above their true worth – never placed them in competition with the indulgence of the kind affections – I have never ceased to hold that the true treasure of existence was love – I have never wavered in that faith – never, for many minutes, been unconscious of its sustaining and redeeming power — I feel therefore in my inmost heart that I can never have enough of love – and that the best of all gifts is given me when pure and thoughtful hearts are resolutely willing to ally themselves with mine — My life you think is not in accordance with this creed – perhaps it is not – I do not know what life of man is – But it is less a contradiction to it than you imagine – affection cannot occupy a man – and ought not to occupy him – We have heads as well as hearts – and bodies and animal spirits, that must have their occupations also, and by their due exercise minister to our delight and perfection – If I were to live entirely in your wilderness, with you and my gentle hearted cousin, we should be occupied half our time, apart – and for more than half of what we spent together, we should talk of things indifferent – and now and then feel <u>ennui</u> perhaps, from want of external variety – Yet we should not cease to love each other – nor to feel that this true affection was the life of our life – and gave its colour and warmth to its ordinary features – Why will you not believe that it is the same with those who live in towns and toils? If there is occasionally a little too much distraction, and too much interference with quiet and deep feeling in the one, there is apt to be too much languor and self will and dependency in the other – and it is incredible how well all is balanced – and brought to an average – for kindness as well as comfort — It is one of the evils of your contemplative life that you judge harshly of those who are active – I cannot help suspecting at least that you do injustice in your heart to the many kind and devoted and magnanimous beings who are busy and merry – and apparently frivolous – who dine gaily and jostle hardly in business with the friends for whom they would go to the death – friends whose good fortune gives them more delight than their own – whose afflictions weigh on their hearts thro' the sleepless night – and whose dishonour would kill them – I <u>know</u> several such – I <u>believe</u> there are many — Still it is true that as life advances and energy decays, the stir of the world becomes more importunate, and the heart longs more for a resting place, away from [the *tear*] din and tumult of its beaten ways – It is this which gives a charm to the aspect of your desart – and makes your kind and cordial invitation fall with a seductive sweetness on my ear – But is there not illusion in this also? I do not <u>despond</u> on the prospect of approaching age – but I look calmly on its necessary evils – It would be sad you will admit to be surprised by them without such preparation. – I accustom myself to them therefore – and I cannot disguise from myself that they are evils – The great softening I believe is that they come <u>gradually</u> – and that our plastic nature accommodates itself to them insensibly – But would retreat afford any alleviation? – Is not one of the decays that of social interest and affection? If occupation becomes irksome and fame insipid, does not love too raise a feebler throb in the pulse, and stupor and selfishness gradually invade all the being? – If we become objects of pity and scorn to our associates in the common business of life, do we not also slide in the same path from the affections of those to whom we were most dear? Should we wish to be a burden and a spectacle to those in whose memories it is most ~~natural~~ desirable that we should live in our bright-est colours? No my Dear Friend, there is no mysticism will help us out of this – Infirmity and decay are great and certain evils – and hard as it is to amaze their victims with the toys and toils of the world – it is still harder I fear to animate them with generous affections, or to make them the objects of anything higher than a painful compassion – Let us live and love each other while we can – but be prepared to lose most even of our purest enjoyments some time before we die – unless early death prevent decay —— Well, here is a long preachment for you this Sunday Evening – but a dull return I fear for your kind exhortation – But I do not rejoice the less in your affection – nor accept or return it less cordially – It is a delight and comfort to me, unspeakable – and I feel assured that it will not be withdrawn — God bless you – I shall write soon again, about your M.S.[1] and other literary projects – I am afraid your ambition is not well directed – and that you are not tractable – but we shall see. I am for trying to sell the history. – if you will only make it history and write more naturally – There is much in it, valuable, and likely to [?have an *MS torn*] effect — Ever Very Affectly Yours

    F. Jeffrey

    Poor Hazzlitt you will hear died the very day I sent my letter to your brother – my only consolation is, that I did not lose an hour after my return, in sending it – leaving half my letters unread, that I might not be too late at my Banker – It was decreed otherwise – I hope my dear Coz. got my letter on Wednesday – and that she means to answer it – It makes me happier and better to think that she loves me —

National Library of Scotland, Acc. 8964, no. 42.
1.   The literary history of Germany.

TO JANE WELSH CARLYLE

date 9 October 1830
from Craigcrook

Craigcrook 9th Octobr 1830

My Dear Child – a thousand thanks, and <u>blessings</u>, to you, for your letter – tho' it drew tears from me – and I prefer the happiness of smiles – I have carried it about with me ever since I received it – and the very smell of the musk with which you had perfumed it seems to spread an atmosphere of purity and tenderness around me, which nothing base or unholy can enter – O if the sense of my love and affection could give you but half the comfort and delight that yours has afforded to me, it was indeed a blessed chance which brought us acquainted – and has led <us> on to trust and intimacy — Yet, inexpressibly thankful as my heart is to you for all this, you must not be jealous if I add that I am almost as thankful to your Mother – You know, I take it for granted, that she has sent me <u>the</u> picture[1] – and with a letter so kind and touching – sent it to me, not in loan, but in gift – tho' under certain conditions at which I should be a brute if I could murmur – and to which I have felt it my duty to add certain additions, in the answer I immediately sent her – But in the mean time, that precious picture is my own – in my quite lawful possession at least – and with the full free and unconstrained consent of all who have anything to do with it – Assure me at least that this is the case – and that your mother in particular has not been wrought upon, either by my importunity, or by your's, to part with a valued object which she would rather have retained. Tho' it is but too gratifying to me to think that you might have been importunate with her in this cause – still it would be more soothing to my heart, as well as my conscience, to believe that I owed it to the spontaneous kindness of the owner – Tell me then truly how it stands – and how it came about ——

Tell me that you are quite well again – and that you will submit to take a little care of yourself – Tho' there may be heroic minds <still> in the world, I am afraid that they are not generally matched with heroic bodies – and that it is not altogether a good regime to sit 3 or 4 days in a warm house – without ever stirring out [–] and then to make amends, by riding 3 miles in the rain [–] There is less ~~rain~~ rain however – and we have the sweetest autumn weather in the world — broad light and deep colours and above all that holy, tender dewy <u>calm</u>, which has always appeared to me the most touching and soothing of all outward existences – But you do not care for anything outward – and I must say one word to you on interiors — The deep truth and tenderness of that part of your letter which chiefly affects me, cannot force my assent to the part with which I must still disagree — It is a real pain to me to see you cherish so strange a notion as that the essence and necessary character of human life is sadness – I do not consider this a matter of reasoning or opinion but of <u>fact</u> – Is it <u>true</u> that men are generally sad? or that thinking cultivated affectionate men are sadder than others? As a matter of observation, I would answer most certainly not – I cannot help thinking too, that the best proof of what we <u>ought</u> to be – and what we were <u>intended</u> to be, is what, generally, and thro' a succession of ages we have actually been – Can you really believe that this bright world, with its laughing Sun and sparkling stars – its brilliant flowers and rills and fountains, was made for the abode of sadness? – What has sadness to do with the dimply smiles and airy hands of childhood or the light hearted frankness, cordiality and daring of youth or the social benevolent cheerfulness of maturer age? Whenever outward circumstances are favourable – or even tolerable, the <u>natural</u> bent is to cheerfulness and joy – Afflictions will come no doubt – and hours of deep thoughtfulness and earnest love will interpose <u>serious delights</u>, that are, in my opinion, as little akin to sadness, as to heartless levity – to the sadness at least which I mean to combat – and to which I do think you give too much indulgence – There are deep colours no doubt in life as well as gay ones – and emotions which partake of grandeur besides those that belong to mirth – But is it not a sad mistake to attend only to the former? – or to suppose that the pleasure which is ministered by the latter partakes of degradation, or can even be rejected without arrogance and ingratitude? You must not take it amiss therefore my Dear Child that I wish you to be as happy as possible and to possess all varieties of happiness – I do not think we differ seriously as to the relative value of its possible constituents – and I for one do not believe that there is any repugnancy among them – Do then indulge more liberally in smiles – (I will excuse you for not laughing much) – and let me hear that you can think even of habitual cheerfulness without scorn — I shall never be persuaded that you were intended to pass the bright years of your life – a life of your own choice, and yet crossed with but few misfortunes, in tears and unfathomable sadness! – Oh no – Yet do not suppose that I will not "take you as you are" heaven knows with what heartfelt gladness I accept of that offer – But I have room for no more – and it is as well – Tell C. I shall write him soon – about his manuscript, and other things [–] Heaven keep and bless you – Ever Yours   F Jeffrey

National Library of Scotland, Acc. 8964, no. 43.

1.   The portrait of Jane mentioned in the letter of 19 September 1830, above, which was sent to Jeffrey (as he explains here) by Jane's mother. The picture became a fetish for Jeffrey, who would constantly return to it, and to his possession of it, in his letters to Jane. Later, as the relationship between Jeffrey and the Carlyles cooled, it would become a point of contention for Carlyle, who complains to Jane on 31 August 1831, for example, that 'there are two things I vehemently desire: first that I had £60 to pay him; secondly that I had my Wife's picture out of his hands, which I cannot but think are nowise worthy to hold it' (*Carlyle Letters*, vol. 5, p. 382).

TO THOMAS (AND JANE WELSH) CARLYLE

date 28 October 1830
from Craigcrook

Craigcrook 28 Octob[r] 1830

My Dear Friends — Why do neither of you write to me? It is vacation time <still> with me – and my thoughts have more freedom to turn to what most naturally interests them – But you I hope are more pleasantly and profitably occupied – and I wait patiently till my turn comes — I have now read nearly all your M.S.[1] – and confess that I have great doubts whether it will readily find a purchaser – just because I fear, if it were published, it would not readily find many readers – The radical error I still think was in going back so largely into remote periods. The public cares very little about German <u>antiquities</u> – whether historical or literary – There is I am persuaded, a great and a growing curiosity about the Genius and literature of that great country – but it is about its new or recent genius – not its old – It is very likely that the two are very closely connected – and even very probable that no just account can be given of the former – which does not trace back its chief characteristics into the latter – But this should be done rapidly and in a general way – without details and minute historical deductions – in the style, for example, of those admirable paragraphs in which you pass to the age of Charlemagne and pourtray the new character which was then impressed on the temper and society of Europe — I must add that even if the subject and scale of the work were less objectionable I do not think the execution such as to promise, or deserve, success – The learned details are given without vigour or any tone of mastery over the subject – and are often broken and incoherent. The abstract of the old poems is the best – but the gayety which invades them – tho' often very engaging in itself, is not generally in harmony with what the author says earnestly in his own person – while the doctrine or spirit of the whole estimate, is not only, in my humble apprehension, misguided and partial – but is nowhere delivered with that unity and fulness which would be necessary to recommend – or even to make it intelligible to ordinary readers – Then you have fits of spleen and peevish scorn which are altogether unreasonable – and unseemly – What for instance can be much more absurd than your proem on the want of public patronage for Poetry?[2] – and your complaint that while other crafts have Deacons, and dignities in town councils – and corporation privileges, poor poets must fight their single way to wealth and honor? — You know well enough that those abominable monopolies are mere discouragements to merit, and contrivances for jobbing and injustice. Would you really have a corporation of poets, out of which no one should be allowed to practise the art, – and into which no man should get, except by serving a 7 years' apprenticeship – or marrying a freeman's daughter, and paying a sum to the Box? If you do not mean this, and if you know that genius, and merit of every sort, has the best possible chance when the field is most open, and there is neither public patronage nor public persecution – what is it that you do mean? – and why begin a calm historical work with so strange an ebullition of temper? – If your work is ever printed, you will deal most unfairly by yourself if you do not alter and correct it unsparingly – but this idle prologue <u>must</u> at all events be suppressed – or you make sure of damnation — Something too much of this, tho' — I do not know why I write it[3] – but I am very sure <u>not</u> to vex and annoy you – and I am nearly as sure that you will not think so – The practical result is, that I do not see how I can be of any use in the obstetrical department, to which I once aspired, in behalf of this conception of yours – but that I shall be most happy to do anything which it may occur to you can still be done for it.

Well – I hope you are all well – and enjoying this fine epilogue to the summer, which compensates for all its dulness – It has made me very idle – and I do not know how I shall be able to buckle to my drudgery next month – but the plastic nature will accommodate itself – and in the mean time I think my health is better for it – I hope you take care of yours – and are moderate in the use of tobacco, and other dangerous sensualities [–] Let me know what you are about – and whether your <u>genuine</u> work is begun – and what it is about – God bless you – Ever Yours   F Jeffrey

And now my fair cousin this little corner is for you – why do you not send me another <u>musk</u> letter? not that the perfume of the other is evaporated yet – but because it gave me so much pleasure that I think if you knew it, you would not grudge me a second – In the mean time I cannot tell you what comfort and delight I have in the miniature or how grateful I still feel to your mother for it – I hope she does not repent of her generosity. Never mind my heresies about sadness – I am satisfied that we do not substantially differ, on that or any other serious subject – But pray write to me and pray for me

    Very Affectionately Your's

    F.J.

National Library of Scotland, Acc. 8964, no. 44.

1. Again, Carlyle's unfinished history of German literature.
2. The first chapter of Carlyle's history was a general discussion of literature and of writing literary history – see *Carlyle's Unfinished History of German Literature*, ed. H. Shine (Lexington, KY: University of Kentucky Press, 1951).
3. Carlyle was understandably stung by Jeffrey's comments, which in a letter to his brother John of 12 November 1830 he called 'a long, unasked, abusive and almost ill-bred Criticism' of his work: 'On reading Jeffrey's Letter, the first thought was naturally to *wash him away*, which could be done with unspeakable ease, I believe; but reflecting then on the man's intrinsic kindliness, also on his sufferings and even miseries some of which I have seen into, it appeared clear enough that he had been only in a sad fit of depression, whence this acetous fermentation of small-beer; so I wrote him one of my friendliest Letters, and mean to be as kind to the worthy little Poet as is possible for me, let him kick against the pricks as he may. A warm loving heart, yet now when he is growing old, I question if there is on Earth one real Friend for him, only millions of Commensals and Compotators, and perhaps he feels this! Let us pity the poor white man; – and rejoice that *Dilettantism* will ere long be kicked out of Creation, in all probability for a century or two' (*Carlyle Letters*, vol. 5, p. 190).

TO THOMAS CARLYLE

date 13 November 1830
from Edinburgh

Edin[r] 13 Nov[r] 1830

My Dear Friend – I have seen Gibson Craig – and he is well disposed towards Gordon[1] – and engages, if no worthier candidate appear – (and he has yet heard from one). to support him – But they are not yet in a condition to make any appointment – The deeds under which they are to act – have not been completed – and there are disputes about Legacy and probate duty, which may retard them yet for a while – However he assures me that the place will be given to the person whom they really think best qualified – and that they are all pledged neither to job or tolerate jobbing in the matter – and so it must rest for the present –

My brother[2] is still very unwell at Craigcrook – and I am far from being easy about him – Tho' he has no bad or violent symptoms, he is very low and weak and is <only> supported by frequent drafts of wine – to the amount of a bottle in a day – while the febrile excitement still continues – However the Doctors are not apprehensive and I do what I can to believe them – tho' Faith, you say, is not among my virtues —— My Charlottes too are both gone to bed with headache – and sitting alone over my midnight fire I cannot keep visions of infection and desolating fever quite out of my mind – so I turn to warm my cold heart at yours – and feel proud that you should know that neither business nor anxiety can make me forget to do a little good on your suggestion – I wish you could show me how to do more —— Our campaign has begun as usual[3] – and I have already had two days speaking – my voice is not very good – but it is better today than it was yesterday – and I think it improves rather than suffers by exercise – It blows so ferociously than [*for* that] I have not been able to ride – but, as Sunday is always calm, I shall go to see John tomorrow – or even if it should blow, it will put me in mind of my last jog at Craigenputtach.— I wish I had time to explain to you the [*over* why] grounds of my horror of radicalism – It is nothing but the old feud ag[ains]t property – more formidable by the greater intelligence and conceit of those who have none – the encrease perhaps – (for I am not sure that there is any encrease) of their distresses – and the glimpses they have had of temporary prosperity – But there is no remedy, but the utter destruction of the right of property altogether – and the establishment of a great cooperative system – which no sane man will seriously consider as practicable — Everything short of that – sumptuary laws – maximum of allowable accumulation – compulsory charity – agrarian repartitions – obviously tend, not to make the poor better off – but to make all poor, of the very lowest description – and that by no long process – besides importing the entire destruction of all luxury, elegance, art – and mental cultivation – and in short reducing the whole race to the wretched condition of savages toiling and scrambling for mere animal subsistence – It is only by protecting and assuring the right of property that we have emerged from that condition, and <are> still kept out of it – and tho' its ultimate establishment produces many evils – and a most revolting spectacle of inequality, I do not see how you can touch it, without bringing in still greater evils — In short I think it is quite plain that the greater portion of all societies must be always on the brink of extreme poverty – and waging a hard battle with all sorts of fears and sufferings – In a mere worldly and physical point of view they gain but little perhaps by the establishment of property – tho' they are more secure from violence and outrage, and even for the most part, from actual starvation – But indirectly even they gain a great deal – in the share that comes even to them of that mental culture which is consequently diffused thro' society and in the hope and chance of rising to a higher place in it – which is a source of enjoy[men]ᵗ even when not realised – But it is their very wants and urgent necessities which first roused the spirit of invention and improvement – and it is only – as it would appear – by their fears and miseries that their multiplication to a still more frightful extent is prevented – If men could have lived merely by breathing, and required neither clothes[,] house, or any other accommodation, I take it to be quite certain 1ˢᵗ that they would <very soon> have multiplied till they had not room to lie down on the surface of the earth – and 2ᵈ that they would have so lived and propagated in as brutish a state as the very lowest of the animal creation — Your very rich man after all spends almost all his income on the poor – and except a very little waste of food among his servants and horses, is a mere distributor of his rents among industrious and frugal workmen – But if you ever touch his overgrown wealth, it is manifest that there is no stopping till <u>all</u> private accumulation or property is divided and made common – and with it all the advantages of working by large capitals, destroyed – But this is as tiresome as mysticism – and perhaps as unintelligible — I should like much better to <u>talk</u> it to you – only pray, if you are about to be a politician, set about it modestly and patiently – and submit to study a little, under those who have studied it much longer and quite as honestly — Well – tell me about your book – and what you are doing – Good-night – I must go to bed now – Moir[4] has your M.S. No my fair Coz I do not forget you! – no not for an hour! – God bless you – You will write when you think it right? Ever Affectly Yours,

    <u>F. Jeffrey</u>

If you are a radical, why do you keep the horses that produce nothing? Why should you waste on two brutes the food of six starving human creatures, that your feet may be kept out of the dirt, or your diaphragm healthfully agitated? riding horses, which you patronise, interfere[s] with the subsistence of men 500 times more than partridges which you abominate. Do you adopt the radical doctrine about <u>machinery</u> too – which is the true parent of the whole? and do you not see that, upon that principle, we should burn our ploughs and carts – aye, and our spades too – and end by only allowing men to work with <u>one hand</u> – or perhaps with their feet only, in order that the necessary work may give longer employment to more persons? all this I think may be strictly demonstrated – Yet you seem to think a radical insurrection very justifiable, and its success to be desired – tho' that is their great practical maxim and would be their first enactment. Do you really think it desirable that machinery should be proscribed, or that the overseers of the poor should be obliged to give 12/ or 20/ a week to anyone who cannot – or says he cannot, earn so much by the labour he has been used to? Yet it is avowedly and expressly for <u>these objects</u> that insurrection is threatened or begun – radical reform of Parl[t] is now sought only as a means to these ends – and indeed <is now> very generally disregarded by the true radicals who have other and quicker means in contemplation – and – on their principles, they are right.

National Library of Scotland, Acc. 8964, no. 45.

1. James Gibson Craig (1765–1850), a writer to the signet and zealous Whig friend of Jeffrey's, held a number of public offices and was obviously approached on behalf of Carlyle's friend John Gordon, who was seeking 'a certain desk Secretaryship' (see Carlyle to his brother John, 19 December 1830, *Carlyle Letters*, vol. 5, p. 204).
2. Jeffrey's younger brother, John Jeffrey, a merchant. The Carlyles would get to know him in London in 1831 when he was courting Elizabeth Hunter (his first wife having died in 1806, not long after the death of Jeffrey's first wife Catherine) and would nickname him 'Saym Relish' from something said over the dinner table.
3. The Whigs' (successful) bid for office; see the next letter.
4. Carlyle's friend George Moir (see note 5 to the letter of 3 November 1829, above).

TO THOMAS (AND JANE WELSH) CARLYLE

date 18 December 1830
from Edinburgh

Edin[r] 18 Dec[r] 1830

My Dear Friend — O yes – alas, I am Lord Advocate! – and about to be M.P.[1] – and to be plunged into a vortex from which my soul recoils – and upon which nothing but a strong – tho' it may be most mistaken sense of duty, could have induced me to venture — It is not to you that I need make explanations or seek to justify a decision to which heaven knows, I have come with infinite reluctance – and too painful a feeling of the sacrifices I make, and the risks I encounter – You do not understand those things – I cannot say that I perfectly understand them myself – but when I say that I have yielded in this case to the judgment of friends to whom I have often left matters of as much importance to[2] as worthy persons – and that my motives in taking up this heavy burden have not been tainted with any mixture that I can detect of worldly ambition or self-interest, I know that I shall be believed by all those about whose belief or opinion I take any care and feel that I may safely refer to the coming on of time for the redemption of any pledges that my past conduct may be supposed to have given for my future –

God help us – why do I write all this to you? – I have written 23 letters since I came home from court – and it is a relief to say a word to those I love and trust in – without the intervention of a Secretary or the necessity of any politic reserve – and to refresh my jaded spirits with even an ideal gasp of the pure still air of your desart — My brother I thank you is nearly well again[3] – after 4 weeks confinement to bed he was moved into town last week and is in a fair way of recovery – The rest of us are well – with the exception of my chronic infirmities – tho' the trachea has given me rather less disturbance than usual this winter – My child is blooming, and always gentle and cheerful – and I think affection-ate and happy — Why does not my fair cousin write to me – She is not inditing a genuine work too – and at all events why not indite a genuine letter to me? I look every night at her picture – and have her image often before me thro' the day – I am a little hurt – perhaps more than a little – at her neglect of me – You have been sparing of your notice also – but I do not take pets or suspicions – and shall only go on loving and serving you, at such distance as you chuse to be of me [–] We shall understand each other better in another world – to which I shall go first – to get things in order for you –

Can I do anything for you or for any cause or person in whom you take inter-est, in my new vocation[?] – Nothing vexes and disturbs me so much as the kind of patronage that belongs to it – which I would gladly give all its honors to be rid of. – And then we must all go to London I fear about the end of January – and live a life there so alien to all my habits and wishes that nothing could reconcile me to it but the prospect of returning – <u>solutis</u> negotiis[4] to the unbroken quiet of Craigcrook – or Craigenputtach — In the mean time pray for me my Dear Friends – and love me – This is the balm and cordial of my existence – and I think it is not in your natures to grudge or withhold it from me [–] Write to me too my Dear Child – if it were only one line of soothing and assurance – which will drop like balm upon a heart fevered and distempered by the troubled atmosphere in which it seems destined to beat out its few remaining beats — When shall we meet again[?] I scarcely wish it to be in London – for I know my life there will be one whirl of public and professional obligation – There is a difficulty about getting a Seat for me – at which I am glad enough in my heart – tho' I fear my being out of Parl[iamen]t will not long be allowed as an apology for my not repairing to headquarters – and now God Bless you – Do not be so long of writing again – and tell me all you are doing – not much cold yet – but a plentiful lack of day light – good night

   Ever Affectly Yours

   F Jeffrey

National Library of Scotland, Acc. 8964, no. 46.

1. The position of Lord Advocate was, nominally, that of chief Scottish law officer. In reality and certainly by Jeffrey's time, it carried a curious mixture of legal, political and bureaucratic responsibilities (requiring election to a seat in the House of Commons, for example) which made its holder in various ways representative of Scottish interests in Westminster. When the Whigs were asked to form a government under Earl Grey (1764–1845) late in 1830, electoral reform – which involved a rationalization of electoral representation, the elimination of corruption and an extension of the franchise – was highest on their agenda, and one of Jeffrey's most onerous tasks was the drafting of the Scottish counterpart of the famous Reform Bill, which finally came into effect in June 1832. From a personal angle, this letter begins Jeffrey's protracted complaints about the demands of office, about his having been uprooted late in his career, and about his being out of step with what he recognized as important historical events then taking place.
2. The preposition 'to' is redundant; he means: 'I have yielded in this case to the judgement of friends to whom, as worthy persons, I have often left matters of as much importance'.
3. See the previous letter, 13 November 1830.
4. Latin: liberated from business.

1831

TO JANE WELSH CARLYLE

date 9 and 11 January 1831
from Edinburgh

Edinburgh Thursday
Evg 9th Jan^y

Well – you are a very good child – and though I have been angry at your silence, I forgive you – and bless you for your fantastic humanities – you will do no good to your lymphatic – but you do good to yourself – and to all who see or hear of you, by the example of your devotedness – and so I <u>do</u> bid God speed you – and wish that I were a little more mad than I am, to be so soothed and pet-ted! – It is your vocation – and Carlyles to prescribe your panaceas to incurables – instead of stooping to alleviate medicable ills – and I can never cease to forget this – and to murmur at the throwing away of your lenitives and cordials – where they are neither prized nor operative —

But it occupies you – and not ignobly – in a life otherwise rather barren of occupation – and as the Alchymists found many valuable things — You see what I mean – and it is too <u>fade</u>[1] and tiresome to write it down at full length – and so I bless you again – and thank you, with all my heart, for your little <u>shred</u> of comfort – which I shall wear near it – and try to believe in, as long as you will let me –

But you never say a word of coming here – or what you propose to do – and you know that we shall be engulfed in the mighty Babylon in the first days of Feb[ruar]y – Therein to abide our new penance, for a time, and times – and you care not ————

Saturday 11th — I have not <had> a moment to finish this till now – and now only to finish [–] God bless you — I have a line from Mrs Austin[2] this morn^g I grieve to say in very poor spirits — Her own health but her husband's very much worse – and so bad that she anticipates that it will be utterly impossible for him to deliver his lectures – which were to begin in a few days – and could not be delayed – so that this incapacity would lead to a resignation of the office – and throw them all back into the distress and anxiety from which they were so much relieved by the appointment — I cannot tell you how much I lament this – and to see her buoyant heroic spirit half confounded by it – But I trust things will take a turn*

---

* The remainder of the letter has been lost.
National Library of Scotland, Acc. 8964, no. 47.
1.   French: dull, drab.
2.   Sarah Austin (née Taylor; 1793–1867), a translator of German and an acquaintance of the Carlyles. Her husband, John Austin, was Professor of Jurisprudence at University College London.

TO JANE WELSH CARLYLE

date 16 January 1831
from Edinburgh

[Edinburgh Jany Sixteen 1831*]
My Very Dear Child – I will not send you my first frank[1] without a line from myself in the inside – But it must be a line only today – I am frightfully busy – and very sick of my work – Heaven bless and protect you – and pray do love me always – always and well! – It is my chief solace to rely on this – and I know you will not deceive me — It is gloomy and cold – but we may have brightness inward – Do you read my speeches on my Electioneering – The last is that at my <u>Dinner</u> – not in the Hall – at Forfar[2] — I have a great chance of being unseated in March or April – and then I shall get down to Craigcrook earlier – and I cannot say the prospect afflicts me greatly — The only thing I grudge, is the expense of defending a seat[3] which, with all its uncertainty, the ministry <u>compelled</u> me to take — But you care nothing about this – and I, not much – Have you any Sun at Craigenputtach? any of that soft sweet low sun which used formerly to brighten our winter afternoons? – Here we have little but frost fogs and smoke [–] O how I thank you for that picture! – but alas it is not to you I owe it – but your mother – No matter I have it – and with your assent – Will you not come to London while we are there[?] – Write soon or we may have gone first – our hours are numbered – and I may be called up any day – Again God bless you   Ever Yours
      F Jeffrey

---

* This written on the cover, above the name and address of the recipient.
National Library of Scotland, Acc. 8964, no. 48.

1. As an MP Jeffrey was entitled to 'frank' letters, marking them with his name or insignia and thereby securing them free passage (in the early nineteenth century the recipient bore the cost of postage). Jeffrey's franking was useful to his friends – and especially useful to the Carlyles – who could use his frank on their own letters to family and friends. 'Throw the poor Duke a word sometimes', Carlyle would write to Jane on 29 August 1831, 'for his franks are very precious' (*Carlyle Letters*, vol. 5, p. 380).

2. A Royal burgh in the valley of Strathmore, 21 miles north-east of Dundee. Jeffrey sought election for the Forfarshire burghs in order to qualify for a seat in the House of Commons. He was jostled by crowds rather badly on a couple of occasions and subject to abuse because his opposition, a Captain Ogilvy, was a candidate on the popular side. But Jeffrey eventually won – only to have the seat revoked in March on a technicality regarding the constitution of the electorate (see note 1 to the letter of 26 March 1831, below).

3. Jeffrey was a wealthy man at the beginning of the 1830s, and he would always be comfortably off, but he sacrificed £2800 a year in handing over the editorship of the *Edinburgh Review* in 1829 and his considerable income as an advocate when accepting the post of Lord Advocate in 1830, only to find that his efforts over the next three years to gain, and regain, a seat in parliament would cost him around £10,000 (again, see note 1 to the letter of 26 March 1831, below).

TO JANE WELSH (AND THOMAS) CARLYLE

date 1 and 2 February 1831
from Stevenege, London

Stevenege Thursday Evg
1st Feby 1831

I told you how it would be – You loiter and loiter about writing to me, – and behold I am gone without a blessing or a parting word from you [–] You should reproach yourselves for this – but I will not reproach you – We have been toiling up, thro' snow and darkness, for four long days – with this shattered carcase – and this reluctant and half desponding spirit – and are here within sight of land – and to enter tomorrow – if the snow drifts will let us – upon our new career of strange work among strangers – We have had a rough scramble today ag[ains]t heinous and driving snows – and have with difficulty made out 60 miles – with 4 horses, in 14 hours – However we are safe housed for the night – and are sipping weak black tea, in a very tolerable state of comfort – by a good fire – in a good parlour as neat and small, and as tranquil almost, as that at Craigenputtach, which so often rises before me, for comparison or contrast! – Cold as the journey has been I think I am better for it – I had a heavy lingering cold, ever since Forfar – but this scramble has removed it – or at least the cough – and much of the feeling of fever and I shall arrive in the line of battle, much fitter for work than I expected – I never went to London with such a weight on my spirits as now – partly no doubt from some apprehension as to my fitness for the new work which waits me there – but mostly I think from the uncertainty of my detention – and the consequent feeling of indefinite exile from my country and my friends – and cherished scenes and habits – But my nature is not desponding – and I shall break my spear in the strange lists, with courage and composure enough — The Mails have already passed to the North tonight so I shall take this to town with me, and finish it after we cast anchor – I shall then be able also to tell you our address – which I do not yet know – God bless you – Is there anything I can do for you in London? Is there no chance of your coming up to see us there? But at all events you must send me advices to warn and protect me – and kind wishes to draw down blessings – and assurances of love and trust to soothe and support me – and so good night – and all these bright stars rain their bright influences on you! –

London ~~Thursday~~ <Wedy> 2d – no bright influences today! – all smoke and sleet and thick darkness – There was more snow in the night and we had a weary tug thro' it – We are only in time for the post now – so I must barely add that our address is 37 Jermyn Street – and that I hope soon to hear from you — I have just seen the Chancellor[1] and am going to dine with him – and tomorrow I take my seat and then an end to peace and quiet – and all but recollections and anticipations – which are the better part of existence I fear generally – and so heaven bless and preserve you

Ever Affectly Yours
F Jeffrey

This letter is to you, Fair Child – I am not in spirits to write to the Man friend – or could you find that out?

National Library of Scotland, Acc. 8964, no. 49.

1.   Jeffrey's friend Henry Brougham had been created Lord Chancellor when the Whigs gained office at the end of 1830 (see note 1 to the letter of 17 October 1827, above). All subsequent allusions to 'the Chancellor' refer to Brougham.

TO JANE WELSH CARLYLE

date 20–8 February 1831
from London

London 20 Feby 1831

Oh what a far cry it is from here to Craigenputtach! – to that mist veiled shrine in the desart – to which my heart turns daily, at the shut of its weary day. – But you have brought it nearer – and I bless you for the kind thought — tho' it would have been better if you had made the journal – and poured its balm on the accumulated fever of a week – instead of asking me to chronicle these idle beatings of the heart which will not be stilled by soliloquies – I cant describe my life here to you – and I need not – well, but yesterday I saw your Mrs Montagu – a thoughtful amiable looking woman – a little <u>mannered</u> and sententious – but yet gentle and indulgent watching you with more intense observation than suits modern manners – or to say truth, the ease of society – and yet gentle, as I have said and only a little <u>bluer</u> than the blue sky of heaven – I gave her C's card and she smiled and put it up in her case – and we parted very good friends[1] – good night! – I am giddy with watching and will not turn the leaf

21st or 22[d] rather – being 3 o'clock in the morning – In the Lords arguing appeals till 4. revived with a lovely cup of Coffee in the garret – and then to H[ouse]. of C[ommons]. till now.[2] walk home in a sort of sleet – and after sipping a glass of sage and lemon juice – and reading 14 letters – say good night to you – and wonder how this setting moon is gleaming over your uplands – and how your slow pure breath is exhaling like incense from those lonely and chilly heights – and so light my watch lamp and commend myself to kind dreams – good night. I cannot compose myself to gossip with you – it is too painful – –

23[d] I have been at the Levee to-day – and after, at a great Cabinet dinner.[3] The last delighted me greatly – so much frankness, simplicity – mutual confidence – and entire absence of all distrust, eagerness or self assurance – I do not believe there ever was so honest a ministry – so unambitious – so truly anxious to do good – If they fall – <u>which is likely enough,</u> – it will be a great public calamity – and the inlet to greater calamities – I wish C. could have seen the brotherly gentleness and mutual forbearance with which everything was discussed – and the brevity and clearness with which all opinions were proposed – and opposed – and <yet> the farthest from indifference – or want of due estimates of the hazards that are impending — Well – but would you rather hear of the Leveé? 1500 fine looking men, mostly in gorgeous uniforms – and I in the midst of them with my damask gown and lace cravat – kissing kings' hands, and whirled away in the Lord Chancellor's state carriage, with his mace and 3 train bearers! – a vanity of vanities! – But this same Chancellor is no mere pageant – but a master spirit – and a prodigy – to whom all these things are but as the flushing clouds that glare round the rushing course of the naked Sun – God bless you –

24th – This is the Queens birthday – but I had not courage for the Drawing room – and worked all day at my reform Bill[4] – till just before dinner when I took a lovely run in the park, and communed with the setting sun – Then I went to a great Dinner at Lord Melbourne's[5] – with all the Judges and the King's Counsel &c rather a dull dinner – with plenty of guzzling and gossip and all in full dress. The Chancellor took me afterwards to Devonshire House[6] – a vast assembly – and perhaps the finest <u>spectacle</u> in London – and now I am at home, weary and giddy – and must look over law cases to be argued in the Lords tomorrow – what can you do for me? There is nothing for it – but on and on – like a squirrel in his cage

Sunday 27th — I have had an oppressive cold for 2 days and am only beginning to recover — Yet I have been obliged to go out —

Monday – I was called away to a Cabinet Council just as I was beginning those lines yesterday— and have scarcely rested since – for my cold kept me awake most part of the night and I have been this whole morning altering my reform Bill – to suit the foolish fancies of the English artists – who know nothing of the business – tomorrow or Wedy – will probably settle the fate of this great question – and also I should think of the Ministry which brings it in – The substance of what we are doing I think, will be popular – But much of the machinery and preparation, very much otherwise, — However if the people think we mean well, they will forgive the rest – and you will do so too, for other and greater things than this or any other political question – I am terribly afraid of my voice – and shall despair altogether if I am not better tomorrow – Despair! O no – God bless you – Kind love to Carlyle – and to yourself – what? – what but kind love also, and constancy and gratitude – as it was in the beginning, is now, and ever shall be – world without end – Ever Yours

    F Jeffrey

National Library of Scotland, Acc. 8964, no. 50.

1.   Mrs (Anna) Montagu (see note 1 to the letter of 5 June 1830, above) was similarly impressed with Jeffrey: 'there is a look of unpretending goodness, and natural warmth, about him, which I am sure has preserved him from all the dangers of successful, and somewhat malicious roit – You told me to forget the *Reviewer*, I never once thought of him till I came home' (as quoted in *Carlyle Letters*, vol. 5, p. 246).

2.   Commons did not begin each session until late in the afternoon and when there were urgent issues pending, as there were throughout the early years of the new Whig ministry, a session might last all night.

3.   All part of the formalities surrounding the swearing in of a new government.

4.   The Scottish counterpart, that is, of the Great Reform Bill, for which Jeffrey, with the assistance of Henry Cockburn as his Solicitor General, was responsible (see note 1 to the letter of 18 December 1830, above).

5.   Melbourne House, Piccadilly, London residence of William Lamb, second Viscount Melbourne (1779–1848), Home Secretary under Earl Grey in the new Whig ministry.

6.   One of the main centres of aristocratic Whig society and (along with Chatsworth) home of William Cavendish, the sixth Duke of Devonshire (1790–1858).

TO JANE WELSH CARLYLE

date 5–12 March 1831*
from London

Library House of C.
Saturday one o'clock Morn[g]

I have just made my first speech[1] – not altogether to my satisfaction – but with cheering and applause enough to satisfy any moderate ambition – I was not in the humor for speaking – and <u>know</u> I can speak better – so that I may now be at ease as to the place I might fill here – if I had opportunity and inclination to seek for it – But I have slipped away from that clamorous and ambitious crowd, with the din of their acclamations still in my ears, to this quiet – and now solitary and cell like retreat, to say a word to <u>you</u> – and to wash my soul clean from those vanities and idle strivings – and take you and this calm sky to witness how lightly I prize them – and how little they interpose between my heart and its old, youthful – and unchangeable aspirations – It is with a strange and half melancholy feeling that I now look out, from the latticed windows, of this deserted room, on the broad calm waters of the river, and the soft fleecy moonlight that hangs over them – with the recollection of that hot, crowded, turbulent, and loud shouting assembly – which is still clamouring within a hundred yards of me – and yet appears like a dim and half forgotten vision to my stilled and abstracted thought — I could not make a nightly entry since the date of my last letter to you – for I have had a friend who walks home with me from the house and sits drinking soda water till we are both more than half dead with sleep — If they make an intelligible report of my speech I will try to send you a paper – tho' I know you are far above caring for what only involves the peace and prosperity of a nation – some clumsy and dull extravaganza of Willhelm Meister[2] – about dramatic truth or impossible education, seems to you far more lofty and reasonable – But this is for your husband, and not for you – at least I hope is not for you – It would be a real pain to me to know that there were <u>two</u> such castaways – But God bless you – I must go back to my post – we stand ticklish enough – but are connected like brothers – and are cheerful, and confident, in pure purposes, and unimpeachable honor – bless you–

Monday night – or rather Tuesday Morn[g] 2. another stormy debate – and a quiet walk home [–] I cannot write to you in this state – it will not do. – and I must not attempt it – It only makes my head whirl more – you must let me work my spell – and not speak to me – Blessings! –

Wedy or Thursday Morn[g] 3. at last our debate is over – and I have come home pensive in a thick fog – no division – yet — My speech has had great fortune – and they are going to publish a corrected copy of it, in a separate form [–] I had a long walk in the park this morning – a lovely spring day – all the shrubs in half leaf – and the grass far greener than any season ever showed in Scotland – and the sky so bright – and not a curl of smoke on the whole bright horizon on to Windsor – it sent peace and purity into my soul – and yet holds the sway of it – Goodnight –

Thursday night – I deserted my post tonight – and went to dine with the Chancellor. He is as gay as a schoolboy – and has a step daughter, who is really a school girl – and I have been gayer myself than I have been for a month nearly – and now I have been two hours signing official returns – and answering solemn letters – and turn to ask your blessing — O that picture![3] — I have not brought it with me – I had brought it down to my study, to be in the way – and in the hurry of packing up, it was forgotten – and there it languishes in a dark drawer – and I languish for it here – no matter – I shall get back to it I hope soon – I can remember you without it – I have seen no more of Mrs Montague [–] I have no time to see anybody – I do not get to bed till after 3 – of course I rise late – and have letters and papers to write all today – and back to the House again before 4 – It is like a busy campaign – and I have something of the spirit of a campaigner – God bless you – I am too old for campaigning – and languish often enough for tranquillity and slow beats of the pulse again.

Friday H[ouse] of C[ommons] 4 – I have got your letter – and it has hurt me – I would not have so miscontrued you — What is this half line, and this simple fact of your blue friend?[4] – so insignificant – and yet important enough to make you undo a weeks work of kindness – and to take a tone of distrust and distance – which I was never so far from deserving? Is it that, to my own hourly pain and mortification – I was unlucky enough to leave your picture behind? – and is it in this way you console me? – Well – I cannot quarrel with you – but you cannot prevent me from mourning – and then to write me all that trash about reforming women – and the weak men in Parl[iamen]t – and not a word of kindness! – Why should not you be above taking pets – and why should I be distrusted? I am very deeply hurt – and have several times thought of sending your letter after your journal – But that musk odour has redeemed it! It breathes of something still sweeter than these flowers which you despise – and soothes me, in spite of <the> harsher spirits which breathe there also – I write this fresh and fasting – but I suppose I shall relent after midnight – and at all events I shall not send this off till I have slept upon it – Bless you! anyway – I would give the world to have half an hour's fair scolding with you – face to face – but do not treat me so another time –

Saturday — a little better – but not right yet – nor shall I be, till I get some penitence and soothing from you — To show you that I have no malice, I send you, under 2 other covers, and this, a corrected report of my speech – which tho' not very correct after all – will give you a better idea of it than the news paper – It is published separately at the request of the ministers – along with [?an]other two only – But you do not care about it – nor about me, I fear much, now – But that is peevish and untrue and I retract it — God forgive you [–] It is cold and bleak today — but I must have a run out – I have no horse – and no bathing – and if it were not for famishing I suppose I should die outright – as it is, I am in reasonable force, of body at least – My Charlottes have gone to see sights in the city — after writing each a long letter to poor Kitty⁵ – whom you know we left – dying I fear, at Edinᵣ. They cry almost every day about her – and often wish to be home chiefly to be of comfort to her – I mention this just to show that living in towns and going to court – does not necessarily harden the heart – which I know is taken for granted at Craigenputtach – You have much to learn – and luckily much charity – which need not have been

O these separations of those who should have been together! What would life be, I wonder, if we could boldly put an end to them, and defy scandal and ridicule – and [** *MS torn*] live as we like – and actually might – and perhaps [** *MS torn*] ought? It would be a bold experiment – But do not you prattle any more about women being <u>slaves</u> and <u>idols</u> – and so forth — They are no such things – but very much what they should be – and certainly what they <u>must</u> be – and therefore I take it, were <u>designed</u> to be – But you mystics are sad fault finders – and think it modest and reasonable to be quite positive that you could make a much better world, and infinitely better people, than God and all generations of men have made before you – for my part I say God mend you – and me also! – and I must add – love me and bear with me and write to me Ever Yours

　　F Jeffrey

---

* Postmarked 12 March 1831.
** One or more words may have been lost to the tears in the MS here.
National Library of Scotland, Acc. 8964, nos 52, 51.

1.　Jeffrey's maiden speech on the principle of, and necessity for, electoral reform was published as *Corrected Report of the Speech of the Rt Hon. Lord Advocate, upon the Motion of Lord John Russell, in the House of Commons, on the first of March, 1831, for Reform of Parliament* (London, 1831). Taking all the first-hand evidence into account, one has to conclude with Henry Cockburn that 'as a debating speech, it fell below the expectations both of his friends and of himself' (*Life of Jeffrey*, vol. 1, p. 314), for a number of reasons. (Cockburn puts it down to anxiety about his voice but this is surely only part of it.) In his letters, notebooks and reminiscences, Carlyle made Jeffrey's failure in parliament a central theme of his account of Jeffrey during these years, no doubt encouraged by the woeful letters he was receiving from Jeffrey himself.

2.　Goethe's novel *Wilhelm Meisters Lehjahre* (1796), whose translation by Carlyle as *Wilhelm Meister's Apprenticeship* (1824) had been reviewed by Jeffrey in *ER*, 42 (August 1825), pp. 409–49.

3.　A great fuss appears to have been made over Jeffrey's forgetting to bring the picture of Jane to London with him (see, for example, his next letter to her, 26 March 1831). Even Anna Montagu got into the act, writing to Jane on 21 February 1831: 'I called yesterday upon the Lord Advocate who had obligingly paid us a visit the week before ... but, it required all his wit & smartness, and all his wifes simple kindheartedness to reconcile me to one fact, that of his *having left your picture behind him!* fancy my vexation ... it was *yourself* that I was cheated of ' (as quoted in *Carlyle Letters*, vol.5, pp. 245–6, n.).

4.   Jane had taken offence at Jeffrey's reference to Anna Montagu as 'blue' (i.e., a bluestocking) at the opening of his letter of 20–8 February 1831.

5.   A servant of the Jeffreys.

TO JANE WELSH CARLYLE

date 26 March 1831
from London

London 26 March
1831

Well, well, my wrangling little, earnest kind child – you need not rail any longer at Parliament and court people – for I am done, for the present[,] with both – my committee have unseated me[1] – and this is the last day of my franking – till I can get in again – and so, in spite of all your pertinacity and ill usage of me, I hasten this gratis sheet upon you, for which I daresay you will be less thankful than any other human being, upon whom it could have been bestowed – But such is the weakness of my heart — I hope there will be a dissolution – and then I shall deserve no more commiseration than the man who has drowned the day before the deluge – But it is not on that account that I hope for it – but on public grounds – and also for this other private one – that if it takes place I shall return immediately to Scotland – and perhaps continue to see you for a moment – which I shall certainly bestow in scolding you – not at all discouraged by the issue of our last bout – of which I recollect nothing more than that it ended – as I shall be well contented that all our quarrels should end – in our kissing and being friends, on the mediation of your worthy husband — You see my head is in a sort of a whirl today [–] I did not get home from the House till 4 this morning – and I have not had (nor have now) an instant of leisure since I got up —

You really are but a better kind of great baby after all – a smart intelligent child certainly – with sweet dispositions – and a good and a <u>great</u> heart – but a little spoiled – and not quite so deeply seen in the mysteries of human nature as you fancy yourself – but if you were a little less scornful and more indulgent I should care less about your false judgments – Why should you have so many more confident opinions than I have? and upon matters too that depend not a little on observation and experience of life in all its varieties? and above all, why have you contempt and intolerance for those whose tastes and opinions differ from yours? This you may depend upon it is a blemish and an error – and I hope you will come to think so by the time you get out of your teens. – for the present I lay my account with your wrangling very prettily in defence of it — after all tho' I thank you for your penitence – and I do forgive you with all my soul – and I will not scold you – if you do not wish it notwithstanding the termination to which I have allowed myself to look forward – But your picture is not in a <u>damp</u> drawer – nor did I ever say so – I said a <u>dark</u> drawer – how could you possibly fancy that I should place it for a moment in the damp? But young women are so extravagant and thoughtless — O would to heaven I could see you again! – but for an half hour! It is not true that I want faith – but I do long and languish for proofs tangible and visible – and of that you can never cure me —

Heaven bless you – Do write to me again here – our time is uncertain – but there is scarcely a chance of our going – except for 3 days into Hampshire [–] for ten days I think to come — I must leave you now – God bless you   Ever and ever Yours

F Jeffrey

National Library of Scotland, Acc. 8964, no. 53.

1. His election committee. Part of the electorate of the Forfarshire burghs that brought Jeffrey into parliament had been disfranchised, and when in March 1831 this was confirmed he lost his seat. After another outlay of great personal expense, he was returned on 7 April 1831 for the seat of Malton (itself a large English market town 21 miles northeast of York), in the gift of Lord Fitzwilliam. Within a fortnight, however, parliament was dissolved, which meant seeking election all over again. His third election campaign, started on Jeffrey's behalf by ill-advised friends, was for the coveted seat of Edinburgh, which he lost. Eventually, in early June 1831, he was returned for Malton, considerably out of pocket (see *Life of Jeffrey*, vol. 1, pp. 312–18).

TO JANE WELSH CARLYLE

date 5 and 6 April 1831
from Ferrybridge, York

Ferrybridge – this Monday evening, the 5th of April – aye Ferrybridge – half way to Scotland – and yet not on my way to Scotland. O my Dear Child – this pulls hard at the heart strings – This lonely room on the <u>home</u> road – brings that home so painfully before me, that I am tempted to leave Malton[1] and my electors on one side – and Parl[iamen]t and reform and ambition behind me, and to run on and on, without thinking – desperately down a steep plane – till I am landed at Craigenputtach! But it must not be, yet for a season — I am on my road to Malton – where I shall arrive early tomorrow – and hope to be elected on Wednesday or Thursday – and then post back to London – and fretting and fevering again! I grudge the toil and tumble of this not a little – but I am sordid enough to grudge the expense still more – I don't myself believe the Parl[iamen]t will last a month – and here I am obliged to travel 500 miles – to call, severally, on 600 people – to mount upon a tall horse, and harangue them from the saddle, in the open market place – rain or fair weather and, last and worst, to spend better than £500 in giving a miserable dinner to this preposterous constituency – I pressed hard to be left <u>out</u> till it was seen whether there was to be a dissolution or not – but I was told I must get me another seat <u>immed[iatel]y</u> – and this being got for me – I was compelled either to comply – or to draw back the hand I had put to the plough – and desert a cause in which I have an interest far above what can be measured by money or toil — But you do not care about all that – only, as I could not help writing to you, I was under the necessity, you see, of giving you to understand how I happen to be here – on what errand – and in what frame of mind and posture of Spirit – But that last remains to be told – I have had a long, lonely day – with more leisure to recollect myself than since I left home – and tho' something desolate, yet not undelightful – It was bright and calm – the hedges and young trees green, and large fields full of bleating lambs. I gazed and mused till the light dazzled my eyes – and I fell half asleep half a dozen times – and had odd half dreams, mingling with waking fancies in a bewildering sort of way that had a kind of fascination about it – and made me unwilling to be roused to too distinct a sense of realities – and it was in the course of this that I thought and fancied so much about you – that I cannot try to sleep till I have said a word of kindness to you — Why did you not write to me tho'? I told you there was a great chance of my moving – and that I wanted a few kind lines, without wrangling or dogmatism, to soothe and compose me – Did you take another pet at that letter? – There was no wrangling in it I think – but something perhaps too scornful of wranglers – O no – nothing the least like scorn in reality – only a little childishness – and fond wishing that you too could submit to be a little child. – of such – aye and the happiest in this world also – But it <is> no matter now – Do not be angry with me. — Life – <u>my</u> life at all events – is too short to be so thrown away – and [?on *omitted*] quarrels for uncandid vanity too – o miserable – God bless you – I have come 100 miles today – and I must go another 30 before breakfast tomorrow – I shall be in London again I think on Saturday – may I hope to have a letter from you then? not in answer to this, I fear – but soon after – and no reproaches or argufyings — I shall take this to York with me – since it cannot [?go *omitted*] tonight – and perhaps add a line before sending it off – Think often of me fair infant – and only as kindly as I do of you – good night –

York Tuesday morning — cold, cold, – but I must hurry on to Hatton – and here are my four horses at the door – They say I shall be elected tomorrow – but I could not let you wait for a frank –

> Ever my very Dear Child   Ever Yours
> F Jeffrey

National Library of Scotland, Acc. 8964, no. 54.
1.   See note 1 to the previous letter.

TO THOMAS (AND JANE WELSH) CARLYLE

date 4 May 1831
from Edinburgh

Edin^r 4th May 1831

My Dear Carlyle

Hard work this Electioneering! — You will have heard of my splendid defeat here yesterday – and of the glorious and disastrous victory of my opponents – and on Friday I must go back to my old Perth district – and try my fortune once more on that unlucky field – So that I am home without an hour's enjoyment of home – and home in vacation, without a moment of leisure —I feel[1] however that I ought to have found, or made leisure to answer your last letter – I honor your feelings – and do not dissent generally from your principles – But I am not satisfied that you have made out a case for their application. If a man have really <u>no chance</u> – or no tolerably probable chance of succeeding – so far at least as to be independent of future assistance, in the experiment he <now> requires aid to pursue, it may be wrong in him to ask that aid, and foolish or even pernicious to give it – But surely there are many cases in which the most valuable and impartial of all aid may be given to carry on such an experiment – Before deciding on your brother's case therefore I wished – and I wish still, to know a little more particularly the grounds on which he thinks it probable that, in one or two years more, he may be enabled to establish himself on a footing of independence – and this, with your leave, I would much rather learn from <u>his</u> information than from yours [–] I intended therefore, to have had an interview with him, and to have investigated the grounds of his scheme of life – with some rigour and cold bloodedness – tho' I trust not without indulgence – and to have decided accordingly – certainly not in scorn of your high minded remonstrances – but probably with some mitigation of their severity – and some larger trust in fortune and providence than you may think it allowable to indulge – Our sudden dissolution and the tumultuary movements which preceded and followed it – and which have cast me back here – have prevented this – So that, as I can for the moment do nothing farther in the business, I have only to entreat that you also would forbear to do anything in the mean time – and allow your brother and me to settle our little matters in a calm business like manner, when I return to London in the Spring – It may be very wrong for a person in his situation to insist on waiting on the brink of the pool till an angel should stir the waters – but is it therefore right that a man of education – because his prospects are not very good during his first year of waiting for employment or a profession, should therefore substantially renounce that profession, and set himself down to eat potatoes and read German at Craigenputtach, or elsewhere? I have no disposition to throw away money – (especially after having been forced to spend so much, so very unprofitably)

– without a fair prospect of doing good with it – but I scarcely know any use of it which is likely to do so much good, as that which enables an able and industrious man to surmount the obstacles that beset his early career – and to float him over the shoals and bars that obstruct his course into the fair way and flowing tide of this world — Trust me then my Dear proud friend in this matter – and do not fear that I will either wilfully or thoughtlessly do anything either to injure or degrade your brother – I will have the fear of your philosophy before my eyes – and have little apprehension of ultimately giving you pain by my decision —

And so you are writing a book[2] – and why will you not tell me what manner of book it is? and how much of it is written – and when anybody is to see it[?] – I would to God you were not so impracticable – and arrogant – No man who despises and contemns educated and intelligent men, at the rate you do – will ever have any success among them – unless indeed a witty Satirical [one *omitted*] – I wish I could persuade you that you are not an inspired being – and never will be the founder of a new religion – and then your eloquence ingenuity and fancy might be of far more use to you and to others — But that solitary life and bad stomach of yours have spoiled you to such a degree – all but the heart – that I despair of the success even of my rough course of unspoiling – Well, God mend us all – Good night – write me soon and think kindly of me.

Ever Affectly Yours,

F. Jeffrey

Well, little one – are you still pouting and petting – because I will not reason and wrangle with you? O folly folly! – Why else did you not write <u>to me</u>? — But I have got back to your picture – and there is not an atom of mildew or anything else on it – and it looks so gentle and pure and patient that I cannot find in my heart to say even a teasing word to it – nor to you either – for its sake – and so Bless you my very dear Child – and do anything you chuse with me – only let me feel that you love me – and write to me mildly and softly – and indulge my weakness so far as to let me fancy you are happy – and not the less happy because you are sure of my love — Bless you

Ever Yours F. J.

National Library of Scotland, Acc. 8964, no. 55.

1. Carlyle copied the bulk of this letter – from 'I feel, however, that I ought to have found' up to and including the phrase 'why will you not tell me' at the opening of the second paragraph – in a letter of 8 May 1831 to his brother John, whose prospects Jeffrey is discussing in anticipation of being able to assist him (*Carlyle Letters*, vol. 5, pp. 269–70). Carlyle told John on [18] April 1831 that he had written requesting Jeffrey's help (*Carlyle Letters*, vol. 5, p. 263), but seems to have been anxious that his brother had already applied to Jeffrey, not for advice or preferment but for a loan, which worried Carlyle, as in the past John's borrowing from Carlyle's friends had worried him (R. Ashton, *Thomas and Jane Carlyle: Portrait of a Marriage* (London: Pimlico, 2003), p. 96). Carlyle com-

municated his anxiety to Jeffrey. This letter represents Jeffrey's considered response both to Carlyle's request for help for his brother and to his anxiety about John's borrowing. Jeffrey did indeed subsequently discuss the matter with John: 'Having thus talked over the whole matter, & with much toleration & frankness expressed his opinion, he ended the conference by renewing his former offer – professing his entire readiness to give me any sum I might demand to put any of my plans in execution', John wrote to Carlyle on 7 July 1831 (*Carlyle Letters*, vol. 5, p. 295, n.). Jeffrey eventually was able to secure John 'an appointment to be Travelling Physician to a Lady of great rank, the Countess of Clare, with a salary of 300 guineas a year all travelling expenses included', as Carlyle wrote to his mother, 26 August 1831 (*Carlyle Letters*, vol. 5, p. 366).

2.   The book was *Sartor Resartus*, at this stage most often referred to by the Carlyles as *Teufelsdreck*, after the main character (Teufelsdröckh in the final version).

TO THOMAS CARLYLE

date 16 May 1831
from [Edinburgh]

Edin^r 16 May 1831

My Dear Friend — It cannot be a greater comfort to you to receive a letter from me than it is – in itself – for me to write one – But it is a pleasure now but imperfectly at my command – I am hurried enough, as you see – and besides I have been suffering under a very painful affection,[1] of a local nature, ever since I left London – Yet I must say something in answer to your last – a line at least, if not a letter in return – I feel the full value of your deference to my counsels about your brother – and hope to give you no cause to repent it – But you alarm me about yourself – Do not dream for mercy's sake, of the Cynic's tub – and that unseemly romance of encountering the primitive lot of man – with your habits of mind and body – and a young and delicate wife – whose great heart and willing martyrdom – could only make the sacrifice more agonising to you in the end – and it is not necessary – nor anything like necessary – let us draw you from your seclusion – and inspire you with more humane thoughts – You shall have aid – and effective aid – which you shall one day repay, if you will, tenfold – never fear – we shall find something for you to do – neither inglorious nor unprofitable – You are fit for many things – and worthy of many things – and there are more tasks and things worthy of you – than, in your Cynic moods, you are willing to believe – I made a proposition to you once before, which I told you, tho' rejected at the time – was to stand waiting your acceptance for the rest of our lives – and which you <u>shall</u> accept without more ado, if you ever speak to me of the Cynic scheme again [–] I think too that you are humanising apace – and gradually drawing nearer to those of your own blood and lineage – to whom you <should> belong – I have been reading your paper on Taylor

in the last Edinburgh[2] – and am more satisfied with the patient and (<u>compara-</u><u>tively</u>) indulgent <tone> of much of it, than with any of your former writings
– Empson[3] mentioned it to me in London, with great praise – and said that
Macaulay and several others (who laughed at your <u>Mechanical</u> age – and some
of your ravings ab[ou]t the ravings of your German novellists) were very much
struck with the force and originality of the writing [–] Give yourself but fair
play – and the world around you fair play – and you will make your way in it
very well – Learn to respect and esteem men who are your equals in intellect
and honesty, tho' they dissent entirely from your creed in taste and philosophy
– and temper your bigotry so far as to think it <u>possible</u> that people may differ
from you in all your fundamentals, without being in a <u>damnable</u> error – Imagine
it <u>possible</u> in short that you should be wholly or partly in the wrong – and that
it may be <u>your</u> fault and not theirs, that they laugh at some of your idolatries [–]
I tell you again that, in all my life, I never met a good and sensible man so scornful and intolerant as you are – and it is even amusing to see how it breaks out in
the middle of your professions of humility and charity. – Even in this last letter
– what a foolish vainglorious diatribe, about those who have no significance but
by juxtaposition! – and I know not what – Alas, alas, what is this little <u>signifi-</u><u>cance</u> upon which we value ourselves? Some trifling accident of excitability and
ambition – which makes a certain fever and stir – and leaves us neither happier
nor higher than our neighbours – for my part the more I see of philosophers
and men of genius the more I am inclined to hold that the ordinary run of sensible, kind people, who fill the world, are after all the best specimens of humanity
– and that the others are, like our cultivated flowers, but splendid monsters, and
cases of showy disease — How many <u>significant</u> people do you suppose there
are in the world? – or rather in our parish, or the circle of our acquaintance?
<u>unus atque alter,</u>[4] I fancy at the most, – and a social, humble minded being, who
should love his brother – (even tho' he does not give that endearing name to the
women) is to scorn all the rest – or to keep aloof from all equal intercourse with
them – and, looking with a most ridiculous supercilious pity, upon the worthy
reasonable people around him, who do not care about his vagaries, give himself
airs of condescension when he says he wishes them well, and would be glad to
assist or befriend them – but truly, as for companionship of mind or fellowship
of pursuit, they are no more mates for him, than the beasts of the field! — O fie
on this filthy pride, and foolish straining after ideal unsocial elevation – Pluck
it from your heart my friend – and cast it from you, – and you will be happier,
and more amiable – and not a little wiser – But I did not mean to lecture you
– and I will not. Let me know a little practically what scheme of life you have in
view – and rely on my counsel and aid – There is scarcely anything I have more at
heart than your comfort and happiness – and I think you know this — For that
fair child, I have a love which is overpowering – and not the less for that <u>she is</u> a

child – in some things – tho' I allow her the heart of a heroine – and the courage, I doubt not, of a martyr – Heaven guard her from the fate of one! – Why does she not write to me? – my heart is athirst for kind words and words cost so little! – no matter – I have faith. – There is a gleam of Summer today – and the long summer twilight spread away so softly to the North – with that dewy Venus dancing above it – that a little stream of love and softness shot into my heart as I gazed at it, thro' all the earthly influences of business and bodily pain — But now good night! – God bless you little one – Would to God I too could be taken for a child! – and your childish womanhood is offended at it—O folly!

Ever Affectly Yours,

F. Jeffrey

National Library of Scotland, Acc. 8964, no. 56.
1. Still standard usage at the time, meaning a bodily reaction.
2. Carlyle's review of William Taylor's *Historic Survey of German Poetry*, *ER*, 53 (March 1831), pp. 151–80.
3. William Empson (1791–1852), reviewer and professor of 'polity and the laws of England' at the East India College, Haileybury, who would become Jeffrey's son-in-law in 1838 and, in 1847, editor of the *Edinburgh Review* after Macvey Napier.
4. Latin: one and besides another.

TO JANE WELSH CARLYLE

date 27 May 1831
from Edinburgh

Edinr 27 May 1831

Bless you then Beloved – for your kind words – and your kind <u>heart</u> [–] But do not tempt me – I will not say from my duty – but from my <u>fate</u> – do not make me murmur at what I cannot change – I might have kept out of this tossing bark – but here I am, fairly abroad, at the mercy of the winds and currents – and you must not beckon me to the safe and pleasant shore! — I have no time now for anything but Elections, and election riots[1] – and am blamed if I ride out but for an hour to air myself – or venture to dine at Craigcrook on a Saturday — O you need not tell me what a poor thing ambition is – nor how much better <u>love</u> is than noisy acclamations – which pass for fame – No hermit ever was truer to that creed than I have ever been, in the bustle of the world – no active champion in the <u>meleé</u> less forgetful of the virtue and wisdom and happiness that can only be found aloof from it – I think I am not spoiled, for affection and calm enjoyment, by the tasks and toils that have too much engrossed me – and I am sure I have not lost any relish for them – God help me – when I breathe the odour of my dewy sweet briars in the evening at Craigcrook – and hear the loud chuckle of the blackbirds among them – and listen to the faint shrill distant warble of the high larks over my head as I ride reluctantly back from it in the morning – I look on <u>my actual life</u> with a start at its strangeness – and almost as if it were the picture of some unhappy victim of enchantment – I do not know what I would not give up, to have one – two [–] three or four hours of calm lonely unbroken talk with you – in some remote place, where not merely the intrusion of busy or foolish people was excluded – but the very idea of it – and all sense of their existence – I should not ask even for <u>talk</u> I think – and am not sure that I should not rather prefer sitting silently gazing on you – and letting my heart repose, as in its proper home and resting place – Why then do I not come? – You see <u>partly</u> why I do not – and why I say I <u>cannot</u> – Yet you see but a part – and the least part, of this why – I <u>could</u> come certainly – without physical injury – or infamy – utter ruin[?ation] to my worldly interests or enjoyments. – I might encounter – and perhaps should do well and wisely to encounter, the wonderings, and ridicules – and impatient enquiries which such a starting off – of such a person at such a moment, would produce – I might even disguise or evade some of those – and be a great gainer on the whole — But I have stronger impediments in my own family – My Charlottes would not come with me – They are so delighted with being at home again – and really so engrossed with poor Kitty, that I could not propose it – and knowing my engagements here – and prizing very kindly the comparatively great share they now have of my society – and not quite understanding the state of my heart, I see that, if I were to propose running away for 3 or 4 days, at this time, without them – I should excite painful feelings – which I do not think I ought to excite – – and which I know <u>you</u> would not approve of my exciting [–] This then <u>is</u> a consideration of duty – and I know you will not tempt me to desert it – I will come tho' – in*

---

* The MS breaks off at this point.
National Library of Scotland, Acc. 8964, no. 57.

1.   See note 2 to the letter of 16 January 1831 and note 1 to the letter of 26 March 1831, above.

TO THOMAS (AND JANE WELSH) CARLYLE

date 5 June 1831
from Edinburgh

Edinʳ 5 June 1831

My Dear Carlyle
      You cannot overrate my will and anxiety to serve you – But I must not mislead you as to my <u>power</u> — when I said we should find work fit for you, I fear

I only expressed my strong but vague and general conviction that, with a little patience and accommodation, some fitting occupation might be found, or made for you – I still hold that trust and conviction – and exhort and encourage you also to hold it – But I have nothing tangible or immediate to propose – nor do I know, much more than you do, where to look or apply for practical assistance – Certainly the fittest work for you – would be that which required the talents you possess – and gave scope to your ardour and enthusiasm – but that I fear you must make for yourself – at least I do not see where it is to be found – for other humbler toils – that sweat of the brow – or of the brain, whereby it is man's lot – (not his curse I think) – to earn his bread – I cannot but think that some might be found – not unworthy of you – and not too irksome – and yet You are a ticklish animal to harness I fancy – and apt I should suspect, not merely to kick at and break away from your yoke fellows – but even to take an irreverent fling now and then at your driver — On the whole however you should know your own trim best – at least for a very general settlement of departments – What would you like best? ([dislike *omitted*] least, rather, I fancy I should say) – some sort of mercantile, book keeping arithmetical drudgery under buyers and sellers? – or official clerkships in some public office – about stamps – excise – post office or so forth? – or independence on the law, as keeper of records – writer in chancery engrossments? – or anything about education in colleges or seminaries? – or as librarian or museum keeper – arranger of manuscripts and curiosities and so forth? – or calculator for insurance companies or boards of longitude? I do not mean any of these literally – but which of the kinds of thing – (to borrow from the vulgar tongue) – would you least eschew and abhor? Before making any application, or considering in what quarter it could be made with likelihood of success, it is really necessary to have some sort of notion, however large and loose, of your inclinations in this way – For you must feel yourself, that an application for some pleasant and profitable employment – for a man of education and good moral character – of a studious disposition – with much knowledge, and rather too much admiration of German philosophy – with a certain tendency to scorn the existing race of men, and all existing institutions and establishments – would not be very likely to indicate one fitted for any particular place – or to suggest any particular employment as well fitted for him —

I daresay you do right in going to London – certainly in leaving Craigenputtach – before winter – and in going to London to look about you – I shall see you there too – and we can talk all things over – that is always a comfort anyhow – and petite cousine does not come with you[?][1] – perhaps it is better – but she will be lonely at C[raigenputtoch]. – If we had been at Craigcrook she might have rested in that ark – while you were out looking for olive branches — I fear you must write next to London – for we move I take it on Thursday – address to J. W. Barber's 123 Pall Mall – as I do not yet know where we will find a biding for our heads — I half fear for your book[2] – especially the radical part of it – tho' that is more likely to attract notice than the religious part – what I <u>most</u> fear is the <u>vilipending</u> of existing things and people – which I hold to be your radical error – Do not you think as much sense and genius might be shown <– and in a more amiable way –> in pointing out the mass of good feeling and deep sense which lies under the apparent frivolousness and selfishness of our <u>exterior</u> – busy trifling life – and in explaining how that exterior is <u>necessary</u> – and by what <u>necessary</u> and inward fermentation the vital leaven of wisdom and virtue is leavening the whole lump – <u>all</u> the <u>elements</u> and aspects of which are equally necessary and useful? Is there no chance of <u>this</u> being the <u>true</u> as well as the kind and pleasing view of our condition? – and that the despair and contempt with which you look on it, is but a narrow, peevish and shallow view, as well as an arrogant and offensive one? — Well, well[,] we shall settle all that when we meet – in the mean time do not think you do well to be scornful –

Thank you – fair one for your flowers – I have them in my purse, with the old musk smelling note – But you must write me – a letter all your own – and all to myself – as the children say

> God bless you both
> Ever Affectly Yours
> F Jeffrey

National Library of Scotland, Acc. 8964, no. 58.

1. The 'little cousin' was, of course, Jane, who remained at Craigenputtoch when Carlyle went to London to find a publisher for *Sartor Resartus* in August 1831.

2. *Sartor Resartus.*

TO THOMAS CARLYLE

date 4 July 1831
from London

London 4 July 1831

My Dear Carlyle – I have no tidings for you – tho' I have pressed my inquiries in all the quarters I could think of. – However I have set several likely enough people to be on the lookout – and if anything occurs I shall not be forgetful of you —

I have seen your brother[1] – and find him on the whole very reasonable, and practical – I mean to speak to some of my medical friends for him – and have hope that we may be able either to get him a situation – or opening in some provincial town – or, what he could like better, an engagement to go abroad with some rich family as a medical friend and attendant — This is a situation which leads to a great deal of good practice among the English abroad – and is perhaps the very best ultimate introduction to good practice at home – His foreign travel and knowledge of the tongues,[2] will be a great recommendation to him in this way — But we must not be too impatient –

It is rather hot here – tho' we have not had a great deal of hot work in Parl[iamen]t yet – But we begin tonight – and shall probably have a hard week of it – But I think we shall divide on Friday Ev^g – I hope so. My health I think is better than when I was here last – But the approaching campaign will try it — How often shall I envy you the cooling breezes, and long evening's leisure of Craigenputtach [–] I can scarcely think of green fields – and the quiet listening to late thrushes – and the midnight odour of moist honeysuckles that used to soothe me at Craigcrook – without crying – I do not think I am quite made for this stirring world – tho' few people have stirred more in it – or <u>appeared</u> more satisfied with the stirring part that has fallen to them —

Well, what about your book? [–] and when are you coming up with it? and with what hopes? I trust your health is better – I cannot quite reconcile myself to your being buried in the smoke and stir of this huge anthill – and that fair thoughtful creature! It does not seem a sphere for her either – But Heaven knows – and all I hope will be for the best [–] I must say a separate word to that dear Cousin

Ever Affectly Yours,
F. Jeffrey

National Library of Scotland, Acc. 8964, no. 59.
1. John Carlyle (see note 1 to the letter of 4 May 1831, above).
2. John knew German and had worked in Germany and travelled through Austria and France.

TO JANE WELSH CARLYLE

date 4 July 1831
from London

London Monday 4 July
My Very Dear Child – I am rather mortified that you do not write to me – I thank you for your flowers – but I cannot read the Persian flower language – and could make no more out of them, than poor Ophelia's "thoughts and remembrance suited"[1] — However they were very dear to me – They were brought to me in The House of Lords, where I was attending some appeal cases – and I could not help kissing them – and placing them on my breast – before the very

<u>being</u> of the Lord High Chancellor himself – who does not understand much of these matters —

It is lovely weather – even here most lovely – and the parks and gardens – have an enchanted look on a fine Sunday – with all those endless groupes of gay dressed, calm, happy looking people, gliding on the noiseless turf, under the broad spreading trees and by the gleaming waters – Yet the heart of the exile feels lonely – and a bout of sadness and pity predominates – and then the tasks that are before us – and the clamour and heat and stir of these fierce contentions are what we are this very night to enter – O what would I give, instead, to think that I should see this Sun set over your lovely moors – and stand by your side in that wild ravine which leads down from your lofty world – and see your mild eyes turned to the dewy stars – and hear the soft notes of your voice mix with that gurgling torrent — Ah me – I must not think these things! – altho' <u>they are</u> – and are the only thing I really love to think of – only not now – but surely some time – and I hope soon – a hope worth living for – In the mean time I have that precious picture – I lent it for a week to Mrs Montague – and I believe they have been copying it – You do not grudge that? She says she had fancied you would look nearly so – I do not believe it – nobody ever anticipated that peculiar countenance – Those very lovely, but <u>too thoughtful</u> eyes – and that half <u>obstinate</u> half capricious lip – which does not agree very well either with them or with itself – I have studied the enigma carefully – and think I half understand it — We have seen but little of those Montagues – They have influenza in their house and rather foiled the access of friends. I should like them very well I fancy, if I had time – But I have no time – even to write to you – and you cannot <u>wish</u> that I should write – or you would write sometimes in return – surely there is nothing in what I last*

---

* The MS breaks off at this point.
National Library of Scotland, Acc. 8964, no. 60.
1.   Said of Ophelia, that is, by Laertes: 'a document in madness, thoughts and remembrance fitted', *Hamlet*, IV.v.179.

TO JANE WELSH CARLYLE

date [?July 1831]
from [London]

Nay do not be ill, my very Dear Child – anything, almost, but that – I think you are sad too – and I am sad and anxious about you – and look on your picture, till I fancy it looks reproachfully on me in return – and yet there is no cause for reproaches – It cannot be half so great a pleasure for you to hear from me, as it is to me to write – But alas I have no time for pleasures! – Thank you for your mild words – and your little fragrant rose leaves – which, withered as they were, perfumed all your letter – and breathed their sweetness in to my heart – I never doubt or distrust you – and you do not fancy it – They are but idle words of pet and longing – trying, not very successfully, to mask themselves in playfulness – "the half forced smile, while struggling for the full drawn sigh"[1] [–] Well – then we understand each other again – and you do not take me for a worldly underling in the vulgar cause of ambition – or a heartless partaker of the heartless dissipation around me — O never, in any period of my existence, was I less in danger of falling into those snares – never so deeply in love, with love and nature. – It is strange with what eager fondness I cling to the glimpses I can catch of the loveliness and grandeur of the universe, in the middle of this universe of man's vanities and crimes — Do you remember that pathetic and deep-meaning line in an old Scottish song? – "And werena my heart light, I would die!"[2] – I cannot tell you how often that feeling comes to me – during my present life of exile and bondage – If it were not for my love of nature, I think I should die too – It is an especial mercy of providence I think that our House of bondage[3] is placed among objects of grandeur and beauty, with the majesty of the old Abbey on one hand – and the smooth expanse of the river on the other – with the groves and towers of Lambeth beyond[4] – If we had met near the Bank or the Royal exchange[5] I do not think I could have survived it – As it is, I rush out, and walk on the bridge – or place myself at a window in our calm library, and look out on the white moon light, and the shadows of the massive trees pencilled so sharp and dark on the turf below – and then muse – as you would wish me to muse – and then start, and back to that hot, glaring, tumultuous room again – where I pass for a gay sarcastic, patient acute sort of person – and so I am —

It is still beautiful weather – something showery – and cool for July – but balmy and bland – I am to have a walk I hope – But we must not make sure of anything in this world – Last Saturday I had refused all engagements – and proposed to myself the imminent refreshment of* a long day spent down in Surrey and the carriage was actually at the door to take us away – when a mandate was delivered to me to assist at a conference at the Home office at half past 4. and I was detained till near 7. and had to write official instructions till midnight —— Yet it is a great drama that is acting – and even we, who have little to do but to look wise, like the Senators in Venice preserved[6] or at least to prompt a little from behind the scenes – derive a sort of importance from its greatness – But what is the good of importance?

Be well – What are you to do when C. leaves you? You must not stay alone in that solitude – If you were quite well, I should rather like you to try it a little – But if you are not well let me beg of you not to think of it – Will you go to your mother – or to any other dear friend? – I shall be least jealous of your mother

– But at all counts let me know – that I may write to you – Here are people
– God help me – Farewell Dearest
        Ever Yours
        F. Jeffrey

---

* At some stage in its transmission, this letter became sundered at this point and the two
sections now appear in separate accessions in the National Library of Scotland (compare the
letter of 4 and 5 March 1833, below).
National Library of Scotland, Acc. 8964, no. 61; MS 787, f. 92.
1.   George Crabbe, 'Sir Eustace Grey' (1807), ll. 9–10.
2.   Not so old, though certainly Scottish: 'And werena my heart's licht, I wad dee!' is the
      refrain from the much adapted and anthologized lover's complaint of the same title writ-
      ten by Lady Grisel Baillie (1665–1746).
3.   I.e., the House of Commons.
4.   Westminster Abbey, the Thames and Lambeth Palace, all visible from the Commons.
5.   In the City or commercial district of London.
6.   An allusion to the impotent Venetian senators in Thomas Otway's tragedy *Venice
      Preserv'd, or A Plot Discovered* (1682).

TO THOMAS CARLYLE

date 24 July [1831]
place London

London – (37 Jermyn
Street) Sunday, 24 July
    My Dear Carlyle – And you are really coming to this resort and mart of all
the Earth – with your manuscript in your pocket, like Parson Adams[1] – that
fair woman pining in unsettled health behind you — ~~and~~ dim visions of good
and glory before, and mingling impulses of scorn, pity and hope for mankind
around you — Well – come – we at least, in this little dwelling, shall be most
happy to see you – and be of such comfort as we can to you – There is an air,
it seems to me, of more than usual sadness in your last letter – and in <u>her</u> little
postscript also – Is this fancy in me? or accident? – or is it indeed so? I hope her
health is not more seriously affected than you mention [–] But I have fears, and
anxiety about both of you, which I cannot easily get rid of — Write at all events
without delay – and let me know – I do not see why you should linger if you are
ready – But there will be people and business <enough> in London, long after
the middle of August – Heaven knows <u>when</u> we shall get thro' these Bills – or
<u>how</u> they are to be got thro' – I do not believe they will be out of the Commons
before the middle, or even the end of September – and the crisis[2] – which makes
the bravest hold their breath, even to think of (I mean of those who can think)
will be after that. The prospect any way is frightful, of the probable proceeding of

the Lords – I believe they have a majority of 50, firmly and fiercely hostile to the measure – &, up to this hour, resolute in their mad purpose of defeating it. They may yet take council of their fears – but I do not confidently expect this. The least perilous case they can take for the country – and fortunately, I still think the most probable – is to throw the Bills out at once, and totally. We shall then know <u>our</u> course and have a better chance of keeping the country quiet till we can follow it. The greatest embarrassment will be if they cripple and deface the measure by amendments – and send it back in such a state as we cannot accept, it and as the country will not bear – This will not so visibly justify extreme remedies – or so certainly reconcile those who must be reconciled to the use of them — But enough of this – It is a sweet Sabbath morning – and even here the Heavens look mildly on us – we must trust and wait — I am for a long walk, out among the green fields – and there I shall think neither of London or Commons – but of Craigcrook and Craigenputtach – and of peace, love and mysteries

God bless you – I see you clearly standing thoughtful at your door, gazing on the motionless trees above you – or pacing down among the moorland muttons – listening to the larks and curlews – God bless you

F Jeffrey

National Library of Scotland, Acc. 8964, no. 62.

1. The MS was *Sartor Resartus* (see note 2 to the letter of 4 May 1831) and the allusion ('Parson Adams') to the main character in Henry Fielding's novel *Joseph Andrews*, who went to London to try to interest the booksellers in his unsaleable sermons.
2. The blocking of the Whig government's Reform Bill in the House of Lords (with some members of the government, like Henry Brougham, threatening to force the creation of enough Whig peers to 'stack' the upper house and secure a decision in the Bill's favour).

TO THOMAS CARLYLE

date 3 September [1831]
from London

Saturday Evg 3ᵈ Sept

My Dear Carlyle – I have at last seen Murray[1] – quite sober – and I think very well disposed towards you – The short is, that he will take the risk of printing a small Edition of your Book – 750 copies – and decide the profits with you[2] – leaving the property and copyright entirely to you – He says – and I believe truly – that no books sell at present – of any sort or description – and that people read nothing but newspapers – that this printing therefore is a great risk – and that he undertakes it, partly to oblige me – but chiefly out of a strong belief he has in your genius and originality – I gave the best account of you and your work that my conscience would let me – and this is all I could make of it – I fear you will not be able to make more of it – But Murray says he is anxious that you should try whether you can make a better bargain elsewhere[3] —

If you are really anxious to have it out, I fancy you will be obliged to close with this offer – I do not know what to advise you – I fear the work is too much of the nature of a rhapsody to command success – or respectful attention – and I cannot but expect you to look it over scrupulously, either before printing or in the proofs – – and especially to take the trouble to recast and abridge the first 10 or 12 pages [–] You have no idea how large a proportion even of judicious readers may turn back from the vestibule, if they meet with anything there to repulse or distaste.

Remember I shall always be happy to see you – when I am visible – – In my last cover from Mrs C. she says she has written to you that she wishes to join you here – and to remain – This will require some consideration – I wish to heaven I could make such considerations less matters of anxiety – God bless you

      Ever Yours

      F. Jeffrey

National Library of Scotland, MS 787, ff. 62–3.

1.   Carlyle had arrived in London with the MS of *Sartor Resartus* on 10 August 1831 and had immediately consulted Jeffrey, who thought 'Murray (in spite of the radicalism) would be the better publisher; to him accordingly he gave me a line saying that I was a genius and would likely become eminent; farther that he (Jeffrey) would like well to confer with him about that Book' (*Carlyle Letters*, vol. 5, p. 318). Writing to Carlyle from Craigenputtoch, Jane quoted from a letter of Jeffrey's (now lost) written some time between 11 and 15 August 1831: 'Jeffrey writes me that you "look very smart and dandyish – have got your hair cut and a new suit – and are applying various cosmetics to your complexion" – Moreover – that he "will *do what he can for the book* but fears its extravagance and what will be called its affectation"' (*Carlyle Letters*, vol. 5, pp. 345–6). Nothing happened for a couple of weeks because Jeffrey's direct intervention was required and as Lord Advocate he was extremely busy. Carlyle understandably became impatient: 'Inquiring for Teuflk [i.e., *Sartor*]', Carlyle wrote to Jane on 29 August 1831, 'the Critic professed that he had "honestly read" 28 pages of it (surprising feat!) that he objected to the dilatoriness of the introductory part (as *we* both did also), and very much admired the scene of the sleeping City: farther that he would write to Murray that very day' (*Carlyle Letters*, vol. 5, p. 376). Jeffrey did finally manage to get a letter off to Murray 'that very day' (28 August) – 'Will you favour me with a few minutes conversation any morning this week (the early part of it, if possible) on the subject of my friend Carlyle's projected publication. I have looked a little into the M.S. and can tell you something' (quoted in *Carlyle Letters*, vol. 5, p. 376, n.) – and to arrange a meeting with the publisher. Murray agreed to publish and this letter sets out his terms (compare *Carlyle Letters*, vol. 5, p. 399).

2.   Murray would offer Carlyle nothing up front, in other words, but would split with him any profits the book might make.

3.   'I mean to set off tomorrow-morning to Colburn and Bentley ... and ascertain whether they will pay me *anything* for a first edition: unless they say about £100, I will prefer Murray', Carlyle to Jane, 4 September 1831 (*Carlyle Letters*, vol. 5, p. 399). In the end

Carlyle did neither. The Colburns were not interested, negotiations with Murray broke down (see Carlyle's letters to Murray of 19 and 24 September, *Carlyle Letters*, vol. 5, pp. 441–2, 446–7), and Carlyle's plans for publishing *Sartor* in the autumn of 1831 came to nothing. It was not published until over two years later, serially, in *Fraser's Magazine* between November 1833 and August 1834. For a full account of the composition of *Sartor Resartus* and of the trials of its publication, see Rodger L. Tarr's introduction to Carlyle, *Sartor Resartus: The Life and Opinions of Herr Teufelsdröckh in Three Books*, ed. M. Engel and R. L. Tarr, The Norman and Charlotte Strouse Edition of the Writings of Thomas Carlyle, 2 (Berkeley, CA: University of California Press, 2000).

TO JANE WELSH CARLYLE

date 11 October 1831
from London

37. Jermyn Strt
Tuesday Evg 11th

My Dear Child — How ill must I be when I had rather not see you?[1] Most of my forenoons are spent in <u>agonies</u> which it would grieve you to witness – and which your presence would rather aggravate than relieve – If I have an hours lulling of the pain before dark I must spend it in dictating <u>necessary</u> letters and in the Evening, I am stupified with <u>laudanum</u> – and so worn out that I am not fit for conversation – So we must wait a little – I shall send to you as soon as I can talk to you – My heart feels the kindness of your offer to come to me – and the truth – <u>Violent</u> pain annihilates everything but itself – but in its remissions it is sweet to think of those we love – May you never be incapable of thinking of them! – There is no evil whatever, to be compared to long continued violent pain – You and C. think this a sad heresy – and God grant you may never be forced to adopt it — I have had a dreadful day — But by dint of opium, my state is now bearable [–] It is a miserable existence – But either the pain or I must soon wear out now – Heaven Bless and protect you

Ever Affectly Yours
F Jeffrey

National Library of Scotland, Acc. 8964, no. 64.

1. Jane had arrived in London on 29 September and they had caught up with each other only briefly on the evening of 6 October before Jeffrey's illness – an anal fistula, which would require laudanum, bleeding and surgery – worsened.

TO JANE WELSH CARLYLE

date 31 October 1831
from London

37 Jermyn Strt
Monday 31 Oct[r]

My Dear Child – I tried, again unsuccessfully to see you yesterday – But as it turned out, it was as well that I did not succeed – for I was taken very ill very soon after leaving your door, and obliged to hurry home – where it was soon thought proper to subject me to a repetition of the operation to which I submitted a fortnight ago – and I have not, as you may imagine, been very comfortable since — Yet upon the whole I think I am better – and certainly suffer less intense pain – If I am in a condition to move I think we shall go to Wimbledon[1] on Wednesday – where I shall have more complete quiet – and a purer air [–] But I must see <you> – before I go, even to that short distance – will you come to tea tomorrow Ev[enin]g? I will send the carriage for you before 8. and it will take you back when you like? – O how little I have seen of you – How do you like London? I am afraid you live too much with crazy – or half crazy people – But perhaps you prefer that – God bless you – neither of us is in a perfectly natural position – but you least of all – let us hope we may be <u>shaken right</u> before the great jumble is over.

Farewell – I cant conveniently sit up to write longer – Do not answer – unless you cannot come – or will not – or what else

Ever Affectly Yours
F Jeffrey

National Library of Scotland, Acc. 8964, no. 63.
1.   Then a semi-rural village on the outskirts of London.

TO JANE WELSH CARLYLE

date 17 November 1831
from Wimbledon

Wimbledon Common
Thursday Evg 17 Nov[r]

My Dear Friend — Have we indeed been two months within reach of each other – and met only two or three times? How, and why has this been? You will say it has not been your fault – But let us not talk of faults – I told you not to come when I was in agonies – and you never came at all – and I was 3 times at your door – and never found it open[1] – and you live and are occupied with people I cannot care about – and I feel, or fancy, that you are cold and scornful to me, and the things to which I am devoted – and this brings ice about my heart – and you do not care that it should be melted! —

Oh the folly of these repulsions – in such a world as this! But I will think no more of them – and am coming to see you – I have been much better (tho' you have never asked and why should I tell you?) since I came here – I am now almost entirely free from pain – and, if I could sleep at night, and rise in the morning, like other Christians, I think I should be almost well — I walk about a good deal, and drive thro' this beautiful country – I have been twice in town – but for a few hours <only>, and on appointments with ministers – which kept me till dark – But I am coming, if I am well enough – on <u>Saturday</u> and hope then to see you – will you send a note for me to Mr Barber's 123 Pall Mall – to say whether you will be home about 2 o'clock – I hope you will come out and see us here next week – You will find something I think to remind you of Craigenput-tach – and I hope by that time the snow which now covers us will be gone – We have no fogs however on these clear uplands – tho' I hear they are darkening all London [–] Well – good night – and Heaven bless you – I hope I shall see you on Saturday – if not do send me a line out here – to tell me what you are doing and proposing to do – With kindest love to Carlyle – for whom alas, I have no tidings, from Chancellors or booksellers[2] — Ever Affectly Yours

F. Jeffrey

National Library of Scotland, Acc. 8964, no. 65.

1. Jane had been ill 'these ten days', wrote Carlyle on 24 November 1831 (*Carlyle Letters*, vol. 6, p. 56).
2. No tidings for Carlyle about either jobs or publishing.

TO JANE WELSH CARLYLE

date 21 November 1831
from Wimbledon

Wimbledon. Monday Evg
21 Nov[r]

I hope you are better, My Dear Child – I cannot tell you how my heart sank, when I found myself at last inside your of door – but yet kept from your presence by your illness – and that you were breathing, quick and feverously, within yards of me! –

I wrote you a foolish pettish, unreasonable note the other day – I suppose I am not quite recovered, when I write in that way. – Will you – <u>haud ignore mali</u>[1] – allow me this unhappy privilege of infirmity? I daresay I do not deserve it – But we shall settle this, with our other scores, when I can have one half hour's quiet talk with you – When shall this be? Will you come out and stay a day or two with us, on Wednesday or Thursday? I shall come in, either of those days that will suit you best – If you write soon after getting this, I believe I shall receive your answer tomorrow Ev[enin]g – But at all events, I shall call again about 2 on Thursday – and hope then – if not sooner [–] to see you[2] —

It has been a sweet vernal day here – and full of all soft influences and remembrances – I walked for over two hours on the common – in a perfume of whin blossoms – and fresh exhalations of the granully[3] earth – with such a gorgeous frame work of autumnal woods, embossed and swelling all round me, as put reform bills and prorogations quite out of my head – and sent me listening after wild larks and robins and distant bleatings of black faced sheep –

God bless and keep you – It is a sweet, dewy balmy night – with a low wind bearing the low clouds softly over the moon – and singing in the high trees that skirt our corner of the common [–] There is nothing of winter – or sadness in its aspect – and I feel as if I should go happily to sleep under it – Good night, my Dear Child — I half expected a line from you by todays post – But perhaps it is better not – I shall hear tomorrow – or Wedy morning – Ever Most Affectly Yours

    F. Jeffrey

Does not Carlyle know yet that you is a plural pronoun? Or dual at all events? –

National Library of Scotland, Acc. 8964, no. 66.
1. Latin: not to blink at evil.
2. By late November or early December Jeffrey and the Carlyles had resumed regular intercourse, with Jane writing in an undated letter to Carlyle's mother that 'The little Dear is well again, and as gay as a lark; and trudges over to us twice a week, without women or equipage. Always losing himself by the way, and needing Carlyle to take him home' (*Carlyle Letters*, vol. 6, p. 44).
3. I.e. granular.

TO JANE WELSH CARLYLE

date [29 November 1831]
from Wimbledon

Wimbledon. Tuesday Evg

I could not come to town today – But I hope to see you tomorrow – My time is not much at my own disposal – and the shortness of the day, and my distance here, limits my use of it still further – after this week we shall be in Clarges Street

– and I hope that may do some good – ~~But if you speak again to me, as you did when I last saw you I will~~ – no matter – I hope to see you tomorrow – Ever Most Affectly

     Yours

     F. Jeffrey

National Library of Scotland, Acc. 8964, no. 67.

1832

TO JANE WELSH CARLYLE

date 11 January 1832
from London

13 Clarges Street
Wedy Evg 11 Jan^y

My Dear Child — Why did you not write to me at Malshanger?[1] – But above all, how are you? We only got back here after dark – and I have such a mass of letters to answer – and official appointments to keep that I fear I cannot come to you tomorrow – Send me a note therefore, by the early delivery, saying that you are well — I found the enclosed in a blank cover on my arrival

With kindest remembrances to Carlyle
Ever very Dear Infant
Affectly Yours
F Jeffrey

National Library of Scotland, Acc. 8964, no. 68.

1. An ancient seat 5 miles west of Basingstoke in Hampshire and home of Jeffrey's friend Jane Grant (sister of Elizabeth Grant), married to a Colonel Pennington. See Elizabeth Grant of Rothiemurchus, *Memoirs of a Highland Lady*, 2 vols, ed. A. Tod (Edinburgh: Canongate, 1992), vol. 2, p. 192.

TO JANE WELSH CARLYLE

date 6 February 1832
from Warwickshire

Weston House Warwickshire[1]
6 Feb[y] 1832

My Dear Child – How are you? I am haunted by the vision of your pale, slight form – and am impatient with myself for not urging you to write to me here with some account of yourself – But it is now too late for that – However if you wrote on Sunday or Monday addressed at <u>Malshanger</u> near <u>Basingstoke</u> I shall receive it on Tuesday – and on Wed[y] Ev[g] I expect to be in London again [–] We got to Oxford in good time on Monday – and came among its antique domes and towers just as the gas lights were beginning to prevail over the last gleams of a winter twilight – You know I think this the most picturesque city in the universe – and it is this with which I have the greatest number of youthful and romantic associations[2] – I sallied out, after tea to indulge in these, and in a long lamplight ramble met the ghosts of more departed feelings and fancies than I expected ever to encounter again in this world – I was very nearly suffering in the flesh however for this unearthly communion for I had an alarm about my <u>trachea</u> in the night – and was very near hurrying back to my bed and Doctors in London – But the sun broke out gloriously in the morning – and I met [*for* made] a daylight survey of my old haunts and came on here in reasonabl[y] good ease in the afternoon – and have since been tolerably so and so — This is a vast new house – in the palace style [–] a great deal too big for the family – (or their friends) – and a great deal too fine for their really simple and <u>comfortable</u> habits – However we have plenty of fire, hot air[,] books – leisure and good humor and have come on very much to the general satisfaction – tho' we shall all be glad to get round our own fireside again

God bless you – my very Dear, heroic – too thoughtful – and too fastidious infant –

I hope Carlyle is busy – and not too busy – and that he begins to think that it is not utterly base to care about ones own happiness and that of those one loves – I am very impatient to see his new hypermystical lucubrations [–] I praised him very much to Rogers the poet[3] last Sunday – who gave me a fair opportunity by praising his life of Schiller[4] – and wondering what manner of man the writer would be – I must not add a word more   Ever Most Affectly Yours
     F Jeffrey

National Library of Scotland, Acc. 8964, no. 69.
1.   Near Long Compton, and the home of the Sheldon family.

2. Jeffrey went to Queen's College, Oxford, after he graduated from Glasgow in 1791, for slightly less than a year. What he does not confide in Jane, interestingly enough, is how miserable he was at the time.
3. Samuel Rogers (1763–1855), famous for his *The Pleasures of Memory* (1792), was also a banker, patron and art connoisseur, and was well known in society, especially though not exclusively in Whig society.
4. Though originally published in instalments in the *London Magazine* (1823–4), Carlyle's *Life of Schiller* was his first book (not counting his translation of Goethe's *Wilhelm Meister's Apprenticeship*) when it appeared complete in February 1825.

TO JANE WELSH CARLYLE

date 9 February 1832
from London

13, Clarges Street
Thursday 9ᵗʰ Feby

My Dear Child – I am uneasy about you – and have felt quite provoked not to have been able to come to ask for you either yesterday or today – and I have an unlucky committee to attend tomorrow at 2, which makes me despair for it also – I cannot but be very anxious about your health – and what I must call your foolish distrust of medical advice – But I confess some of the sentiments you expressed when I last saw you, have left a more painful impression on my mind even than your illness – Pray let me hear that you are better and more cheerful – and more contented to pass thro' life without working out any heroic task – and as most amiable and happy women have done before you – I shall begin to hate this mysticism in good earnest, if besides filling your head with unintelligible notions it weighs down your heart with a fantastic feeling of unworthiness

God bless and keep you
Ever Yours
F Jeffrey

National Library of Scotland, Acc. 8964, no. 70.

TO JANE WELSH CARLYLE

date 4 March 1832
from London

13, Clarges Street
Sunday Night – 4 March

My Dear Friend – Do you know that I too have been quite unwell? more unwell, for the time, by a good deal, (I hope) – than you have been – I felt a little pinch at my <u>trachea</u> when I last saw you – and next day I was quite ill – my voice went almost entirely – and a good deal of my breath – and I have been on a regime – and in a sort of durance, ever since. I thought I was getting well on Thursday, and went out – But I had a severe attack in the night – and have since been obliged to be very cautious – tho' I think the formidable symptoms are now gone and the disorder reduced to the character of a vulgar cold —

I tell you all this, to explain why I have not seen you – all this long week – and why I <u>must</u> ask you to write me a line to say how you have been – I wished much to have had you by me for the last two days – when I was well enough to listen – and not allowed to speak – so that you would have had all the talk to yourself — I made Mrs J[effrey]. and C[harlotte]. go out yesterday to a great dinner – and leave me to solitude, chicken broth[,] barley water, and weak tea – with such soothing thoughts and recollections as I could persuade to keep me company – By the help of a little reading – and some light sleep – just solid enough to float a few visions – I got thro' the Evening tolerably well – But I was much indebted to your Idea – and very grateful to you for letting it come — You think it as good as yourself – but I do not go that length. I am anxious to learn how your love affair with Mrs Austin comes on. Empson is very jealous of you in that quarter – so am not I – no not even of her – but feel thankful and gratified at every discovery you make of beings whom you think worthy of your regard – and feel fitted to you affections – my complaint and my regret for you, has always been that you find too few – and made it a matter of duty and dignity to be distant and difficult – and, if not scornful at least unsocial — But Sunday is almost done – and I will not preach any more to you [–] Let me know how you are – mind and body

God bless and sustain you
Ever Affectly Yours
F Jeffrey

National Library of Scotland, Acc. 8964, no. 71.

TO JANE WELSH CARLYLE

date 15 April 1832
from London

13, Clarges Street
15 April 1832

In Heaven's name, why do you not write to me, my Dear Child? You promised to let me hear from you as soon as you reached any of your homes in Scotland – and now, I am, at the end of I do not know how many weeks[,] without one word of remembrance, or any intimation where you have set up your rest – or where my enquiry may reach you. – I am anxious about you – but I am also mortified and hurt, at your silence – for I cannot but believe that you might have let me hear of you, if you had wished it – I had a kind of foreboding, you may remember, that your coming to London was not to be for good – and you lost your health, and much of your cheerfulness there – and I feel as if I had lost much of your confidence and affection! – I do not feel however that I have deserved this loss – any more than you deserved the other – but I cannot help lamenting it, as a misfortune –

I have not been very well of late – I suffered for several days from spasms – which put me in mind of <u>Cholera</u>[1] – if not in fear of it – But I am now better – and, as we are to have a fortnight's holidays this week, I mean to run out of town, probably down to the sea coast – where I hope to enjoy the long lost luxury of a few leisurely and lonely days – in which my pulse may learn to beat calmly – and my soul prune its wings in tranquillity –

Tell me where you are – and <u>how</u> you are – and what you are doing, and designing – I am afraid you have gone to meet the Northern Spring rather before it can keep the assignation – and cannot help hoping that you have not taken post on the heights of Craigenputtach, during those bitter breathings of the East – There is a great flush of verdure all round us here – and a bright budding, at last on the woods and shrubberies – I wish you had staid to see the red blossoms of the almond trees in this neighbourhood – which are far more delicate and brilliant, probably because they come earlier – than our lilacs of July. But I forgot that you despise people who care about blooms and vernal odours – as you do too many other innocent people –

I have not seen your friend Mrs Austin since you went away – I hope you mean to correspond with her – I think I shall go to see her tomorrow for the chance of her having heard from you – for, tho' it will mystify me a little, it will relieve my anxiety – Oh how foolish those pets and jealousies are – in this short, troubled life! – but how much more foolish, those confident opinions – and insolent assumptions of superiority which make still wider breaks in the great family of mankind! –

Our public affairs are not in a very clear or secure state[2] – But, even if they go well, they will not go fast – and I fear we have little chance of getting thro' out task before July or August – a disaster may liberate us sooner –

Give my love to Carlyle – I think he liked London better than you did – and yet he profited little, I fear, by the <u>practical</u> lessons it might have read to him and probably still holds that the great sufferings of society are owing to the want of poetical abstractions in the great body of the nation – and to a depraved taste for preserves of pheasants and partridges among the rural proprietors – which is about as near being true, as the visions of the astronomer in Rasselas.[3] O cæci hominum mentes[4] – It always provokes me to see him throwing away great talents – In about five years after my death, he will come to think more as I do –

God bless you – Write to me – frankly at all events kindly if you can with truth – O surely not unkindly – Ever Affectly Yours

    F. Jeffrey

National Library of Scotland, Acc. 8964, nos 72 and 73.

1.   The previous year, 1831, had seen a cholera epidemic spread across Britain from London and the south-east, claiming victims mostly among the lower classes.

2.   A reference to the protracted battle of the Whigs to get their Reform Bill through the House of Lords. See note 1 to the letter of 18 December 1830 and note 2 to the letter of 24 July 1831, above.

3.   Samuel Johnson's *The History of Rasselas, Prince of Abyssinia* (1759), a didactic philosophical fable on the vanity of human aspiration and ambition. The deeply learned astronomer whom the philosopher Imlac meets is discovered to have an insane belief that he is responsible for changes in the elements and the episode leads Imlac/Johnson to a discourse on 'the dangerous prevalence of imagination'.

4.   Latin: O blinded is the mind of man.

TO JANE WELSH CARLYLE

date [?7 and 8 June 1832]*
from [London]

**never enjoyed so intensely the soft langour of spring – Poor Sir Jas Mackintosh is dead[1] – Sir W. Scott is coming home,[2] I fear no better – I see Empson very often – and Macaulay, who is to have Mackintosh's place[3] – tho' all places are too precarious at present to be worth accepting [–] The English Bill is passed – and the Scotch will pass[4] – I am waiting here for its going into committee – But the King is sore and sulky – and I think will have us all out before the end of July – and try the desperate experiment of balancing a democratical House of C[ommons]. by a Tory cabinet – For myself I care nothing – and shall be glad to be released – for my friends not much – But I cannot but be anxious for the country — But you are like Martha[5] and care for none of these things – Well I have been reading the memoirs of Sir Ed^d Seaward – Do try whether your Dumfries Libraries can furnish you with it and read it too – There is a sweet Quakerish grace and tenderness about <u>her</u> character,[6] which is winning and ~~anglel~~ angelic beyond anything modern — It is said to be edited by Miss Porter – But tho it certainly is not old – I cannot think Jane Porter capable of anything so good[7] — I have been reading other books too – but I will not tell you anything about them [–] You despise my taste so much – and I have not forgiven the scorn with which you received my recommendation of some parts of Miss Mitfords Village[8] which I still maintain, notwithstanding, to be exquisitely beautiful – and far superior to anything that your raving Germans have ever inflicted on the world.

How is Carlisle? I hope his health is good now –

H[ouse]. of C[ommons]. Friday 8th — I have not had a gasping time[9] since I was called away at the bottom of last page – and can only say God bless you, tonight – Is Carlisle very busy? – and with what? I thought he was humanising towards his fellow creatures faster than you were while he was here – and I hope he has abated something of his insane preacher[-]like antipathy to the good natured and generally kind hearted who spend some 40 or 50 days in the year shooting at partridges – His tone about them is such as might have been natural to a man maimed and beggared and orphaned by the savage execution of the old forest laws — sad doings in France![10] – the people of that country will never cease I think from trembling — Lovely weather still — I long and pant after a few green days of solitude and leisure – and have strange poetical visions when I walk home in the light and breezy dawn, from this house of hard labour – How is your mother? give my love and thanks to her – I think I can see this setting sun streaming down that steep and wild pass which leads up to your desart from the old square house below – and hear the brawling of the torrent – and the sharp note of the grand lark and bleating of your wild flocks — and then the yellow light on the tops of your old mossy trees and white chimneys! – Well – God bless you – send me a rose leaf for old love   Ever, <u>ever</u> very

    Affectly Yours

    F. Jeffrey

---

* '?July, 1832 HWM' in pencil (NLS), but 8 July did not fall on a Friday. 'We had a fiddling sort of Letter from the Advocate', Carlyle wrote to his mother on 12 June (*Carlyle Letters*, vol. 6, p. 169).

** The opening of the letter has been lost.

National Library of Scotland, MS 787, ff. 89–90.

1. Sir James Mackintosh died on 30 May 1832.

2. After a stroke in 1830, Scott had sailed to Malta and Italy for his health. He died three and a half months after this letter was written (21 September 1832).

3. Macaulay took over Mackintosh's position as a Commissioner on the Board of Control, then investigating the affairs of the East India Company.

4. The English Reform Bill and its Scottish counterpart, after much haggling and compromise, finally went through in June 1832 (see note 2 to the letter of 24 July 1831, above).
5. Luke 10:38–42.
6. Lady Seaward's, that is.
7. This fictional 'edition' of *Sir Edward Seaward's Narrative of His Shipwreck and Consequent Discovery of Certain Islands in the Caribbean Sea, with a Detail of Many Extraordinary and Highly Interesting Events in His Own Life ... as Written in His Own Diary*, nominally 'edited' by the poet and novelist Jane Porter in 1831, has also been attributed to her brother, William Ogilvy Porter.
8. See note 9 to the letter of 4 January 1829, above.
9. Meaning perhaps 'I have not caught my breath' (if I read it correctly).
10. The violent suppression of republican uprisings in Paris and Lyons by the reactionary ministry of Marshal Soult.

TO JANE WELSH CARLYLE

date 22 July 1832
from London

13, Clarges Street
22ᵈ July 1832

My Dear, Dear Friend – Why do I not write to you, like a friend? why is there this "numbing spell" upon our spirits? I feel as if it were no fault of mine – and yet I do not feel that I can fairly tax <u>you</u> with having placed this icy barrier between us — I received your sweet, innocent, and touching verses, with an inward thrill of sympathy and delight – and kissed your rose leaves with a devotion, <with> which a more exacting person than you, could have been satisfied – and I have mourned ever since over the account both you and Carlyle give of your still impaired health – and a day has not passed in which my heart has not been with you in your desart – or in which visions of that loveliness have not come, with the witchery and the agony of a <u>possession</u>, over my watchings of the night – But still, there is a repulsion and a distrust – I live indeed in another element and another sphere – and it is a strange and tantalising – and almost a fearful thing, to catch these glimpses of your strange and enchanted solitude athwart this driving vapour of faction and folly and contention, by which all with which I am in contact are enveloped, and partly borne along – But I feel as if you despised me, and withdrew from me, for this – and I feel that such alienation is unjust and undeserved – and that I could not so have withdrawn myself from you – if I had not something in me above & beyond this, I should not have had this feeling – and a sense of injustice and resentment mixes with a deep feeling of desertion and pain — I do not know that there is any use in saying this – perhaps I ought not to have said it – but the feeling is there, – and it is said – and I have done —

My life upon the whole has been, since you left us, very much as it was before – The return of Summer and the sweetness and beauty which it sheds over the lovely country in this neighbourhood – have given it something of a softer and gentler character – I do not recollect when I have been more awake to these vernal delights, or more disposed to melt down or wash away worldly cares and contentions, in that deep and overpowering sympathy with nature to which I have always clung as the grand medicine of a Soul hurt by too rough a contact with the world – and the sure witness of its undivorced communion with something better and higher. I have spent many <u>green days</u>, and half days, among the fresh shades and deep verdure of this old inhabited – but quiet and lovely region – and among the soft lawns of Roehampton, and the airy uplands of Richmond[1] – with its trooping deer and its antique oaks and still older witch thorns and rock and lovely underwood, I have lain and sat for hours, as completely abstracted from the cares and vanities of London as you could be at Craigenputtach —

Tell me tho' of that lone and melancholy upland – and tell me of your health and spirits – I like to think of your gallopings – but not of your musings at home – I will not – <u>indeed I will not</u>, tease you anymore with my maxims – nor wrangle with you about yours – But you must allow me to regret that you are not more cheerful and more social – that you are not more satisfied with what you do – and are obliged to seek pardon and indulgence for not performing more adequately a task which has never been laid upon you but in fancy — O my Dear friend be happy; and believe that all opinions <u>must</u> be false which tend to depress an innocent spirit, and to impose upon a conscience void of offence a conviction that it is chargeable with blameful want of exertion –

But I trespass in this sort no more – I shall wish a brighter change in the spirit of your dream – and would <u>pray</u> for it – if prayer was a part of my ritual –

I called the other day on Mrs. Austin. Is not she imaginative and mystical enough for you? Yet she wears her mind open to the enjoyments and even to the <u>vanities</u> of the world you despise – She asked me to frank a cover for you – and I believe it is partly a deep stinging feeling of resentment, that my handwriting on the outside,[2] should only bring you kind words from a stranger which has impelled me to write to you tonight

Good night then – and God bless you — Write again soon – very soon if you expect to catch me here – In ten days or less I hope to get away – will you not come to me at Craigcrook – and be what you were to me when I last saw you there?

Kind love to Carlyle – I rejoice in his brothers punctuality – It justifies what your friend does not think justifiable – adieu

Ever Yours

F. Jeffrey

National Library of Scotland, Acc. 8964, no. 74.

1. The first is in south-west London, the second outside London on the River Thames in Surrey.
2. See note 1 to the letter of 16 January 1831, above.

TO THOMAS CARLYLE

date 22 September 1832
from Loch Long, Argyllshire

Glenfinnert[1] – Loch Long
22d Septr 1832

My Dear Carlyle – Your <u>money</u> letter only found me out, in my deep retreat at Loch Lomond the night before last – where it seemed particularly absurd to be settling accounts, and endorsing banker's papers! – But it is common honesty to give you a receipt, which I hereby do, of all debts and engagements whatsoever – and so, since you would have it so, that matter is settled![2] –

I am sick of Electioneering and not quite well in health – But I never forget you – nor that dear fair Lady! – tho' she once cared more for me than she has done lately – No matter – a little love is still better than none – and the dregs of that cup are sweeter than the sparkles of any other –

I wish I could come to Craigenputtach! – and it is a delight to think that you are coming to Edinburgh – I trust we shall not be assembled till after New Years day – and I hope not till the end of Jan[y] – Much may happen before that time –

God bless you – What are you busy with now? I cannot but wish you more philanthropy – and more respect towards those from whom you differ – But you fulfill your destiny – like the rest of us –

I have recovered my nationality (which was something impaired) in the Highlands – and have learned to love and to be proud of my country again – in the midst of these bright waters – and wild woods – and rocky mountains – all <u>filagreed</u> over with silvery torrents, interlacing their green bosses, and ringing, in the evening and noonday calms, with the swells and falls of an Eolian harp – Why is that fair creature so delicate – and so little social? I am, and have been, more uneasy than I shall tell, about her health, and it is not comfortable to hear that, when the year is again turning, she is again unwell – Bring her soon to Edinburgh – It must be winter at Craigenputtach before the end of Octob[r] — I shall write again very soon, to one of you – Today I have not heart to say more –

Ever Affectly Yours
F. Jeffrey

National Library of Scotland, Acc. 8964, no. 75.

1. Glen Finart, 8 miles north-west of Helensburgh in Argyllshire between Loch Ech and Loch Long.
2. '[T]he repayment of his debt', wrote Jane to Carlyle's mother around 25 September 1832, 'is a great load off our mind' (*Carlyle Letters*, vol. 6, p. 233). Jeffrey had loaned Carlyle the £60, here discharged, on 22 May 1830 (see Jeffrey's letter for that date, above). As the Carlyles' financial situation had begun to improve over the early months of 1832 Carlyle had longed (to quote a letter to his brother John of 31 August 1832) 'to clear scores with

the Advocate, and sign myself *Nemini debens* [indebted to no one]' (*Carlyle Letters*, vol. 6, p. 216).

TO JANE WELSH CARLYLE[1]

date 18 and 19 November 1832
from Edinburgh

Edinburgh 18 Nov[r] 1832

My Dear – Dear Friend – I must write to you again! – I hear you are coming here – and I feel, by the beating at my heart which that intelligence <has> occasioned, that we must not meet as strangers – I am not going to tell you now why I have not written – I shall tell you when we meet – only it is nothing for which you <u>can</u> hate – or for which (I think) you ought to blame me — I have been gazing on your picture for near half an hour – and I am not in a mood to wrangle – How this little foolish life of our's does run away –! Ay, little and foolish <u>always</u> to the liver – even if it should, now and then[,] be of some moment to his generation – Are you old enough yet to be quite familiar with that deep and soothing feeling of utter nothingness, to which all reflection, sooner or later, brings all reflecting minds? a feeling not merely of the insignificance of our poor personality – and all our paltry business, and triumphs and mortifications, and fine assumptions of superiority – but of the swift approach of that inevitable <u>close</u>, which every hour brings so much nearer – a few more struggles and fond aspirations – a few more throbs of the heart and strivings of the brain – a few more dreamy days and sleepless nights – and the dream of life is ended – and the deep sleep from which it was exhaled receives it again into its bosom! Very trite philosophy you will say! – yet not, if it be deeply <u>felt</u> – and familiar. The truth of course I <u>knew</u> always – but the <u>feeling</u> has possessed me but lately – and, unless sickness and solitude have brought it <u>prematurely</u> to you, I cannot easily believe that you feel it, as I do.

But no matter – tell me of your health! – I cannot bear to think of your pining and wasting away, in your prime of youth – and so sadly too – and unjoyously – & you shall never persuade me that you have treated either your mind or your body rightly, till I see more health and animation in both – But say that you are better – I have been tolerably well – and, but for politics, more than usually idle – my long absence has pretty much put an end to my business – and I enjoy the leisure infinitely – If I could with honor throw off the <u>other half</u> of my shackles, I should be far happier [–] But they will fall off by and bye – My Charlottes are very well – Mrs J. has been very uneasy about her father – who has had a sort of paralytic attack – and tho' he is much recovered the distance makes her con-

stantly anxious – How soon are you to come? Geo. Moir says about the end of
this month – That is now at hand – I hope you will stay, at least
till we go – which will not be I hope till,*
I hear often from Empson – who sometimes
and makes good reports of Mrs Austin –
after you went away – but I do not [?   ]
much to anybody – Tell me about [?Carlyle's]
his hand now and then in the Reviews –
it were traceable by other marks
occasioned me a little pang – especially
was done on <u>your</u> instigation – but I
foolish – and I do him justice, and honor him

It has been a lovely, deep calm, autumn day – and I walked out for two hours
towards the shadow of Pentlands – and saw the sun set, grand and tranquil on
the Ochils[2] – If it were not for these escapes from this life of courts and office
hunting, the fever of it would kill me – and you are killed by having no worldly
tasks, or connections – God help us! – it will all come right enough – and now I
take one peep of your picture – and to bed —

Monday 19th

Where are you to be when you come here?[3] I remember you were very amiable when you were in George Square – Ay, and when you left Craigcrook to go
there – and I thought you very happy there also – Why have you changed? Is it
indeed necessary that we should all change? But I shall see [you *omitted*] wher-
ever you may be – and that will be something — How is your mother? I never
think of her without a glow of gratitude for her sending me that picture

wished me to send back! – Well at least I do none
– nor deserve (much) I think to be then
– you will be here at my Election – and
for a day – will you not? I hope al-[?ways]
shall be elected, and that you will wish for my success
you — Write me a line

Yours Ever
F Jeffrey

---

* The top right-hand corner of the second sheet of this letter has been badly torn, resulting in
large gaps here and in the concluding section.
National Library of Scotland, Acc. 8964, no. 76.

1.   Carlyle's reference to a 'silly scrawl' from Jeffrey in a letter to his brother of 2–3 Decem-
      ber 1832 may possibly refer to this damaged letter, especially as Jeffrey was writing less
      frequently, though what we can reconstruct seems comparatively inoffensive (*Carlyle
      Letters*, vol. 6, p. 273).

2.   The Pentland Hills is a range of hills extending from a point 3 miles south-west of the centre of Edinburgh for 16 miles through the counties of Midlothian, Peebles and Lanark; the Ochil Hills is a range of hills in south-east Perthshire extending 25 miles south-west from near Perth, on the Tay, to near Bridge of Allan in Stirlingshire.

3.   'If you see Jeffrey pray tell him when I am coming – for I shall not have leisure to answer his inquiries – that is I am not in a writing vein and *fancy* I have not leisure', Jane wrote to Eliza Stodart from Templand on [20 December 1832] (*Carlyle Letters*, vol. 6, p. 282). When the Carlyles did arrive in Edinburgh, Jeffrey remained unaware that they were there, and but a 'stone-cast' away (*Carlyle Letters*, vol. 6, p. 292).

TO JANE WELSH CARLYLE

date 21 December 1832
from Edinburgh

Edinburgh 21 Dec^r
1832

Why do you not write to me? Your silence gives me pain and uneasiness – especially as I can learn nothing of you from any other quarter – In the midst of all my occupations, I watch every day for the coming in of the Carlisle mail – and feel a sinking of the heart, when I find there are no letters from you

I have been elected,[1] you will see – and returned – and now, on my coming back from my <u>chairing</u>, to my daily disappointment, I sit down to murmur these low words in your ear – and to ask, earnestly and anxiously, why you have hidden your face from me? I will not – I <u>do not</u> suspect you of any paltry pet, or idle resentment – I <u>know</u> you have nothing to resent – and you should know that too – and therefore I fear that you are ill – Why else do you not answer my call to you? I should have been ill indeed, before I had been so long neglectful of your's –

I have no time to write – But I can no longer bear this long expectation – Send me but one line, to say how you are – and when you are coming — I have been pretty well – tho' not very robust yet – It will be a comfort to know that you are even so well – and so God bless you – I am not sure whether I am entitled yet to frank, or not – but I shall make the attempt – tho' I shall make my letter but single – remember me most kindly to Carlyle – he might have written I think – if you were unable – Ever Affectly Yours
      F Jeffrey

National Library of Scotland, Acc. 8964, no. 77.

1.   Jeffrey's election (with his friend James Abercromby) on 17 December 1832 to the seat of Edinburgh in the newly reformed parliament crowned a lifetime of reforming activities in Scottish politics and in the pages of the *Edinburgh Review*.

TO JANE WELSH CARLYLE

date 28 December 1832
from Edinburgh

Edin^r 28 Dec^r
1832

Mrs Austin has sent me the enclosed to be forwarded to you – I am half tempted to send it merely <u>with my Comp[limen]ts –</u> and if I had anything in me of the <u>pettish</u> nature of your sex, I certainly should – But my heart will not let me – I am very deeply hurt by your neglect – or alienation*
whatever it is – and I do not see any se[?nse]
or dignity in pretending that I do not ca[?re]
But if I have no power to influence
your sentiments, I certainly have n[?o power]
to control your expression of them
as if I were, at all events entitled
at parting. God bless you –
Still Af[?fectly Yours
        F Jeffrey]

---

* From here on, between one and three words – though in one or two cases, possibly none at all – have been lost from the end of each line to a tear down the right-hand side of the sheet. National Library of Scotland, Acc. 8964, no. 78.

1833

TO JANE WELSH CARLYLE

date 5 January 1833
from Edinburgh

Edin^r 5th Jany 1833

My Dear Child – I thank you for your letter – tho' I have mourned over it more than I shall tell you – I cannot bear to think of your ill health – For your mental langour or depression I feel confident there are cures – and I hail as the best possible symptom, your encreased willingness to be happy, and to listen to friendly counsel on that subject – I fear my gentle friend, that I have no <u>specific</u> to offer – but there are certain <u>tonics</u> which I can recommend safely. – and certain vices of <u>diet</u> which I can still more safely condemn – and with a little gentle exercise, instead of constant fatigue – and a fine exposure to the genial airs of heaven, instead of the pent up vapours of the study, I shall look confidently to your active and speedy restoration – Why should you be changed from the times you mention? But I trust now you will change back to them – and scratch your eyes <u>in</u> again, on your second leap into this great furze bush of a world —

I write now only to beg that you would let me know where and when I can see you? I cannot promise you much help in the <u>dancing</u> part of your scheme – But I shall be glad to join you at Battledore[1] and if your roofs are not high enough for that work, I hope you will come to mine – I half expect Empson down next week – He asks after you often – and I have never been able to tell him anything! – and So God bless you my Dear Infant

Affectly Your's
F Jeffrey

National Library of Scotland, Acc. 8964, no. 79.

1. A game in which players using bats or racquets keep a shuttlecock (a cork or rubber core surrounded by a cone of feathers, from which the game gets its alternative title) from falling to the ground.

TO THOMAS CARLYLE

date 14 February 1833*
from London

35 Charles St Berkely Sqre
14 Feby 1833

My Dear Carlyle – Thank you for your kind letter – I kept Mrs Austin's letter till yesterday, that I might deliver it in person – But the <u>Barbata Belissima</u>[1] had gone forth – and I did not see her — I Her destiny, I now hear, is likely to be changed from Berlin to Paris where there is a negotiation to place her husband as Professor of Political economy, in place of <u>Saye</u>,[2] who is dead – There is also still a talk of making some arrangement by which he may still be kept here[3] —

I am very sorry that my fair friend is still so unwell – But she is visibly so much better than when we parted here, that I am not nearly so uneasy about her – I do hope she gets somebody (of as sound principles) to play at Battledore with her — I have had a very sharp attack of illness myself, The very night I arrived, I was seized with a fit of <u>trachea</u> which forced me to call <u>a cupper</u>[4] out of bed, and be bled at one o'clock in the morning – and I am only now recovering – (tho' I <u>am</u> recovering) from the effects of it —

These wild Irishes work us much evil – tho' the admirable success of our first move on the Irish Church[5] will enable us I hope either permanently to mollify or at least to set them at defiance – The measure in my opinion might have been more extensive – But as it recognises no perilous principle, and leaves everything open for future improvement – it is perhaps wiser to make such a beginning – we have entered the end of the wedge – and may drive it home, at our leisure – We have got a more airy and spacious house than we had in Clarges Street – and I hope you will come to see us in it – I left home this last time, more sadly and reluctantly than last year – partly perhaps because I had settled more down to my old habits and occupations, and partly because I feel more sensibly how fast Life is ebbing away with me – and how little I can reckon upon any long period of enjoyment, after another return – Oh this strange dream of life – and this starting at the sleep – or the waking rather – in which it is to end

I have seen Empson several times – he enquires very kindly after you – I am called away now – and can only add God bless you

Ever Yours
F Jeffrey

---

* David Alec Wilson, quoting from the last paragraphs, misdates this letter 14 August 1833. National Library of Scotland, Acc. 8964, no. 80.
1.   Italian: beautiful beard (Mrs Austin had facial hair).

2. Jean-Baptiste Say (1767–1832), French entrepreneur and political economist who with Pierre-Louis Ginguené and François-Stanislas Andrieux had founded the influential newspaper *La Décade Philosophique* in 1794. Say was a member of the circle known as the Idéologues, which shared many ideas and values with Jeffrey's *Edinburgh Review* set.

3. University College London, where John Austin was Professor of Jurisprudence (see note 2 to the letter of 9 and 11 January 1831, above). Austin was unable to work, often afflicted with psychosomatic illness, and Sarah Austin provided for the family with her literary work.

4. An apothecary, who would apply a suction cup to bring the blood to the surface before applying leeches to bleed the patient.

5. Catholic Emancipation had taken place in 1829, allowing Roman Catholics access to some institutions of power (such as parliament), but the Church of Ireland remained a Protestant church funded by taxes levied on the predominantly Roman Catholic population of Ireland. The controversial 'Irish Church' policy to which Jeffrey alludes involved attempts to redress this iniquity and reform the Church of Ireland by suppressing certain bishoprics and using some of the church funds for secular purposes.

TO JANE WELSH CARLYLE

date 4 and 5 March 1833
from London

H. of C. Monday Night
4 March 1833

My Dear Child – Your life is so unlike mine, that the very contrast would bring you often to my thoughts – if there were no kinder remembrancer – Here we are, late in the 4th night of a painful and acrimonious debate,[1] in which everybody is sick of listening and drunk with the desire of talking – and in which, for the last two days, there has been nothing new, and nothing true, or reasonable, or candid – and have I not done well therefore to slip away into this quiet library – and look out on the calm river – and the dim moon – and to think of your still parlour, and your books and your work – and the high aspirations and mystical colloquies that are born there – and should not be allowed <there> to perish? — The scene would be still more soothing, if I could see you moving in it with an air of finer health – and a more cheerful and sociable spirit – and I hope you will tell me soon that, if my second sight were truer, I should so see you — I will hope that it is so – and had indeed so far persuaded myself, till the other day when I saw Mrs Austen – who told me that in your last letter to her you had reported but poorly of your health and spirits – When I last saw you, I think you had resolved on making conquests – and charming all those who had prejudices ag[ains]t you, with love and admiration – a most worthy and admirable design – in which I generously encouraged you and cordially wished you success – and I hope still to hear of your feats in that way —

I have not been able to see much of the bright and bearded beauty I have just mentioned – tho' Empson and I have walked up several times to her distant bower – But I am more and more pleased with what I have seen – she is so full of elasticity and hope and confidence, and so indulgent as well as generous that it is a delight to look on her, and I know nobody to whom I could send you to school, with so much assurance of your profiting by it — Carlyle's stoical sublimities, and my more frivolous and humble dissertations on good and happiness, have not answered quite well with you – and your best chance perhaps would be with a female preceptress, who would enliven her lessons with a dash of female gayety, and blend, less suspiciously than we* could do, an occasional apology for a few female vanities, for which you are all the better —

I began a letter to Carlyle more than a fortnight ago,[2] and, being interrupted in the middle of it, carried it in my pocket for two days, till despairing of ever finding time to finish it, I sent it off, in the shape of an interesting fragment – in which light I hope he made it welcome, – tho' he has not condescended to send me over the fragment of a reply – I hope you will be more generous. I have not yet seen Mrs Montagu. We called there last week – but found that Mrs Proctor had just been confined – and the whole female part of the household were busy in attendance —— I think I told you that I had seen Harriet Martineau and was not captivated – My chief objection to her – (besides her extreme ugliness) was, that she admired no lady, and talked slightingly of people far superior to her – and to whom she had been greatly aligned – Yet I have since heard that she is a simple and kind hearted creature – and in hopes of finding that it is so, I mean to go to her again[3] –

Tuesday 5th – I was called into the House from this comfortable gossip last night – and did not get away till near 2 o'clock – and at breakfast I had the great pleasure of a very welcome letter from Carlyle – Welcome both for its kindness and cheerfulness – and for giving so good an account of your health, and dissipation – I thank you with my whole heart, for being better, and something more gay – It seems to me so unnatural that you should be otherwise than well and happy that I cannot but ascribe it to mismanagement – and feel something like anger accordingly – very absurd and unreasonable – I admit – tho' not altogether so unnatural or unkind as you may fancy – and you begin to like John much better than me – and to think his life much the most rational! Very well, likings cannot be control[le]d – and opinions will be as they must – However I defy you – both of you, or all three, and that just because I believe in fate – and that none of us have no choice – as to a rational life I must, just at present – decline any competition – for scarcely anything can be more irrational than mine – I mean if you look on its exterior only, my only consolation is that scarcely any of it is voluntary – and that I have my good dispositions for very rational pursuits[4] – It is very hard that we can so seldom do what we like – and so seldom like what we must do – The reverse of that, I suppose is the definition of Elysium – to which it is to be hoped we are all hastening – tho' by something of a rough road –

I wish I could tell you anything to amuse you – But you do not care to hear that I have been at a drawingroom and the State Dinner – and that I think ladies in full dress very pretty things – or that poor Lord Dudley is at last dying[5] – and Lady Lyndhurst (it is to be hoped out of sympathy) very sick[6] or that I have made a friendly acquaintance with <u>Croker</u>[7] – or that Lady Stafford is in my judgment the most beautiful creature in the world[8] – or even that the spring has already breathed its sweet breath on us, in this Southern land – that the grass is as green as green can be – and all the young trees and early shrubs studded with buds of green and yellow – and the almond flowers peeping out – and bunches of violets everywhere – all this will come to you too, by and bye – But what will all this signify if you go moping and pining – with cold feet, and heavy eyes and faint smiles of endurance at the idle mirth of good people about you? – O, but you have changed all this – and are a maker of conquests and a trier of new favourites – I trust it is so — But I can say no more to you today – I am going to threaten Carlyle in the cover – and my post will be overweight if I allow anymore paper to you – God bless and guard and cheer you My Very Dear Infant

    Ever AffectlyYours

    F. Jeffrey

---

* At some stage in its transmission, this letter became sundered at this point and the two sections now appear in separate accessions in the National Library of Scotland.

National Library of Scotland, Acc. 8964, no. 81, and MS 787, ff. 93–5 (compare the earlier letter, conjecturally dated [?July 1831]).

1. On the Irish Disturbances Suppression Bill; it would continue to preoccupy both houses for some time.

2. This must be the previous letter, dated 15 February, which ends abruptly enough to qualify.

3. Harriet Martineau (1802–76) was a radical journalist and social commentator and campaigner, whose *Illustrations of Political Economy* (1832–4) was making her reputation at this time. Compare this with Jane's account in a letter to Eliza Stodart, [9 March 1833]: 'Jeffrey writes to me that he has seen Harriet Martineau and does not like her at all – "first because she is most excessively ugly — a[nd] secondly because there is nobody good enough for her to admire" – not even himself I presume' (*Carlyle Letters*, vol. 6, p. 342).

4. The phrase 'as to a rational life' begins a new sentence.

5. John William Ward, first Earl of Dudley (1781–1833), a politician, traveller, scholar, writer and eccentric.

6. Sarah Copley (née Brunsden; *c*. 1794–1834), wife of John Singleton Copley, Baron Lyndhurst (1772–1863), Lord Chancellor under the Tories. She died in January 1834.

7. John Wilson Croker (1780–1857), a prominent Tory politician and controversial contributor to the rival of the *Edinburgh Review*, the *Quarterly Review*.

8. Harriet Leveson-Gower (née Howard), the Duchess of Sutherland (1806–68).

TO THOMAS CARLYLE

date 5 March 1833
from London

London 5 March 1833

My Dear C. I had written the greater part of the enclosed <u>to your wife</u> last night – partly because I was a little in a <u>pet</u> with you – for not writing – and supposed she was more graciously disposed towards me. – and now I find that <u>you</u> are the kind and true one – and that she is false and perfidious – grudges me a scrap of her writing, and sends me mortifying messages, which I shall find a time to resent and repay hereafter! – But I must thank you in good earnest, for your indulgent acknowledgement of the little scrap, which I have always been reproaching myself with palming on you – and still more for the tone of cheerfulness, and improved <u>humanity</u> which reigns in your whole letter – I am much obliged to you for liking my brother – and not a bit <u>jealous</u> – either of you, or your capricious spouse – altho' she hopes to make me so – I thank you too for putting me on seeing L. Hunt.[1] I shall go certainly – and am sure it will be gratification to me – especially if I find that my visit affords any pleasure to him – I have always thought him a man of genius – but spoiled by too high an estimate of his own powers – and some affectations to which it has led him [–] If I can in any way be of use to him – it will be a real gratification – I have sent your enclosed letters – Do not fancy that people repell you – I believe the [? *MS torn*] verb is in the other relation – But I can see that you are improving – and have good hope that, in time you may become almost as tolerant of your fellow sinners, as the Sinless Being who made them! – Talk gently to those from whom you differ – and do not vent dogmas as axioms – and above all being British born <do not> talk to men of your own race as if they should own the superiority of any other — The Paris scheme I think is over for the Austins – and I hope they may still be kept here – If they do go to Germany it will now be Bonn – and not Berlin[2] — What are you writing or meditating – I saw <u>Murray</u>[3] the other night, not very drunk – nor very like a Bankrupt – have you any more M.S. to offer him? Remember me kindly to your brother when you write – Have you any thoughts of being here this year? – The mystics I hear are on the decline in consequence of your desertion – Ever Yours
    F Jeffrey

National Library of Scotland, Acc. 8964, no. 82.

1. James Henry (called Leigh) Hunt (1784–1859), a prolific writer of poetry and of critical and political prose, and editor of the often radical middle-class *Examiner* (founded with his brother John). Leigh Hunt lived in Chelsea and befriended the Carlyles when they were settling in London.
2. See Jeffrey's letter of 14 February 1833, above.

3.   The publisher John Murray.

TO JANE WELSH CARLYLE

date 13 March 1833
from London

35 Charles Street – 13 March 1833

My Dear Child – – This is from Mrs Montagu – I called again on her, but have not got in – I have seen Leigh Hunt, and find him pleasing and sociable (you know I think <u>that</u> a great virtue) and with a buoyancy of spirit, which stands him in better stead, in his circumstances, than all the lessons of all the philosophies – I hope there is a prospect of his extrication – and I shall do all I can to help it — God bless you, my Dear, wayward, high minded Infant! – I pray always for your health and happiness – and I place health first, because I think most of the depressions you occasionally suffer are maladies – and require physical rather than moral treatment – Dr Hamilton[1] I believe will do you more good than Dr Goethe – at all events less harm — Let me hear soon from you – I am very busy – and not particularly satisfied with what may be called the posture of our affairs [–] But things will be as they must – and I hope you must always care a little about me – and think sometimes

Ever Affectly Your's
F Jeffrey

National Library of Scotland, Acc. 8964, no. 83.

1.   James Hamilton (1749–1835) served as Physician-in-Ordinary at Edinburgh's Royal Infirmary for 48 years (1775–1823), while also serving as a physician at George Heriot's and two other Edinburgh hospitals. He was author of one of the standard medical textbooks of the period, *Observations on the Utility and Administration of Purgative Medicines in Several Diseases* (1815), which is probably what Jeffrey has in mind.

TO JANE WELSH CARLYLE

date [?May 1833 (?1834)]
from [Edinburgh]

*in autumn, when I shall have more time – and more apology – and probably alone – tho' that of course must be uncertain – and perhaps you will come here first – or even to London perhaps tho' I somehow dread that – as a step which may not soon be retraced – and which may lead even further – But we are in the hands of fate – and must work at our destiny —

Now, have I not been candid with you? – and not unkind – surely not unkind on your most pettish – or <u>childish</u> apprehension – O never unkind – heaven knows how very deeply and truly the reverse! –

Well – God bless you again my Dear Child – There is something sad and uncongenial in these long partings of those who could be so happy to be together – yet they are tests and purifiers of a true affection – and make one both more confident of ~~the~~ its strength – and more assured of its character – I think this <u>picture worship</u> a sure sign of inward religion – and if it last long enough, of a certainty no idolatry – no worshipping of stacked stones – I have unspeakable comfort in the picture – and assuredly shall not travel again without it – not for fear of your taking the pet at me again – you will never do that – but for a far weightier reason

Now write to me once again before I go – and that means very soon we shall probably have to move on the 8th or 9th of June – if Parl[iamen]t actually meets, as I think it will, on the 14th or 15th — I am not quite well yet – but bear a good heart – and have been less troubled than usual – with trachea and varicosity – If the East wind had any variableness or shadow of turning, I think we should be better – but there seems no hope of that – and now farewell – I have 10 letters to answer – and 5 prorogations to send and here am I, idling away my time and the time of the country, in idle gossiping with a babe –

Heaven Bless you
Ever yours
F. Jeffrey

This little seal is the top of the pencil I stole from you – on which I have had my crest cut – and I still carry in my purse the little note you sent to me, with the (broken) promise of a Journal

---

* The opening of the letter has been lost.
National Library of Scotland, MS 787, ff. 87–8.

TO JANE WELSH CARLYLE

date [?]
from [London]

*last wrote to you that can make it painful or difficult for you to reply – Alas for truth and love if they check at such crosses as these. But I do not encourage such unworthy fancies – and rely on, and believe in your love, with a faith without bounds or speck – I cannot tell you what a comfort that faith is to me – nor how much I feel that I owe to you – and yet easily paid –

And now God bless you – write me a kind line – The chancellor shall know nothing of it – I send you a little carnation leaf which I gathered yesterday at Holland House[1] – and which you cannot go wrong in decyphering – I must see you soon – and then there will be no need of cyphers — Heaven bless you – my gentle and deep hearted friend – Ever Yours

F. Jeffrey

---

* The opening of the letter has been lost.

National Library of Scotland, MS 787, f. 91.

1.   The London home of Henry Richard Fox (later Vassall), third Baron Holland (1773–1840), and Elizabeth, Lady Holland (née Vassall; *c.* 1771–1845), and the centre of Whig intellectual and artistic culture.

TO JANE WELSH CARLYLE

date [13 September ?1833]
from [?]

Saturday 13th

But one line today my Dearest Friend – and that only because it is Saturday, and I cannot write tomorrow – and because I want to ask a question which I should have asked before – on what day or days do you now receive your letters? – It is so provoking to write in a hurry in order not to miss the post – and to find that the letter lies 4 or 5 days after its post journey is concluded – I wish you were nearer the post office – But is that worth wishing? – or if wishing would do any good I should wish you near me – and forever – It is still Sept and hot – and we are going to row up above Richmond, and bathe our thirsty souls in the deep verdure of the country – Heaven Bless and guard you – Ever and only Yours

F. J.

National Library of Scotland, MS 787, f. 97.

TO JANE WELSH CARLYLE

date 14 November 1833
from Edinburgh

Edinburgh 14 Nov[r]
1833

My Dear Infant – Am I forgotten yet? or suspected of being forgotten?[1] I have not the least fear of either – only we have been silent long enough – and I long now for some outward manifestation of the inward Life — Do not ask me what I have been doing – tho' I am willing enough to tell you – as truly as at a Saint's confessional. It is enough that I am not changed – and have not been changed – either at nurse – or in the ripening –

I have thought of you – as constantly and as kindly as ever – and feel assured that I too have been remembered —The affairé[2] official of Whitehall has a heart as mindful as the recluse of Craigenputtach – and if the recluse objects to this article of faith – her creed is the paltrier of the two – The imposed tasks of life have little to do with its voluntary movements – and the treadmill is the same distraction (or degradation) whether it grinds out fine sifted speculations on Diderot or Goethe, or responses to pragmatical Town clerks on the working of the Burgh Reform Act[3] – if you demur to this, you are still in the outer court of the Gentiles – and your spirit is dark within you —

But we need not discuss those points of learning at present – You know (or do you care to know?) that I left London a good deal damaged in health – in August – recreated a great deal in a devious journey, and series of visits homewards, and got to Craigcrook in Sept[embe]r – nestled afterwards with my sister in an upland retreat in Ayrshire – and have been here, dining with my constituents – superintending the hatching of town councils – and (of late days) parading with gown and wig in the courts, since the middle of October – I am pretty well in health again – and tranquil and resigned in spirit [–] Mrs Jeffrey has been sadly affected by the death of her Father – of which she heard about six weeks ago[4] – but is now very much restored to her usual cheerfulness – The younger Charlotte is quite well – and I do not think has lost any of her constitutional tendency to happiness – by her long exile from Scotland – We shall be home I hope till the end of Jan[y] at least, – and perhaps longer – are you not to be here also? – tell me at least where you are to be? and for how long and why, and for what reasons, you are where you are – and to be where you are to be? My answer to such a catechism is easy – that I am, and shall be, where I must be – tho' if the question is, why I must? the answer might seem more difficult – and yet be the same in truth – viz. because I must! —

I have heard nothing of you, now, for a long, long time – last I think from my cheerful friend the D[r],[5] recently before leaving London – and he spoke favourably of your health – Do let me know that it is good – or how it is – and if possible too, of your improving cheerfulness, and encreasing toleration for such people as God has thought good enough for the general population of the world – and the bearing his image upon earth – I do not see why you should be more difficult – But this is learing[6] again – which I readily admit to be foolishness –

I hear of Mrs Austen from Empson – she has been at Boulogne – and is returned to London – We are friends, I hope for life – and I mean to write to her – She has taught me some lessons – I mean by her life and example only – and I think might teach you some – But I am more docile – perhaps because I need more teaching —— Best love to Carlyle – I hope his dyspepsy and misanthropy are milder – remember me too very kindly and gratefully to your mother – and write me a line soon –

God bless you My Dear Child – no one can be more affectly Yours
F. Jeffrey

National Library of Scotland, Acc. 8964, no. 84.

1. Four months earlier, in July, Carlyle had written to Leigh Hunt that 'It is months since we heard a syllable of him, except by the Newspapers'; again to his brother John on 1 October 1833: 'Jeffrey has never yet written' (*Carlyle Letters*, vol. 6, p. 419; vol. 7, p. 8). After they had received this letter, Carlyle wrote on 18 November 1833 to his brother John: 'He now writes to Jane in the frostiest, most frightened manner; makes honourable mention of you; to me hardly alludes except from a far distance. Jane will have it that he took many things to himself in the Article *Diderot*; a possible thing, which corresponds too with the cessation of his Letters. I love the Advocate, and partially pity him, and will write to him in such "choicest mood" as I can command at present' (*Carlyle Letters*, vol. 7, p. 42). This letter proved to be the first of the spate of 'some five or six letters' that Carlyle mentioned to John on 23 December 1833 (*Carlyle Letters*, vol. 7, p. 63).
2. French: busy.
3. The reform of election to, and conduct of, the councils of the many and various (and ancient) burghs of Scotland, concerned with local administration – powerful, often corrupt and largely self-selecting bodies – had been a central policy of the Scottish Whigs in the 1780s and 1790s, and had become so again after Waterloo. After the improvement that occurred as a by-product of the Scottish Reform Act, Jeffrey continued throughout 1833 to press for their reform, making access more democratic and introducing triennial elections. Of all his achievements as a politician throughout the years 1830–4, it was in burgh reform that Jeffrey took most pride.
4. Charlotte Jeffrey's father, the New Yorker Charles Wilkes, had died in August.
5. Carlyle's brother John.
6. From the Scots (and Northern English dialect) verb to lear, to teach or instruct (here, lecturing).

TO JANE WELSH CARLYLE

date 4 and 5 December 1833
from Edinburgh

[Edinburgh December Five 1833*]

My Very Dear Infant – I thank you a thousand times for your letter – It is very kind – very reasonable – and above all, very <u>tolerant</u> and very <u>cheerful</u> — I thank you too for being well – at least for being better — and for having given me a brighter and lighter picture of your existence – than I have for long been able to peice out, from my own memories and fancies — God bless you, my large hearted, high minded child – for you are but a child you know – after all – with your pretty bits of lessons and exercises – and your magnanimous purposes of <u>fighting</u> for your pet fancies – or convictions as you call them – Fighting is about the worst kind of child's play – and of such is <u>not</u> the kingdom of heaven – But you do not mean to fight anybody – not even me – It is but a way of speaking [–] But you do not tell me where you are to be this winter – nor, exactly, what your occupations are – now that you can task yourself to occupation – I long to see you again – to look again on eyes no longer heavy – and steps not loaded with waddings[1] – How long is it since we have had a walk together – or even a windy ride, on your moorlands? Will you come here, and let us begin again? – Never mind a grey hair or two – I concern not myself about a whole fell of them – But you talk of growing old, without feeling it – and I grow old, without talking of it – I have many admonitions that it is even so with me – yet more outward than inward – Dyspepsias and tracheas and heart flutterings and head swimmings – and varicosities and dimness of sight – and a very little Lazar house[2] of my own – a nice epitome of nosology! – and yet the restless spirit within partakes but little of this decay – a little lazier I believe I am – and caring less for the ordinary tasks of the day – but as active in fancy – and as much alive to emotion – as much in love with nature – and as prone to affection, as in youth – with no more propensity to die – and with as strong a love for happiness (debasing as you may think it) and as deep a sympathy with it — Well, there is another mark of age – talking so much of self – but I have done –

Do you hear anything of Mrs Austen? – I like her the best of all your favorites – tho' her book upon Goethé – adds nothing to her reputation, or his – I am determined to learn German – and give battle to that race of canting muddy-headed pretenders – I want Macaulay to clapperclaw Niebuhr[3] in the meantime – and Palgrave[4] to demolish Goethé – But they have both better work in hand – But there is a good time coming – and they must bide it ——

And now it is dark December – and the roaring blasts must be dismal in your upland solitude – come down and shelter among human habitations [–] It is not good for either of you to be so much alone – I have a great deal to say to you – perhaps something to unsay – tho' nothing you care for – O no —

Write to me – it is a great kindness – and a great pleasure – I can scarcely tell you how great – and tell me of yourself, gently and calmly – and let us put away all tone of wrangling – I know I offend in that sort – but I will not again and so Heaven Bless you

> Every Affectly Your's
> F. Jeffrey

I shall write to Carlyle one day soon – What is he busy upon now? remember me kindly to your mother – I never look on your picture without feeling a glow of gratitude for her generosity – and, trust in me — again good night!

* Written above the name and address on the outer sheet
National Library of Scotland, Acc. 8964, no. 85.
1.   Laid up bundles of vegetables (e.g., peas and beans); figuratively, burdens.
2.   A hospital or home for the chronically ill.
3.   Barthold Georg Niebuhr (1776–1831), statesman, historian and author of *The History of Rome* (1811–32), which is the work Jeffrey wants Macaulay to 'clapperclaw'.
4.   Sir Francis Palgrave (né Cohen; 1788–1861), the lawyer and historian who published, for example, a history of England in the Anglo-Saxon period in 1831 and *The Rise and Progress of the English Commonwealth* in 1832. He was, like Macaulay, a regular contributor to the *Edinburgh Review*.

TO THOMAS CARLYLE

date 8 and 9 December 1833
from Edinburgh

[Edinburgh December Nine – 1833*]

My Dear Carlyle – You are very good – and very reasonable – and I value your love for me very highly — Why I do not write – (or have not written, for we shall put that in the past tense, if you please) I cannot well answer, to myself – and therefore not to you – only, writing or not, never doubt that I shall always have a great affection for you – with some provocation – and some admiration – and a most sincere desire for your happiness – or, if that word offends you – your well being – right mindedness – strong workingness – or whatever else is your favourite synonyme for a desirable condition of being —

Let nothing shake this faith in you – and I think I shall never do anything to shake it – You say much changes within you – let me hope that some of the changes may bring our views more near to each other – For my part I do not change much – I believe I am more indolent – and consequently less disposed to wrangle about anything – Never having had much of a creed, I think I have daily less – and having no tendency to dogmatism, and no impatience of indecision, I think zeal for creeds, and anxiety about positive opinions more and more ludicrous – and that all discussion which aims at much more than exercising our faculties, and exposing intolerance, is very tiresome and foolish – Do any of your mutations tend <u>this way</u>? I fear not —

I am delighted to hear, from you both, that my fair cousin is decidedly better in health – But what do you do up in that mountain, all winter? or why will you not come down and mix in our Christmas merriments – and thaw your frozen blood at social firesides like other Christian people? You profess to be great lovers of your fallen creatures, and yet you will not look near them – I do not well know what to make of a philanthropy that drives people into the desart, and makes them fly from the face of man –

And what do you read in your treasure trove of a library?[1] – My passion is for historical collections, I mean contemporary documents, and full length samples of the ages that are past – Your speculative history I hold very cheap – unless indeed it be of my own making – and therefore I utterly loathe and contemn the dogmatical dreams of Niebuhr – which is not bricks without straw but bricks without clay – Poetry is the best – but it excites and exhausts too much – and for working days work I prefer Rushworth[2] – and old chronicles – or even a well printed Chartulary or record of authentic charters – It is a fine thing that same authenticity and a rare –

I wish my poetical friend had not troubled you (and me) with that long letter – But I have written to the Chancellor[3] – I could not seem to do an unkind thing – or to refuse even an implied request of my fair cousin – But I have not the least hope of doing any good – The application is far too vague – and I know but too well how such applications – from far higher quarters – are, and in fact must be treated – The Son is peculiarly fitted for any one place, and can find one vacant, or about to be so – something might possibly be done – But it is mere nonsense to say he wants any situation, and is fit for any — all this need not be told his mother – only let her know I have written – and should be most happy to serve her – which is perfectly true —

I hear often from Empson – who always enquires after you – He tells me a great deal of Mrs Austin – her husband is better in health and has honorable occupation in one of those Law Commissions – They have given up all thoughts of leaving England for the present – Macaulay I am sorry to say goes to India as Chief Law Commiss^r – and one of the Supreme Council – in fact to watch over the practical working of the new system – He has £10,000 a year – and will be away 4 or 5 years – It is a great loss to us – public and private [–] But he promises to take care of his health – and to write more than ever for the Review – for my part, I feel as if I was never to see him again – and that it is a very melancholy parting. He is at this moment the man of the greatest and most universal ability in England[4] – not excepting the Chanc^r – and we can very ill spare him — But you care for none of these things —

Do you hear from your brother?[5] – Why are you not as sociable and cheerful as he is? or in what way did so large a tinge of the melancholic temperament come into your patrimony? — It would be a fine thing now, if it should turn out that your lofty self-tasking philosophy, was merely the result of a bad secretion of Bile, – and was all washed away by copious potations of the Cheltenham spring[6] – I think it might be worth while to try the experiment – You now think this would be a great degradation – But you shall not persuade me that your condition of existence would not be more desirable if there was more of gayety in it – even if you did not go the length of exhilarating the ordinary at Cheltenham, with parodies of Goethe and epigrams on Edward Irving[7] – on which I do not insist —

My brother is very well – and settled for the winter again, with his two wives[8] – I start often to think how little I am settled – or can be – and shrink a little from the prospect of <the> stormy discussion about patronage – Conveyancing – Corporations, and other dull and revolting subjects, that await us before the end of the Session – If I grow very tired of them, I shall cut and run – tho' not to a desart – I have worked enough – and have no motive to die in harness.

God bless you – Write to me when you are minded – I shall answer – better at least than in the year 1833 – But at all events let me know whenever you think I can do you – or anybody you care about, any good – My Charlottes send their love to you – and are in no danger of forgetting — I am not sure whether I mentioned before that Mrs J. had lost her father. He died in August – and she has been very deeply afflicted – She had written to him once a fortnight, ever since the day of her marriage — and so good night again [–] I am in my old course of late hours – and am writing to you at 2 o'clock in the morn^g –

　　Ever Affectly Yours
　　F. Jeffrey

Do you want back that letter of Mrs R?[9] – It will make this cover too heavy —

---

* Written above the name and address on the outer sheet.
National Library of Scotland, Acc. 8964, no. 86.

1.　Jeffrey is referring to the access Carlyle had recently gained to the large library accumulated by the late Professor of Divinity at Edinburgh, Andrew Hunter (1743–1809), at Barjarg, an estate with a large manor in a neighbouring parish (*Carlyle Letters*, vol. 6, p. 443).

2.　John Rushworth (*c.* 1612–90), the historian whose eight-volume *Historical Collections of Private Passages of State* (1659–1701) covers the years 1618 to 1648 and makes an invaluable source book for the Civil War.

3.　Henry Brougham (see note 1 to the letter of 17 October 1827 and note 1 to the letter of 1 and 2 February 1831, above).

4.　See note 1 to Jeffrey's letter of 1 March 1830, above, on Carlyle's sensitivity to Jeffrey's praise of Macaulay. Reporting on this letter to his brother John, Carlyle responded to Jeffrey's lament that 'we can very ill spare' Macaulay by saying 'Depend upon it we shall get on, better or worse' (*Carlyle Letters*, vol. 7, p. 64).

5.　John.

6.　Cheltenham was renowned for its medicinal waters.

7.　In this dig at Carlyle's enthusiasms, Jeffrey unkindly links Carlyle's reverence for Goethe and his friendship for the revivalist Irving. Irving had lost his congregation earlier in the year, and would die the following year (December 1834).

8.　John Jeffrey, with his actual wife Elizabeth, and her sister Susan Hunter.

9.　Mrs (Caroline) Richardson, with whom Jane corresponded (see note 2 to the letter of 16 July 1828, above).

1834

TO THOMAS CARLYLE

date 14 January 1834
from Edinburgh

Edinburgh 14th Jan^y
1834

My Dear Friend — It is best to tell you at once that I do not think there is the least chance of your getting the chair of astronomy,[1] and that it would be idle to make any application – In the first place it is utterly out of my sphere and department – and I know I should be laughed at, if I were to pretend to interfere – accordingly, tho' the most hopeful of the candidates now in the field, was my clerk or Secretary, before going to the Cape as Observer,[2] and is entitled to the best general character – he has not even applied to me for a recommendation – it being matter of notoriety that no testimonials will <u>be looked</u> at, except from persons of weight and authority in this particular branch of science – and I am perfectly certain – indeed I may say I <u>know</u>, that Govt will be entirely guided by such suffrages – The place in fact will be given (and it is difficult to say that it ought not to be given) according to the recommendations of Herschell, Airy[,] Babbage[3] and some six or 7 other men of unquestionable eminence in this department, without the least regard to other recommendations – If you can satisfy <u>them</u> that you are the fittest for the place, you may be sure of it. If you cannot, you may be equally sure that it is needless to think of it

I am quite incapable of judging whether you might so satisfy them as to the proper <u>Scientific</u> qualifications for the place, or not – but my <u>second</u> ground for holding that your chance of success is absolutely nothing, is, that you have had no practice in observing – and that nobody will be appointed who has not had <u>much</u>, and much approved practice, and skill in this department – Sir D. Brewster,[4] and Lord Napier[5] I know look upon this as the first and most important part of the qualification – and would abate much of scientific attainment, to secure a large measure of tactical dexterity, and acquired habits of minute observation – and they say that Herschel is of the same opinion – Most certainly they would never trust the handling of their instruments to one who had not served an apprenticeship even to the mechanical part of the business – and I know they are all exclaiming ag[ains]t the mischief which Prof' Wallace[6] has done by his rash and incautious handling of the apparatus – which they say it will cost £900, to and many months work, to set to rights – The place to be given, in fact, is primarily and mainly an observer's place – there being little expectation of its being possible to make a class of practical astronomy, in such a place as Edinr – and you cannot be surprised therefore that it should be an indispensable qualification in any candidate, that he is a skilful and practiced observer —

I am very sorry for this – but still more sorry for certain expressions of dissatisfaction in your letter— They revive and encrease the deep regret I have always felt at your not having the occupation and consequent independence of some regular profession — That of a Teacher is no doubt a most useful and noble one – But you cannot actually exercise it, unless you offer to teach what is thought worth learning – and in a way that is thought agreeable – and I am afraid you have not fulfilled either of those conditions – You know I do not myself set much value on the paradoxes and exaggerations in which you delight— and at all events I am quite clear that no man ever did more to obstruct the success of his doctrines by the tone in which he promulgated them – It is arrogant, vituperative – obscure – anti-national and inconclusive – likely enough to strike weak and ill conditioned fancies – but almost sure to revolt calm, candid and thinking persons – It sounds harsh to say this – but I say it as a witness – and as you begin to experience the effects, you may perhaps give more credit to my testimony than you used to do – You will never find (or make) the world friendly to your doctrines, while you insist upon dragooning it into them in so hyperbolical a manner. – I am glad however that you are tired of your solitude for one great step to your case will be your mixing gently and humbly and, (when possible) gaily, with other men – and if we once had you fairly down from that barren and misty eminence where you reside bodily, I trust we should soon reconcile you to an intellectual subsidence, as wholesome and comfortable –

Well – forgive me all this[7] – I am sick, and somewhat tired of my own compelled activity – and look forward, with more recoiling of heart than I like to own, to the contentious scene which lies before me – I shall be in the main but a looker on however – and instead of embroiling the fray may perhaps help in some small degree to allay it – my calm temper and utter distrust of all extreme opinions, qualify me well enough for this and at critical seasons one quiet and earnest voice, may do more with honest leaders than more vehement argumentations – at the worst, I can always retreat – and retreat when I may, no one can now say that I do it, before I had a full justification in the state of my health and strength —

I am glad that my fair cousin is better – tho' I cannot approve of her taking to nurse lunatics[8]—and shall not feel quite easy till I hear she is out of that perilous occupation — What are you writing now? or meditating? I was glad to hear from your brother that you had been studying our old English prose writers – There were Giants in those days – and one feels taller when mounted on their shoulders – We shall move I think about the 28th – Write before that time – God bless you

    Ever Yours

    F. Jeffrey

National Library of Scotland, MS 787, ff. 64–9.

1.   At the University of Edinburgh, a position which involved the superintendence of the Royal Observatory on Calton Hill in Edinburgh. Jeffrey no doubt knew that Carlyle had taught in the related area of mathematics but is obviously exasperated by Carlyle's seeking his assistance with a job for which Jeffrey takes him to be underqualified.

2.   Thomas Henderson (1798–1844) was trained in the law and had been Jeffrey's secretary until 1831. He was also a renowned amateur astronomer, who on leaving Jeffrey's employ had become a Fellow of the Royal Astronomical Society and, from April 1832 to May 1833, been Royal Astronomer at the Cape of Good Hope. Henderson was indeed awarded the position of Regius Professor of Astronomy at the University of Edinburgh, later becoming the first Astronomer Royal for Scotland.

3.   John Herschel (1792–1871), President of the Royal Astronomical Society; George Biddell Airy (1801–92), Professor of Mathematics, then (in 1828) of Astronomy, at Cambridge University (later Astronomer Royal); Charles Babbage (1792–1871), also Professor of Mathematics at Cambridge (sometimes credited with the 'invention' of the computer) and, with Herschel and others, one of the founders of the Royal Astronomical Society.

4.   David Brewster (1781–1868), the Scottish periodical and encyclopaedia editor who was also a celebrated physicist, the inventor of the kaleidoscope and discoverer of the polarization of light. Carlyle knew Brewster, as it happens, and had contributed articles to his *Edinburgh Encyclopaedia* in 1819.

5.   Charles Napier (1786–1860), decorated British admiral, later naval administrator and MP.

6.   William Wallace (1768–1843), an autodidact who had become Professor of Mathematics at the University of Edinburgh and had been supervising the Observatory on Calton Hill in Edinburgh.

7.   How far Carlyle was able to forgive Jeffrey this refusal and outburst is a moot point. Carlyle wrote of this letter to his brother on 21 January 1834: 'Within the last few days, I have made a proposal for a Public Office, and been rejected! There is to be an Astronomical Professor and Observer in Edinburgh, and no man of the smallest likelihood to fill it: I thought what an *honest* kind of work it was; how honestly I could work at it for my bread, and harmonize it with what tended infinitely higher than bread; and so wrote to the poor Advocate with great heartiness telling him all this. He answers me by return of Post in a kind of polite Fishwoman-shriek; adds that my doctrines (in Literature) are

"arrogant, antinational, absurd", and to crown the whole "inconclusive"; that the place withal is for an old secretary of his (who has not applied to *him*), unless I can convince the Electors that I am fitter; – which I have not the faintest disposition to do. I have written back to the poor body, suppressing all indignation, if there were any; diffusing over all, the balm of pity; and so in a handsome manner terminate the business. One has ever and anon a kind of desire to "wash away" this Correspondent of ours; yet really it were not right: I can see him, even in this Letter, to be very thoroughly miserable, and am bound to help him, not aggravate him. His censures too have something flattering even in their violence otherwise impertinent enough: he cannot tolerate me, but also he cannot despise me, and that is the sole misery' (*Carlyle Letters*, vol. 7, pp. 78–9). That Jeffrey's rebuff did not inhibit Carlyle from seeking Jeffrey's help in procuring him another position is apparent from the very next letter.

8.   A reference to William Glen (1803–52), a classical scholar and graduate of Glasgow University whom Carlyle had met and admired in London. Glen had gone insane and been confined in Glasgow, then sought out the Carlyles for rest and recuperation, arriving at Craigenputtock with his brother Archy in early January.

TO THOMAS CARLYLE

date 4 February 1834
from Edinburgh

Edinburgh 4 Feby 1834

My Dear Friend — We go I believe with tomorrow's dawn – and you may suppose it is difficult to possess my soul in patience tonight – If I were the patron of the Rhetoric chair,[1] I should venture to appoint you tho' with some consciousness of responsibility – But, <u>imprimis</u>, I am not the Patron – 2da The chair is not vacant and 3^tio The University Commission have recommended that, when it is vacant, it shall not be filled again but abolished – as useless – and never likely to prosper – and I have some years ago, countersigned that death warrant – except in the case of some man of great and established reputation being willing to accept of it – in whose person one more Experiment might be made 4to – (tho' is it necessary to say more?) several persons of name and eminence have been recently suggested – such as Poet Campbell and others – and yet Govt – is averse, even for such persons, to continue the appointment – and I am quite sure would not be persuaded to do so, in favour of any one less generally accredited, or with a name less generally attractive —

You are very good natured to me – and set down my vivacities to the right account – I am afraid they do no good – but God knows – they are not meant to hurt or offend you! – But is it not a melancholy and rather provoking thing, to feel – (and again on an occasion like this) that what I cannot but consider as perversions and absurdities, should thus be accumulating obstacles to your ever attaining either the public position or the general respect to which your talents and diligence might otherwise have entitled you? While things are as they certainly will be all my life, I do not think there is the least chance of your being admitted into any regular Seminary, as a Teacher – with such doctrines, and such a tone of inculcation, on record ag[ains]t you, as must be referred to, even in proof of your qualifications —

I do not yet know where I shall be in London – But you may address to me at the House of C[ommons].

> God bless you–
> Ever affectly Yours
> F. Jeffrey

I have[2] vivacities with my fair cousin too – for which – if they vex her – I ask her pardon – But who would not be provoked to see Titania in love with Bottom?

National Library of Scotland, MS 787, ff. 70–1.

1. At the University of Edinburgh, which Carlyle understood to be vacant – mistakenly, according to Jeffrey. Carlyle was right to the extent that the Professor of Rhetoric and Belles Lettres since 1801, Andrew Brown, was ill, and would die two weeks later on 19 February 1834. (This was the second time Carlyle had sought Jeffrey's support for the chair; see Jeffrey's letter of 22 October 1828, above.)
2. Clearly something is missing here, a word or phrase like 'indulged in' as J. A. Froude suggests (J. A. Froude, *Thomas Carlyle: A History of the First Forty Years of His Life*, 2 vols (London: Longmans, Green, 1882), vol. 2, p. 401; see also Wilson, vol. 2, p. 355).

TO JANE WELSH CARLYLE

date 8 September 1834
from Edinburgh

Edinburgh 8th Septr
1834

My Dear Friend – For Mercy's sake let us be friends still – and seem so. – Tho' you have instigated your mother to ask back your picture – and I have sent it – (both because it was in our compact, and because I could never resist a <u>mother's</u> claim) – do not let us be estranged any longer — I daresay I have been too harsh and peremptory – and I humbly ask your pardon if you still think so — Your mother says your health and spirits have been better since you have been in London[1] – It is a greater pain to me than you will believe, to think that they have been so overclouded – and indeed my Dear Child you may believe me when I say, that if I had not thought that the opinions and habits which you cherished were, in part at least, the cause of this derangement, I should never have testified ag[ains]t them as I have done – When I see you well and happy, I shall regard any creed you may adopt, with charity at least, if not with affection – But till then – what can you expect of me? [–] I do not know where you are in London – and shall send this to Empson, who will probably find you – Mrs Austin has gone to Jersey – and I do not know whether you continue to see the Montague's –

Tell me what you are doing – – and what you now think of life – and the human brethren who share it with you? – I pray daily that your estimation of both may be more favourable than it used to be –

For my part I hold by my old creed – that to be happy, and to make happy, is the chief end of man – and I strive to fulfill it as well as I can — The very nature of it makes the will no small part of the deed – and I hope I succeed, in both branches, tolerably – I should be better pleased however, if I could make you happy – and still better if I could hope that you were so by adopting my creed – But things will be as they must – and we may agree at least in thinking that they will all, ultimately be right —

I take reasonably well to my new Judicial functions[2] – tho' I must confess that I enjoy the vacation more than the working time – and that I have not yet entirely ceased to mourn for the loss of London – and all the worth and talent and affection it contains —

Tell me with what, and with whom you are occupied – and what you wish and expect the future – I mean the near and visible future – to produce to you — We are here in a great ferment of Philosophy and Politics[3] – and mighty busy and important in our small way – They say there are 2000 Philosophers, divided into sections – and on Monday we shall have 2000 politicians – all united I hope in principle — I have not been able to hear of one <u>Mystic</u> in the ranks of either – unless you will allow the honor of that name to the Phrenologists – of whom there is a small sprinkling – The least that can be said of the assemblage is – that it is very gay and very goodhumoured – for with great freedom of discussion I have not yet heard a spiteful or sulky word — But you care for none of these things – I wish I knew what you cared about – and perhaps you will one day tell me — In the mean time I hope you will write to me[4] – and let me have the satisfaction at all events of hearing that you are well – and active – and – (you must forgive me for wishing anything so degrading) cheerful and social – and indulgent – to follies opposite to your own   Heaven Bless you my very

Dear Thoughtful Friend
Ever Affectly Yours
F. Jeffrey

National Library of Scotland, MS 787, ff. 80–3.

1. Carlyle and Jane left Craigenputtoch in 1834, with Jane joining Carlyle at number 5 Cheyne Row in Chelsea on 4 June, the house where they remained and which has since become identified with them as a couple.

2. Jeffrey was appointed to a seat on the bench in the Court of Session (the highest court in Scotland) on 7 June 1834, and in the Scottish tradition automatically became a lord.

3. Jeffrey is referring to the first Edinburgh meeting of the British Association, followed on 15 September 1834 by what Henry Cockburn calls 'the most magnificent public dinner ever given in Edinburgh' (*Life of Jeffrey*, vol. 1, p. 366), in honour of Earl Grey, who had retired as prime minister and leader of the Whig party on 9 July 1834. (In spite of his intimacy with Grey, Jeffrey felt that, as a judge and therefore non-partisan, it would be inappropriate for him to attend the actual event.)

4. In January 1835, Carlyle wrote to his brother John of 'one Letter' to Jane – referring to this letter of 8 September 1834, no doubt – 'in the old intolerable strain (reprimanding you, for the thousandth time, for not being "*happy*") which remains unanswered these four months' (*Carlyle Letters*, vol. 8, pp. 11–12). It was after this letter, therefore, that their correspondence appears effectively to have stopped (but see the next letter of Jeffrey's). They still met on Jeffrey's annual visit to London, however, and the friendship was rekindled in 1837, though it never recovered the same warmth. Ten years after this letter, on [10 August 1845], Jane spoke of her having ceased to write to Jeffrey at this time because he had patronized her by complimenting her on her 'bits of convictions' (*Carlyle Letters*, vol. 19, p. 137), though the truth is Jeffrey had been patronizing towards Jane from the very beginning.

1835

[?TO JANE WELSH CARLYLE[1]]

date 27 April 1835
from London

London 27 April 35

My Dear Child – This is my last day — and it is almost as uncomfortable as that of Pompeii – I am hurried and worried – and so are you – and that is your real malady – The pain of parting from what one loves – would be tolerable – and not without its sweetness – if it were not dashed and troubled by the paltry vexations, inseparable from parting from things indifferent – Be of good courage [–] There is nothing wrong with you – The inward light burns as strong and pure as ever – and the clouds that seem gathering without – are more clouds of dust raised by the stir of your moving, than the threats of an angry sky – Be of good cheer then – and wait the coming time – The Spring will have its way yet in spite of the East wind – and the Summer will follow – and winter will not come till the sheaves of the latter harvest are gathered in –

God bless you — I fancied that you were getting into too large a circle – But that was probably selfishness – because I saw so much less of you – and never found your mind at leisure, or vacant for permanent impressions — If it be so however you will enjoy your comparative solitude – and that will be the test – that is if you have not too many and too heavy tasks, to oppress you –

Write to me to Edinburgh – I cannot write any more now – for here are people come in –

Heaven bless you – and all yours
Ever Affectly Yours
F Jeffrey]

National Library of Scotland, MS 10997, ff. 155–6.

1. The recipient of this letter of Jeffrey's must remain conjectural. It is located among a collection of autograph letters and manuscripts of miscellaneous origin in the National Library of Scotland that also includes a stray letter of Jeffrey's to Carlyle of 29 May 1842, and the salutation strongly suggests that it was written to Jane Welsh Carlyle. Jeffrey was certainly in London in April 1835, and visited the Carlyles: 'My little Lord Jeffrey interrupted me since I began this Letter; coming down to enquire if we were "happy". He is here for some weeks enjoying his vacation: a nimble little individual, whom I wish heartily well to, but have no farther trade with, except in the 'Fine-day, Sir' manner. His ladies are with him, but their way is not our way' (*Carlyle Letters*, vol. 8, p. 92). Against its being written to Jane is the fact that there is no other correspondence between 1834 – when Carlyle deliberately neglected Jeffrey's letter of 8 September – and Jeffrey's receipt of Carlyle's *The French Revolution* in 1837. Nor is it obvious what Jeffrey means by Jane's moving to 'comparative solitude'. However, Carlyle and Jane had indeed expanded their 'circle' of friends since settling in London only half-way through the previous year, and were now (as Carlyle's letter makes clear) reluctant to socialize with Jeffrey.

1837

TO THOMAS CARLYLE[1]

date 18 May 1837
from Edinburgh

Edinburgh 18 May 1837

My Dear Carlyle – A thousand thanks for your book of the F. Revolution[2] – It would have been very welcome to me –(whatever its quality had been) – as a ~~mark of~~ <indicating> a return of that old kindness, which I had feared you were withdrawing from me: But it certainly gives me greater pleasure, as it is a work which I feel assured will do you more honor and bring you into more notice than anything you have hitherto produced — It is a book, written most emphatically in your own manner – and yet likely to be very generally read – and which cannot be read anywhere, without leaving the impression that the author (whatever else may be thought of him) is a man of Genius and originality – and capable of still greater things than he has done even here — It is no doubt a very strange piece of work – and is really, as Coleridge I think said of something else, like reading a story by flashes of lightning![3] — It is beyond all question the most <u>poetical</u> history that the world has ever seen – and the most moral also – tho' perhaps not the fullest of wisdom. The descriptions are the finest things in it – and next, the sentiments – especially those of ~~the~~ a soft, indulgent and relenting character – which are generally full of truth and beauty <and it must be owned outnumber all the others —> Your ratiocinations (as those of poets are apt to be) – are less satisfactory, and not very intelligible – You will be called affected – and I fear, in some sense, not unjustly – and by many readers you will <certainly> be found obscure [–] But all the better judges will admire you – and allow that, with many faults, you have innumerable excellences – and above all that you have power, and originality, which atone for everything — I do not myself approve of the style of the composition – It is too odd, broken and ostentatiously singular – But what I object most to, is the tone of <u>mockery</u> – and mephistophilistic <u>humour</u>, in which not only grave but tragic matters are treated – which jars upon our gentler feelings, and, according to my experience at least, is painful and out of place – Your clever Devils may view our poor human doings in this spirit – but not a man, with so a heart so soft and compassionate as yours ——

All this time tho', I have read only the first volume quite thro' – and dipped into a dozen places in the others – I only got the book the day before yesterday – and have neglected my judicial duties to get thro' so much of it – Of course I have heard nothing of it from other quarters – But I feel assured of its success – I mean of its coming to notoriety and being spoken of, and admired, and abused — In good truth it deserves both, pretty heartily —

I will not resume our old points of disagreement – If I have ever seemed to have too little indulgence for what I thought your errors, I hope you will believe that it is far less from any impatience even of dogmatic contradiction, than from a sincere belief that your persistence in them obstructed not only your fame and prosperity – but your usefulness, and authority as an instructor – It will give me great and unmingled pleasure to find that, in spite of all that persistence, you have succeeded in all these things – and I can truly assure you that no renunciation of your heresies could gratify me half so much as this way of justifying them. You have likings and dislikings too (I mean in your book) with which I do not at all sympathise – and seem to me very often to despise and admire very capriciously – tho' it is not your disposition I think generally, to err in overmuch admiring — Why does not your bookseller advertise industriously and puff a little in the journals? You I daresay despise all such base devices – But the trades should not be above them – and tho' they may not give popularity they certainly accelerate it ——— And now I have no time to say any more – I was obliged to give up my London visit this year – It is barely possible – if Parl[iamen]t sit late – that I may still run up about the end of July – But it is most likely not till next Spring – when I shall have great pleasure in finding you famous and flourishing – Have you no idea of being in Scotland before that time?

And my fair cousin! – I hope she does not mean to disclaim me – I think of her often, with the greatest regard – I hear sometimes of her, circuitously, thro' Empson – and am glad to learn that she is well and blooming, since her influenza – Why should she not tell me so with [her *omitted*] own fair hand?

God bless you, my Dear Carlyle – I shall ever think of you but with kindness – and shall always rejoice most sincerely in all your good fortune —

    Ever Very Faithfully Yours

    F. Jeffrey

National Library of Scotland, MS 787, ff. 72–5.

1.   Jeffrey enclosed this letter for forwarding to Carlyle within a short message to Henry Brougham, which is reproduced above in the introduction, pp. xxvi–xxvii.

2. Carlyle's *The French Revolution* was printed in April but not published until 1 June (I. Campbell, *Thomas Carlyle*, rev. edn (Edinburgh: Saltire Society, 1993), p. 105), so Jeffrey was commenting on a pre-publication copy Carlyle had sent him. A product of his wide reading and developing thoughts on history and on social and cultural change – as well as of intensive creative work over the years that he and Jane had been settled in London (including the famous rewriting necessitated by the accidental destruction of a first manuscript while in the possession of John Stuart Mill) – *The French Revolution* was the work which finally established Carlyle's reputation as one of the important individual thinkers of his age.

3. In Coleridge's *Table Talk*, published in 1836, he is recorded as having said of Edmund Kean: 'To see him act, is like reading Shakespeare by flashes of lightning'. See *Table Talk Recorded by Henry Nelson Coleridge (and John Taylor Coleridge)*, ed. C. Woodring, 2 vols, *The Collected Works of Samuel Taylor Coleridge*, 14 (Princeton, NJ: Princeton University Press, 1990), vol. 2, p. 41.

TO JANE WELSH CARLYLE

date 4 September 1837
from Craigcrook

Craigcrook 4 Sept[r] 1837

My Dear Friend

I hope you are now returned to your quiet home – with improved health – and undiminished relish for quietness – and that you have found Carlyle there, in as good a condition – It was a great gratification to me to receive your letter – and to read words of kindness and confidence again from your hand — after so long a cessation — Few things have moved me more than this return – (may I not so call it?) to our first feelings towards each other, both on your part, and that of your husband. Why there was ever any remission in them it is needless perhaps now to enquire. Let us be for the future, as much as possible, what we were in the beginning – For myself I may say that my sentiments have never really varied – and that I feel every day more strongly the infinite folly of allowing differences of taste, or opinion to make any social estrangement amongst those whose principles and affections should bring them together — Our ways of life – and occupations, as well as remoteness of residence, must keep us much asunder – and we may have but little personal intercourse for the remainder of our time in this world – But let us know and feel that we are <u>friends</u> – that we love and respect each other – and wish and hope to meet, where there are to be no more separations – or distrusts, or misapprehensions ——— I was vexed to observe in Carlyle's letter – thro' all its kindness and magnanimity – a tone of despondency – and vestiges if not of a discontented – at least of a painfully dissatisfied spirit – I wish to heaven he could think more favourably and indulgently of his fellow creatures [–] I am sure he would be happier: – and his chance of making them better would at all events be improved – It is a strange view to take of a beneficent govt of the universe, that so vast a proportion of its intelligent occupants, should, for such vast periods of [?   *MS torn*] be left in such a state of intellectual and moral darkness, as to be objects of contempt and compulsion, or at best of painful compassion, to the few who are (or fancy that they are) exempt from the common degradation. For my own part I would rather be without the exemption – if that were necessary to make me believe < – as I firmly do – > that the bulk of mankind are very tolerably happy – and loveable, and respectable – that their existence in short is much more a blessing than a curse – and that the best part of its large actual enjoyment, is in the interchange of <u>deserved</u> love and affection. This is my creed – and I am resolved to die, as I have lived, in it – tho' I shall never wrangle again, to impose it on any other person. I am rather mortified that C. did not follow up the kind feelings expressed in his letter by coming to see us while he was in Scotland[1] – Nobody I am sure could have been more welcome – and I hope he knows that. We were from home a good part of the time, and before we came back, most of those from whom I might get tidings of his whereabouts were scattered – and I could not discover his lurking pl[?ace. *MS torn*] When I come to see you – as I confidently reck[?on on *MS torn*] doing – in Spring, we must arrange for a meet[?ing *MS torn*] in the autumn — In the mean time l[?et me *MS torn*] hear from one or both of you – and above all that your health is now quite restored – and that you are both more resigned to the blindness of the race, and rather more hopeful of its speedy improvement — For me, I labour contentedly enough in my vocation – which I find by no means irksome – and have much comfort in the daily society of many very imperfect beings – in whom I still find a great deal both to love, and to esteem – and occasionally something to admire — My health has not been very robust – but I am still reasonably active and alert – and both my Charlottes (and their little dogs) are perfectly well. My brother John, tho' a little younger than me, has more infirmity, and far more anxiety about his health – than I have. I suppose you have heard that he has lost one of his two wives this year – by the marriage of your friend Susan H. to a Mr Sterling in Dundee[2] – He is now pretty much reconciled however to this calamity – especially as the perfidious lady appears to be very happy in her new connection — I have got a [?cover] for you from the tuneful Sergeant[3] (as I call him) the author of I[on *MS torn*] –(which I hope you have read) he says he saw you [? *MS torn*] at Miss Martineaus – and admired you greatly – for*

---

* The remainder of the letter has been lost.
National Library of Scotland, MS 787, ff. 84–5.
1.   Carlyle had left to visit his family at Scotsbrig in late June and was still there even as Jeffrey wrote, though he would be returning in ten days.

2.   John Jeffrey's sister-in-law Susan Hunter (see note 8 to the letter of 8 and 9 December 1833, above) had married James Stirling.
3.   Thomas Noon Talfourd (1795–1854), at the time a sergeant-in-law (court official) and MP, as well as being a writer and friend of writers. The title torn out of the letter is almost certainly that of Talfourd's poetic tragedy *Ion*, which had been enormously popular on stage and in print since its debut the year before in 1836.

TO THOMAS CARLYLE

date 12 December 1837
from Edinburgh

Edinburgh 12 Decr 1837

My Dear Carlyle – My worthy successor Napier[1] having been sick – I could not see him till today. – He is quite friendly to your proposal – and is to write tomorrow to Longman to recommend their acceding to it.[2] I have no doubt they will – and he is of the same opinion – So that I think you need not hesitate about making your arrangements, as if their sanction was given —

I am not satisfied with the account you give, either of yourself or your wife – and think often of you both, with more tenderness – and more pain than you will perhaps give me credit for. In her I have nothing to regret, but her delicate health – of which I earnestly hope I may soon have a more favourable account – I should be releived if I could beleive that your depression, and distaste with <for> life and all that occupies and interests other men was the fruit merely of a morbid temperament, and I do beleive that it [*for* is] so in a good degree But I fear there are errors of opinion – and heresies as to the grand problem of the <u>Summum Bonum</u>,[3] that contribute their share. I have always wished that you had a profession, to force you more into contact with the common things, in the midst and at the mercy of which, it has pleased Providence to place us – and to give you, by mere habit, an interest in pursuits – which I admit that a philosopher may very reasonably despise – if it do not happen to be a part of his philosophy, that any pursuit is better than a contempt for all – and that an innocent occupation is a part of the happiness, as it appears to be a part of the destiny of our kind. I am rather angry at your not showing yourself at Edin^r – when you were so long – and so idle on our side of the border – I rather think I shall be in London about the end of March – when I hope to find you more energetic, and better reconciled to a world which tho' not the best possible is better I firmly believe than ever it was before – and which you might have a better chance of mending, if you could be a little more indulgent to some of its ways. I cannot say I think the business of an author, the happiest or the most healthful for a person of your temper – But it is better than no business – and I cannot let you give up literature till you get some other occupation – Whatever you were intended for

I am sure it was not to waste your days and powers in a Magnetic Sleep – If your following in literature is not very large, I am assured that it is very zealous and devoted – and that at all events you have attained to the distinction of being a Leader [–] If I could but know that you were gay and good humoured it would be a very great gratification — Remember always that there is nothing I can do for you which it will not give me pleasure to do   God bless you — I write this in our Judicial voting room, that I may not lose the post — ~~Do~~ Give my kindest love to my fair cousin (I hope she does not disclaim our relationship yet) and quicken her tardy purpose of letting me hear of her from herself —— Where is your learned brother? Pray give my kind regards to him when you see him – I think with his general medical skill – his practice in ministering to fine ladies – and his necessary knowledge of your family constitution, he might do you some good, if you would let him doctor and diet, and drive you about — At all events let me hear that you are better — I shall probably write you when I hear of Longmans determination – But I must say adieu now

Ever Very Faithfully Yours

F. Jeffrey

National Library of Scotland, MS 1766, ff. 54–6.

1. Macvey Napier, his successor as editor of the *Edinburgh Review* (see note 2 to the letter of 3 November 1829, above).

2. Carlyle was seeking from Longmans, as the London publisher of the *Edinburgh Review*, permission to reprint articles that had first appeared there in his *Critical and Miscellaneous Essays*, which was published by Fraser in four volumes in September 1839.

3. Latin: the greatest good (as a political and ethical ideal).

TO THOMAS CARLYLE

date 31 December 1837
from Edinburgh

Edinburgh 31 Dec^r
1837

My Dear Carlyle – I enclose you Longman's license to reprint[1] – which I only got from Napier today —

I hope you, and your too delicate wife, have profited by this normal Christmas – – and that she especially is not afraid now for the effects of a winter which begins so mildly. – the odds I understand are, that midsummer day will be colder, than <this> midwinter has been –

Another year gone! and one less to come, for us all – – that one, being a serious deduction from the remainder of a Senior like me! – Yet I cannot say that I feel at all sad upon it – and beleive that I can wish you (as I do) a merry New Year

– as heartily as you can respond to me — I should be merrier myself however – if I could rely more on your responsive merriment –

Do you read Sir Walter Scotts life?[2] – at all events read this new volume – I think the Diary, which is the best of it, will interest you – and give you a juster and a kinder impression of that extraordinary man than you used to have –

I have a gleam of holiday leisure – and my friend Empson, and your astronomical neighbour Mrs Somerville,[3] have come to help me to enjoy it –

I hope to find you all well, and hopeful in April – But should like to hear from some of you in the mean while.

With kindest love to that fair spouse

Ever Very Faithfully

Yours

F. Jeffrey

National Library of Scotland, MS 1766, ff. 57–8.

1. See the previous letter.
2. John Gibson Lockhart's *Memoirs of the Life of Sir Walter Scott, Bart* would eventually run to seven volumes, published serially between 1837 and 1838. Carlyle certainly had been reading it, and writing about it; a rather restrained review he had written of the work appeared in the *London and Westminster Review* a month later in January 1838. (See note 5 on Lockhart to the letter of 16 July 1828, above.)
3. Mary Somerville (née Fairfax; 1780–1872), 'astronomical' because she was a distinguished, autodidactic mathematician and astronomer. Her *Mechanism of the Heavens* – an explication and abridgement of Laplace's massive *Mécanique Céleste* – appeared in 1831, and the year after the preliminary dissertation she had written for it was published on its own.

1839

TO THOMAS CARLYLE

date [?12 July 1839]*
from [?]

Craigcrook Friday Evg

My Dear Carlyle – We shall all be delighted to see you tomorrow But it is right to put you <u>au fait</u> – of our position – <u>Imprimis</u> – I cannot come to Edinr to see you – any way – for – tho' I have not tumbled from a horse, I have ruffled the skin from my shin – and been condemned to rest – and almost continued recumbency for some days — 2do We are to Christen our youngest descendant, tomorrow at 2 o'clock[1] — which ceremony we should be glad to have honored by your presence – But if you do not care to assist at it, we are to send in the officiating Preist in the carriage about 4 o'clock – which could therefore call for you at any after hour – and bring you safe out to dinner (a very quiet family dinner – as we put off the Christening people with lunch) at six — 3^{tio} as our house is full of nurses and children and my niece H. Brown,[2] we can only offer you a makeshift – (tho' I believe not uncomfortable) bed – on a broad drawing room Sopha – to which however we tender you a cordial welcome — 4to If you shrink from these incommodities of the night, why should you not come out to a late Sunday breakfast with us at 10 o'clock? – and stay all the rest – or as much of that blessed day, as you can spare, in my shades? I hope to be "Godlike erect" again by that time – but at any rate we may sit or saunter in the garden, in the cool of the day – and haply hear the voice of God among the trees! — But 5to – and at all events, do not go away without seeing us ——

Now what you have to do is this – send <u>a message</u> – in the vulgar tongue – (not a written note) to 24 Moray Place, before 4 o'clock – intimating when you would like the carriage to call and bring you out – or if you really cannot

come, send a note to say that we may look for you on Sunday —— With kindest remembrances from all here

    Ever Faithfully Your's
    F. Jeffrey

---

* The dating of this letter, inferred from its contents (see note 1), must remain tentative.
National Library of Scotland, MS 787, ff. 76–7.

1.   Jeffrey's granddaughter Charlotte – the third Charlotte (Tarley), after his wife and
    daughter – was 'baptised ... at two o'clock' on 13 July 1839 (*Life of Jeffrey*, vol. 2, p. 303).
    As Carlyle was at Templand in Dumfriesshire at this time, and wondering whether or not
    to visit Edinburgh (*Carlyle Letters*, vol. 11, p. 151), the christening discussed in the letter
    is most likely this one.

2.   Harriet Brown, daughter of Jeffrey's Ayrshire sister, Marion, and Dr Thomas Brown.

1841

TO THOMAS CARLYLE

date 12 [?October 1841]*
from Hertford

E. I. College Hertford[1]
Tuesday 12th

My Dear Carlyle — The worst accounts you heard of me, were nearest the truth: – for 5 weeks I have scarcely been out of bed – and tho' the fever is at last gone, and the cough <too>, I am weaker than an infant's sigh – and not able to sit up alone one hour in the 24 – and do not expect to be fit for anything for many weeks to come – For some days I was as near dead as <u>possible</u> – and am less than half alive, even now – It is a great effort to write even this much [–] But I am much touched by the kind interest you take in me – and we are too old friends, either to distrust <each other>, or to grudge a little effort to releive each others anxiety – I am just going to be shaved for the first time this ten days! – and must recruit strength for the operation – With truest and kindest love to my dear Jane and very cordial regards to yourself

Ever Affectly Yours
F Jeffrey

---

* 'October? 1841' in pencil (NLS).
National Library of Scotland, MS 1766, f. 93.

1. Jeffrey was writing from the College of the East India Company at Haileybury in Hertfordshire, where his son-in-law William Empson taught (see note 3 to the letter of 16 May 1831, above).

TO THOMAS CARLYLE

date 27 October [1841]*
from Hertford

E. I. College Wedy
27th Oct^r

My Dear Carlyle — I thank you with all my heart, for your kind and cordial letter – and am very much touched and gratified by the traits of tenderness and generosity, which it shows forth in so characteristic a manner — I hope I am a little better – but my progress is so very very slow, as to be almost imperceptible – My fever is gone – and the inflammatory cough, which occasioned the fever – But I am dreadfully reduced and low – and tho' I have been now more than 3 weeks, eating nutritive things 6 times a day.! I do not think I have regained <u>one atom</u> of lost flesh – or really improved much on the deadly <u>pallor</u>, with which this frightful attack had covered me – I can sit up longer however – and walk more about the room – and they say am coming on steadily – I am willing enough to believe this – But I am still obliged to have spiced soup brought to me at 4 o'clock in the morning, to keep me alive till breakfast! – and to pass half the day in bed – I [?feel] the full value of your kind suggestion about coming to see me – But I am still too weak and helpless, to see anybody but my kind and attentive nurses – and my voice is often so feeble as to make it painful to speak a dozen words in an hour – <u>quantum mutatus</u>![1] — I could not but smile at the picture you draw of your idle misery – and your working misery – I know you are not so miserable as your words might imply – and that, if you would only task yourself and your fellow creatures a little less highly, you would both be more contented, and more indulgent — But, if you will be miserable, in one form or another, I beg that (, if it does not make any great difference to you), you would indulge oftenest in the laborious view – from which all the rest of the world will profit so much [–] May I ask on what subject and in what form you propose to do your next penance?

If I am able to move I think I shall come to London for a short time about the middle of Nov^r – when I trust we may shake hands [–] You say nothing of your dear wife's health – from which I infer that it is not materially deranged — Do give her my best love – and tell her I often chear my languid hours by thinking of her kindness, and magnanimity – God bless you both

Ever Affectly Yours
F Jeffrey

---

* '1841' in pencil (NLS).
National Library of Scotland, MS 665, ff. 101–2.
1.   Latin: what a great change!

TO THOMAS CARLYLE

date 26 November [?1841]*
from London

4 Lower Berkeley St
Portman Sqre, 26 Nov^r

My Dear Carlyle – I have been better, and worse since I last wrote to you – and have been here, within reach of my Doctors and friends, for the last week. The former however have very much interdicted all intercourse with the latter; insisting that I shall substantially see no visitors, but themselves – or at all events, hold as little discourse as may be with such as may be (rashly) admitted [–] These are severe terms – But I must see <u>you</u>, now that we are within so manageable a distance – Your complying, of course, with the substance of my instructions – and <u>taking the whole talk on yourself</u> – leaving me only to enact the part of <u>audience</u> – which I am always best pleased to do, when it pleases you to be speaker. – I must mention however that I have lately been allowed (or rather <u>ordered</u>) to go out for an hour in the carriage, any tolerable day – and to be returned – not later than 3. o'clock – so that, to be sure of finding me, you should call after that hour, – and before 5 – when I am generally obliged to go to bed, for an hour or two. You will find me still a very poor creature – Tho' they insist that I am making <u>some</u> advances to recovery – and I am willing enough, you may suppose, to beleive them —— With best and tenderest love to your fair spouse – Ever Very Faithfully Yours

    F Jeffrey

---

* '1841' in pencil (NLS).
National Library of Scotland, MS 1766, ff. 96–7.

1842

TO JANE WELSH CARLYLE

date 9 March [1842]*
from London

4 Lower Berkeley Street
London. Wedy 9 March

My Very Dear Jeanie

I heard yesterday of the great affliction which had fallen on you[1] – and I had this morning a line from Carlyle mentioning that you are still at Liverpool – and giving me your address – and with no very good accounts of your health – I have no comfort to offer you – but only to remind you that you have always been a kind and affectionate daughter – and to bid God bless and support you, in this and all other trials! – I should scarcely have written perhaps to say this – But I am most anxious to hear of your health – and of the time when you expect to be back at your quiet little house at Chelsea – and also whether this sad event will affect your plans or movements for the summer – For my part, I continue very much as when I last saw you – and, having been forbidden to meet the Edin[r] East winds till the season is more advanced, shall probably remain here till near the end of this month – and then go either, for a few weeks, to the coast of the channel – or direct to Scotland – where at all events I think I must be, in the first days of May –

If you can let me have one line – it will be a great comfort and relief to me: – and even tho' the effort may be painful, I cannot but think that the exertion may be of use – at all events it cannot be painful to know that one of your oldest and most constant friends is thinking of you with all the tenderness and truth of our first friendship — With kindest remembrances from all this house   Ever Very Dear Child

Very Affectly Yours
F. Jeffrey

* 'Wilson's date' in pencil (NLS).

National Library of Scotland, MS 787, ff. 100–1.
1.   The death of Jane's mother, Grace Welsh, on 25 February 1842.

TO THOMAS CARLYLE

date 9 [March 1842]*
from London
London Wedy 9th

My Dear Carlyle – I had heard of this affliction, before receiving your letter this morn[g] – but had fancied that Mrs C. was already returned to Chelsea – and intended to have gone there to enquire for her today — Instead of that, I have now written to her at Liverpool – and earnestly hope that I may soon hear that her health has not suffered materially from the shock and exertion — I am sorry to find that you are likely to have other annoyances, besides those that are insepa-rable from such a calamity – but trust they will soon be got over – and that the ultimate result may be, to make the future course of your life more tranquil and secure than it has always been, in the days that are past –

I continue very much as when you last saw me – and shall remain here till about the end of this month – when I shall probably go at once to Scotland – or take shelter for a few weeks in the South, till the severity of our Northern Spring is over — I hope at all events I have the comfort of seeing you, before we quit these latitudes — Ever Very Affectly Your's
     F. Jeffrey

———————

* 'Wednesday 9 March 1842. A.C.' in pencil (NLS).
National Library of Scotland, MS 1766, f. 102.

TO JANE WELSH CARLYLE

date 23 [March 1842]*
from Clifton[1]

Bath Hotel Clifton
Wedy Morng 23[d]

I could not come to you on Monday, My very Dear Child – tho' I did make the attempt – the carriage in fact being at the door, when some people came to call, who did not go away till it was too late to think of it — We got on here very well yesterday – doing our 120 miles quite easily in little more than 4 hours – We are in a very airy and beautiful situation here – tho' hitherto rather too cold – There being <u>ice</u> on the pools this morning – and the ther[momete][r] now (at one o'clock[)]) only 38 —— But I have not at all suffered, either from the journey or the cold – and if I continue as well as I am now, I think we shall make out our original fortnight — In the mean time I shall be anxious to hear of you – I quite understand how much your delicate frame, and kind heart must have suffered from this calamity, and its suddenness – But it was an event which, in the course of nature, you must have encountered – and the circumstances which had for many years so much separated you from your surviving parent,[2] – tho' at first they may rather seem to aggravate must in the long run soften the shock – But the most immediate and effectual of all consolations must be, in the thought that you had always been an affectionate and devoted daughter and left no part of duty coldly or negligently performed — Your chief duty <u>now</u>, is to the survivors – who have a claim on your affection – and who have a right to regard any neglect of your health or wilful indulgence of sorrow as acts of unkindness to them – Forgive me this idle lecture – my gentle, thoughtful and <u>heroic</u> child – It would have been better to say only God bless and support you – and I do say this also – I shall be anxious to hear of Carlyle's return – and of his having got comfortably thro' all these annoying arrangements which such an occurrence always occasions – and I trust that the issue of them will be to place your worldly affairs at least on a more secure and comfortable footing than they have always been <on>, since your noble, but somewhat prodigal generosity[3] threw you more on uncertain resources – and so, my Dearest Jeanie – with all kind thoughts, wishes and recollections   Believe me always

    Very Affectly Yours
    <u>F. Jeffrey</u>

All my household – who are here with me send love and sympathy

---

* '1842 March 23' in pencil (NLS).

National Library of Scotland, MS 787, ff. 102–3.

1.   An established 'watering place' on the sides and summit of cliffs above the river Avon near (now part of) Bristol, famous for its hot springs.
2.   Jane's and her mother's mutual irritation, related in part to Grace Welsh's disapproval of Carlyle as a son-in-law.
3.   In signing over the rent from Craigenputtoch to her mother in 1825 (see note 2 to the letter of 9 and 10 March 1830, above).

TO THOMAS CARLYLE

date 29 May 1842
from Edinburgh

Edin[r] Saturday 29 May
1842

My Dear Carlyle – I am much obliged to you for your letter – and will readily do anything I can for any of the race of Burns[1] – Are there not <u>Sons</u> however, of the Poet, in respectable situations? – who ought not to allow the necessities of their Aunt to be releived by public solicitation for charitable aid? The pension scheme appears to me much the best – for it is greivous work wringing pittances from reluctant hands – and I think, if rightly gone about, that it is feasible, and promising enough – I also think your Memorial very good – and see no occasion to add or to alter a word of it. Wilson[2] is certainly the best man to lead and originate the matter here – tho' I cannot make out whether he has yet been applied to in regard of it – I myself have no scruples, official or personal, about coming forward in such a cause; and shall willingly add my name, to the list either of contributors, or Memorialists, in the place where it may be thought most useful – But I am not on such terms with Wilson[3] as to make it fit that <u>I</u> should break the matter to him – If not already done, Lockhart would be the best person for that office. If such names as Hallams and Rogers[4] are put conspicuously to the memorial – and the party presenting it is authorised to say that they take a warm interest in its success, I do not see how it can fail, except for want of disposable funds — I do not see <either> why Milnes[5] should not be a good enough <u>por-teur</u>[6] of such a document – tho' a better might perhaps be found – and I should think it of consequence that Sir Jas Graham[7] should be interested in the cause – He is likely enough to take it up <u>con amore</u>,[8] if properly approached – and if his good wishes are once secured, <u>he</u> would be by far the best person to bring it immediately under Sir Rob[er]t's notice[9] – But no time should be lost — I am willing, if necessary, to give £10 to a subscription – but fear that nothing more will be raised in that way, than a temporary supply – a years maintenance perhaps – but nothing to purchase an annuity – <u>experto credite</u>[10] – and now, this is all the needful — and I have time for no more today [–] I return you the Mem[oria]l

I am sorry to hear that your brains ferment so slowly over the hot worts of Cromwell[11] – Suppose you throw in a little frisk working yeast, in the shape of <the> Miltonic Sonnet, or selections from the Defensio P. A.[12] – or from Cowley's character[13] – and see whether that will not quicken the process?

It greives my heart to hear of the greif that still weighs on the mistress of your household – but I mean to write to her very soon – and I hope the cloud will lighten as the sun is more in the sky – I have a constant and tender remembrance of you both – and So God bless you and Ever Affectly Yours

F Jeffrey

I get thro' my work very tolerably – tho' I am still shaky and uncertain —

National Library of Scotland, MS 10997, ff. 159–60.

1. Carlyle had written soliciting Jeffrey's interest in the plight of the Scottish poet's youngest sister Isobel Begg (née Burns; 1770–1858), widowed with nine children in 1813 and now in straitened circumstances.
2. John Wilson ('Christopher North'), the *Blackwood's Edinburgh Magazine* writer and Professor of Moral Philosophy at Edinburgh University.
3. See note 3 to the letter of 3 November 1829, above.
4. Henry Hallam (1777–1859), an *Edinburgh* reviewer and historian, author of *Europe during the Middle Ages* (1818) and *The Constitutional History of England from Henry VII to George II* (1827); for Rogers, see note 3 to the letter of 6 February 1832, above.
5. Richard Monckton Milnes, later first Baron Houghton (1809–85), one of the Cambridge 'Apostles', and a writer, politician and patron of the arts.
6. French: bearer.
7. Sir James Graham, Baronet (1792–1861), statesman and politician who had become first Lord of the Admiralty in Grey's government in 1830 but later changed parties to become Home Secretary under Sir Robert Peel.
8. Italian: with love or passion.
9. To the notice of the Prime Minister, Sir Robert Peel (1788–1850), who had come into office the year before.
10. Latin: believe the experienced one (the expert) (Virgil, *Aeneid*, XI.283).
11. A pun on worts/words (and possibly warts?): brewer's wort is the infusion of ground malt and other grain prior to the fermentation of beer. Carlyle's current project was an edition of Cromwell's words – *The Letters and Speeches of Oliver Cromwell* – into which he interpolated his own annotation and commentary (it would be published three and a half years later, in November 1845).
12. Milton's sonnet 'To Oliver Cromwell' ('Cromwell, our chief of men') – Carlyle's edition did much to recover the heroic Cromwell of this sonnet – and his Latin prose piece *Pro Populo Anglicano Defensio* [*Defence of the English People*] (1651), written in response to the defence of Charles II by Samalsius (Claude de Saumaise).
13. A prose piece by the Royalist poet Abraham Cowley (1618–67) entitled *Discourse by Way of Vision Concerning Oliver Cromwell* (1661).

TO JANE WELSH CARLYLE

date 4 June 1842
from Edinburgh

Edin^r 4 June 1842

My Very Dear Jeanie – You will be glad to hear that I have been back at my work for the last fortnight – and am none the worse for it – tho' not very robustious yet – and obliged to take more anxious care of this poor old carcase, than I can always think it deserves – But we all cling, I fancy, like long Tom Coffin[1] – to our shattered and stranded <u>craft</u> – and should only pray that we may meet its final breaking up, with as much equanimity! — I was greived to hear from Carlyle, that you were still suffering from the shock of your late affliction – But time softens all shocks – and, tho' working rather slowly, is a better <u>Buffer</u> than any they have yet on the railways [–] The season too, I must hope, will be of use to you – and the final dethronement of that tyrannical East wind, and the triumphal entry of the young Summer among us, should be "able to drive, all sadness, but Despair"[2] — I told him, I think, when I answered his last letter – (and at any rate I now tell you) – that I was but <u>a single day</u> in London, in my transit from Devonshire to Scotland – – and was obliged to give that up to Doctors and Bankers – and other <u>unavoidable</u> personages – so that I could not possibly run out to take my chance of seeing you at Chelsea – tho' I do assure you, I sent many a longing look – and kind wish, in that direction I am very anxious to know what your plans are, for the summer – and I may add, for some of your immediately future years – For I do not think it unlikely that recent events may make some permanent change in your way of life – and I cannot but hope that it may bring it something nearer than it has lately been, to the course and direction of mine – I hope too that at all events it may bring you to Scotland, in the course of the season – as I scarcely think that, after so long an absence, I shall venture cross the border again before the end of the year – Charley goes with her husband to Weisbaden in the course of this month – on account of his health[3] and I am sorry to say that we have but slender hopes of seeing them here on their way back to the college – We have our own dear little Tarley however in pledge – and, as <u>the very little one</u>[4] is also to be sent us, when her parents move, I think, if we positively refuse to part with them, till <u>they</u> come to fetch them they will not well be able to help themselves — But we shall see – In the mean time I live an innocent, domestic and valetudinarian sort of life – to which I am every day more reconciled – and think that the check that declining health has given to the indulgence of those pleasant vices – of which the Gods are sure – they say, to make scourges for us in the end[5] – has so far quickened my sensibility to more blameless enjoyments – as on the whole to make very fair amends – my relish for poetry and beautiful scenery – tho' it was never dead within me – is now more keen I think than ever – and if I do not more enjoy the interchange of kind affections, I seem to feel as if I had more leisure for their cultivation — So you see I may have a tolerably respectable and happy old age, after all – if actual pain and suffering, and the ultimate deadening of the heart – can be warded off, a while longer [–] It is beautiful weather – and I am just going out to Craigcrook for my Saturday and Sundays holiday – I was a little afraid that the soft verdure and rich foliage of Devon and Herts would have spoiled my eye for the more homely beauties of our Northern (lowland) landscape – but my little retreat stands the comparison very well – and I feel as if I could show my Southern friends my walks and views, without fear of their scorn [—] The carriage however has come for me – and as I am to carry out half our dinner in it I cannot venture to detain it. God bless you then very very Dear Child – Do let me hear from you – and if you send me a good account of yourself, you shall have a <u>Sunday letter</u> from Craigcrook – full of the spirit of the day, the place, and the season – in return   In the mean time and always   Believe me with kindest regards to Carlyle

    Very Affectionately Yours

    F. Jeffrey

National Library of Scotland, MS 787, ff. 104–6.

1.   Long Tom Coffin of Nantucket is a heroic sailor who meets his death at sea in the novel *The Pilot* (1824) by the American novelist James Fenimore Cooper.

2.   See Milton's *Paradise Lost*, IV.158–61: 'And of pure now purer air/ Meets his approach, and to the heart inspires/ Vernal delight and joy, able to drive/ All sadness but despair'.

3.   His daughter Charlotte, that is, with her husband William Empson (see note 3 to the letter of 16 May 1831, above). Wiesbaden, in Germany ('the Nice of the North'), was and still is famous for its therapeutic thermal springs.

4.   Jeffrey's granddaughter, Margaret (Maggie), born 1841.

5.   Alluding to Edgar's 'The Gods are just, and of our pleasant vices/ Make instruments to plague us', *King Lear*, V.iii.171–2.

1843

TO THOMAS CARLYLE

date 12 May [1843]
from Lancaster

Lancaster — Friday
Evg — 12 May

My Dear Carlyle – I was particularly sorry not to find either of you, when I called on Wednesday – both because it was distressing to me to have so poor a report of my Dear Mrs C's health to take away with me – and because I came full charged with compliments and discussions about your book[1] – which I had been reading with great attention – and can truly add, with very great interest and admiration — I agree more with it, I think, than with any of your other lucubrations – and have better hope of its making an impression in favour both of your genius – and your doctrines – altho', with regard to the greater part of the last, I must not let you suppose that I am <as yet anything of> a convert – or indeed, other than a decided, and I rather fear an inconvertible heretic – and even as to the matter of genius – tho' there can be no doubt that it has that stamp, both broad and deep, almost on every page, I am yet so far from being satisfied with the taste and style of your writing, that I am absolutely <u>provoked</u> with you – for wilfully putting obstacles in the way both of your fame, and the efficacy of the many great truths you deliver, by obstinately adhering to it – If I had had to deal with your M.S. I should have struck out at least a third – and yet have left you all your poetry and <pathos, and> originality – and most even of your <u>address</u> – which is often very piquant – and awakening – I admit also that you are so far from being generally verbose or diffuse, that the greatest charm of your <u>great</u> passages is their extreme and daring brevity – But you have – (that is <u>I think</u> and feel – and audaciously tell you t̶h̶a̶t̶ <you have>) great masses of rubbish, – of lumbering vagueness – and clumsy repetitions – and uncharitable and absurd <u>abuse</u> – which should be carted away in the gross – as mere obstruction and deformity

— I rather feel I would so deal with the whole of your St Edmundsbury Chronicle or at least with more than 9/10^{ths} of it – tho' I cannot help fearing that you think that the best part of the volume – God help us!

Well – you see my head is giddy with jumbling all day on the railway – and a dish of tea I have been drinking to compose it – and I could not go to sleep (or to bed rather) without venting all this impertinence on you – which I know you have too much real philosophy – and reliance on my old affection and esteem for you – not to take in good part — Indeed all who know anything of my sentiments know that I think you the most original man of our time – and qualified too, to produce a greater and more beneficial effect by your writings than any other man – if you would only give up some whimsicalities of taste and manner, which not only expose you to the charge of affectation, but repel many readers whom it would be of great importance to attract – and perplex and embarrass many others, who might be usefully impressed – if not entirely convinced, by plain reasoning — And so God Bless, and prosper you! – Do cheer your fair spouse – and let me hear soon of her being better, and gayer. – I have been haunted, almost ever since, by the air of suffering and deep depression I observed in her, the last day I saw you together – I am not very well myself – but expect to find relief in the quiet of home and in the regular, and not too heavy – not all feverish occupations to which I am returning — I have long had a notion that you would be both better in health – and more comfortable in every way, if you were sentenced to some such ignoble labour! Is it too late yet, for you to think of it?

With kindest love to your too fragile patient – and her Doctor brother –

Ever Affectly Your's

F Jeffrey

Lady Holland, I believe, has got a successor to poor Allen[2] – who I suppose is not an Atheist – as his father is a professor of Divinity —

National Library of Scotland, MS 1766, ff. 116–18.

1.   Carlyle had published *Past and Present* in April 1843, a meditation on poverty, charity and social responsibility and 'full of the most portentous Speculative-Radicalism ever uttered in Governess-English, or even in *Carlylese* as they call it!', as Carlyle wrote to James Marshall on 1 February 1843 (*Carlyle Letters*, vol. 16, p. 40).

2.   John Allen MD (1771–1843) was a close friend of Jeffrey's and one of his original set of Edinburgh Whigs. In 1801, the year before the launching of the *Edinburgh Review*, Allen had joined the Whig grandees Lord and Lady Holland in Europe as a physician and had remained advisor, librarian and general factotum at Holland House until his death in 1843 (see note 1 to the undated letter, between May and September 1833, above), though he also served as warden and eventually headmaster of Dulwich College from 1811. Allen was notorious for frankly admitting to atheism.

TO JANE WELSH CARLYLE

date [?June 1843]*
from Craigcrook

Craigcrook Saturday

My Dear Child – I have been ill again since I received your letter – and scarcely able to struggle thro' the work of our weary Session – But I did get thro' it, on Thursday – and make an early use, you see, of my vacation, to thank you for your very kind and pleasing communication – O Yes, you are a very practical, worldly wise, and prudent scheming little creature, when you please, I see – and I ask pardon, in all humility, for my doubts of your perfections in that way – My only fear now is that you will not have money enough to put your Mudie project[1] fairly in execution – But you will do some good, I doubt not – and that is a consolation, which many people have not to offer themselves – at the end of a longer life than your's – or mine either —

I am living a quiet, contented and patriarchal life here – with my wife and daughter and 3 blooming grandchildren[2] – Seeing no company, but a few morning and evening visitors among my oldest intimates – and observing – if not quite out of good liking – at least very patiently and chearfully – as temperate and careful a regime – as patriarchs or Jephsons[3] would advise — My malady has been a mitigated return, both of my bronchial infirmity – and of the languid circulation from which I suffered so much two years ago – But it certainly is slighter and I think is wearing off — All the rest of my household is well — We are looking very pretty – and green and leafy here – and so fresh, from the soft showers of the last three days – and with such thick clustering of roses – and profuse flowering of portugal laurels about us as to reconcile one of my taste and fancies, both to the seclusion, and the broken health which has lately fallen to my lot — I hope you will go somewhere before the fine season is over — I have myself a strong faith in the reviving effect of a change of position and occupation in all cases of languid vitality – and think it quite certain that both mind and body are much the better for hearing the rythm of their too uniform movements broken thro' – and the pressure of the perpetual recommence of the same daily distractions taken off – and now I cannot write to you any more today – for here are my neighbours from Belmont[4] – and I shall lose the post if I wait till they are gone — But I mean to be a good boy during these holidays and to write very soon again – I was very much touched by your kind remembrances of Craigcrook – and meant to have said something to you on the subject – at all events I shall love it all the more for that reason – and I am sure you do not doubt that I too have remembrances – and of more localities than this!

Heaven Bless you

always, My Very Dear Jeanie

Ever Affectly Yours

F. Jeffrey

---

* 'W.M. 1839' in pencil (NLS).

National Library of Scotland, MS 787, ff. 98–9.

1.   The writer Robert Mudie (1777–1842) died on 29 April 1842 leaving his widow and five children destitute. The family's plight had come to Jane's attention around the middle of 1843, when she began canvassing for their support. See the letter to Jeannie Welsh of [15 June 1843] (*Carlyle Letters*, vol. 16, pp. 198–9).

2.   Charlotte (Tarley), Margaret (Maggie) and Nancy (born 1843).

3.   Dr Henry Jephson (1798–1878), a famous doctor and philanthropist of the period who treated George IV and Victoria, and whose name is associated with Leamington and its medicinal waters.

4.   The estate neighbouring Craigcrook.

1844

TO JANE WELSH CARLYLE

date 13 May [1844]
from Hertford
E. I. College

Monday Morng
13th May

My Dear Jeanie – I have been very ill, since I last saw you – and have never been able to go to London since that time. I am now recovering – and having my Duties to attend to in the North, I am going up, in half an hour, to <u>the Euston Squ[are] Hotel</u> – where I shall repose and see my Doctors tomorrow – and, if <u>they</u> permit me, proceed by the train of Wedy Morng to Lancaster — I fear I shall not be able to come so far as to Chelsea – and should be unwilling to give my good Carlyle the trouble of coming so far to me – But I do not like to leave these latitudes, and something which feels like your neighbourhood without a word or two of kind greeting to you both – and so Farewell, and God bless you, my very Dear Child

Ever affectly Yours

F. <u>Jeffrey</u>

National Library of Scotland, MS 787, ff. 86A–B.

1845

TO JANE WELSH CARLYLE

date [?1845; possibly 1844]
from Hertford

I am coming again, for two or three days to London, tomorrow – my Dear Child – and am anxious not to be obliged again to leave it, without seeing you – If you could take the trouble therefore to send a line to Coulson's Hotel Brook St, mentioning at what time – after one o'clock – I should find you on Thursday, Friday or Saturday – You may depend on my appearing –

With all kind wishes

Ever Affectly Yours

F Jeffrey

National Library of Scotland, MS 2883, f. 310.

1846

TO THOMAS CARLYLE

date 28 [March 1846]
from Hertford

E. I. College Hertford
Sunday 28th

My Dear Carlyle – I am coming to London to see a few old friends – next Tuesday – for two days only – and as I should be sorry to miss you and Jeanie, when I direct my pilgrim steps for this purpose to Chelsea, I give you this notice that I shall look in on you, on Wed^y or Thursday – at an early <u>London</u> hour – that is somewhere between 12 o'clock and 3.

I grow very old – tho' my health is about what it was when I last saw you – and the vitality, of all but my body – very much I think, as when I saw you <u>first!</u>

I should say something to you of your book?[1] Well – I rejoice as much in its success – and in the large addition it has made to your fame and worldly prospects, as any of those can do who admire its style, and agree in all its sentiments – Why the devil will you persist in scoffing and mocking at your fallen creatures? and fancying that you could order the world so much better than the <many> wiser men, who have failed in doing it very well – or the wise God, who is satisfied with it as it is? —— Yet there is much truth – and much that will do good in your book – tho' much that is mischievous, and more that is very provoking – God help us!

I hope your health is better – and that you feel lighter and more tolerant, after this copious discharge of bile? and my dear Jeanie too, I hope she is more in charity with God's world – and god's creatures, to whom he has chosen to give it?

I shall be at Coulson's in Brook Street <45> – if you should like to fix any time for my coming to you – and Ever Your's

    F. Jeffrey

---

* Dated in pencil (NLS) 'March 1846?', with the later comment '28 Mar 1846 was not Sunday' added in a different hand.

National Library of Scotland, MS 1774, ff. 47–8.

1.   Carlyle's *Letters and Speeches of Oliver Cromwell* had been published late in 1845 (see note 11 to the letter of 29 May 1842, above).

1847

TO THOMAS CARLYLE

date 26 April [1847]
from Isle of Wight

Shanklin – Isle of Wight
Monday 26 April

My Dear Carlyle — Do not let us quite forget each other nor let Lethe creep between us, even before the inexorable Styx comes to separate us! — We are very old friends now – and one of us, alas, also a very old man [–] Yet he does feel warmly towards his old friends – and likes to dream of ["]auld lang syne" – and tho' our ways of life have been much apart – and there is some considerable difference in our tastes, – I should be sorry to think we did not agree more than most people in our estimate of what should be loved and honored in our common nature and what ought to be our dispositions to our fellow men — I am more tolerant of shortcomings, I think, than you and claim – as I probably require – more toleration – but if ~~you~~ we could reform men according to our fancies, I rather think <u>my</u> reformed men would be very like <u>yours</u> – at least as individuals – and tho' I neither hope so highly nor so confidently as you do, of the future improvement of our race, I have a great assurance that they are improving; and that the next generation will be better off – (and deserve to be) than the present — Well – but I did not intend to bore you with matter like this – but only to say that, feeling myself at full leisure here and something nearer you than I generally am, I cannot help wishing to hear from you – and to tell you that I think often and kindly of you – even when I have less leisure to tell you so than at present — We have been here – with all the children and grandchildren – nurses, and ladies maids – a goodly patriarchal household of 14 in number – for the last fortnight and mean to stay a week longer – We have got a very nice house – looking over a pretty little lawn, and its cluttering shrubs and farther woods, to two separate vistas of the blue and lonely sea – to which we can descend by a wooded ravine, thro' the cliffs in 4 minutes and which is scarcely out of hearing all the day long — There is a very beautiful village – without anything like a street – or indeed 3 houses standing together, within it – and consisting almost entirely of detached villa residences scattered among woody swells and hollows – and – for the present at least so generally unoccupied, that the whole place has an air of seclusion and repose, almost as complete as I remember enjoying so much of old at Craigenputtach! and which I still feel to be unspeakably soothing to my world wearied spirit! — We live here very lovingly and happily – without bustle and without ennui – and I almost shrink from returning so soon – to the moderate work, and <still more> moderate dissipation <in> which I must by and bye engage [–] In the mean time let me know how you, and my Ever Dear Jeanie have been – what you have been doing – and meditating – whether you are in any degree weaned from your strange idolatry of old Cromwell – and to what other <u>engouement</u>[1] your constitutional melancholy and enthusiasm is now leading you? Vanity of Vanities, my dear friend! let us agree in that text – and we shall <soon> come to an understanding on all others — But here are the carriages to trundle us up to Carisbrooke[2] – and I must not trespass another sheet [–] God bless you – I fear we shall merely pass thro' London – on our way to Hertfordshire on the 4th – and again on starting for Scotland on [the *omitted*] 13th [–] But if we can stay a day I shall try to see you, and give you notice of my coming – With most kind love to Jane Ever My Dear Carlyle

    Affectly Yours
    F. Jeffrey

National Library of Scotland, MS 665, ff. 127–8.

1.   French: infatuation, craze.
2.   A town on the Isle of Wight 1 mile south-west of Newport.

1849

TO THOMAS CARLYLE

date 23 August [1849]
from Craigcrook

Craigcrook – <u>Blackhall</u>
Edin' 23 Aug'

My Ever Dear Friends! — I shall be so rejoiced to see you! I have been <u>terribly</u> ill for the last 2 months – and am a very poor creature still — so weak and pale and thin! Tho' no longer suffering from my distinct complaint – but only old age, and general decay – which still leaves me, I thank God, all my affections – and most of my intellect and fancy — I doubt whether I shall ever be fit for work – or general society again – but I am not a bit low spirited, or discontented – and, when my voice is in tolerable order – converse as well and cheerfully as ever – M'^{rs} Jeffrey I am glad to say is I think, perfectly recovered – tho' not quite so robust as formerly – and we have the Empsons and all their children with us – and if the constant spectacle of their happiness and everflowing spirits, did not make me forget my own infirmities, I should be unworthy of such descendants — But say when you will come? & the sooner the better – tho' I am in no condition to go from home – and you may be sure to find me at any time — only I hope you will come early in the day – for I am still obliged to go to bed for an hour or two – when other people go to dinner (– between 6 and 7) – But I am up and about at breakfast and lunch – the first before 10 – and the last before 2 — and to one or both of these slight and friendly repasts I hope soon to welcome you ——

A month ago I thought I should die – and not live – and I thought often and very tenderly of you both – indeed I have never ceased to think so of you — Now I think I shall rally to some extent, from this attack – but on a lower level of vitality – and most probably shrink into a secluded, tranquil, domestic existence – no undesirable close of rather too busy a life – if I escape pain – and retain my power of reading – and the objects of my affection

Heaven Bless and keep you always! – The world is very beautiful now all around us — and there are more beautiful worlds, to which we may yet be introduced – and of which I may have to do the honors to you![1]

Ever Affectly Yours

F. Jeffrey

National Library of Scotland, MS 665, ff. 132–3.

1. Francis Jeffrey died five months later on 26 January 1850.

INDEX